African Culture Archive

Over the past forty years, Zed has established a long and proud tradition of publishing critical work on African issues, offering unique insights into the continent's politics, development, history and culture. The African Culture Archive draws on this rich backlist, consisting of carefully selected titles that even now have enduring relevance years after their initial publication. Lovingly repackaged, with newly commissioned forewords that reflect on the impact the books have had, these are essential works for anyone interested in the cultural and literary landscape of the continent.

Other titles in the archive:

Land, Freedom and Fiction: History and Ideology in Kenya
David Maughan Brown

Theatre and Cultural Struggle under Apartheid
Robert Mshengu Kavanagh

Theory of African Literature: Implications for Practical Criticism
Chidi Amuta

About the author

Stephanie Newell is a professor of English at Yale University, specialising in West African literature. Her other books include *The Power to Name: A History of Anonymity in Colonial West Africa* (2013) and *The Forger's Tale: The Search for Odeziaku* (2006).

Wendy Griswold is the Bergen Evans professor of humanities at Northwestern University. Her books include *Cultures and Societies in a Changing World* (new edition 2012) and *Bearing Witness: Readers, Writers, and the Novel in Nigeria* (2000).

Writing African Women

Gender, Popular Culture and Literature in West Africa

Edited by Stephanie Newell

With a new Foreword by Wendy Griswold

Zed Books
LONDON

Writing African Women: Gender, Popular Culture and Literature in West Africa was first published in 1997 by Zed Books Ltd, The Foundry, 17 Oval Way, London SE11 5RR, UK.

This edition was published in 2017.

www.zedbooks.net

Copyright individual chapters © the contributors, 1997
Editorial copyright © Stephanie Newell, 1997

The right of Stephanie Newell to be identified as the editor of this work has been asserted by her in accordance with the Copyright, Designs and Patents Act, 1988.

Cover design by Kika Sroka-Miller.

All rights reserved. No part of this publication may be reproduced, stored in a retrieval system or transmitted in any form or by any means, electronic, mechanical, photocopying or otherwise, without the prior permission of Zed Books Ltd.

A catalogue record for this book is available from the British Library.

ISBN 978-1-78699-069-3 hb
ISBN 978-1-78699-010-5 pb
ISBN 978-1-78699-008-2 pdf
ISBN 978-1-78699-007-5 epub
ISBN 978-1-78699-009-9 mobi

Contents

Acknowledgements		ix
Foreword by Wendy Griswold		xi

INTRODUCTION
Writing African women: gender, popular culture and literature in West Africa
STEPHANIE NEWELL 1

PART I Theory and Politics 9

1 Reading towards a theorization of African women's writing: African women writers within feminist gynocriticism
   NANA WILSON-TAGOE 11

2 Masculinity: the military, women and cultural politics in Nigeria
   BAYO OGUNJIMI 29

3 Women's role in Ghana's social development
   AKOSUA GYAMFUAA-FOFIE 40

PART II Literatures 45

4 A life on the women's page: *Treena Kwenta's Diary*
   JANE BRYCE 47

5 Recovering lost voices: the short stories of Mabel Dove-Danquah
   NAANA JANE OPOKU-AGYEMANG 67

6	Rewriting popular myths of female subordination: selected stories by Theodora Adimora-Ezeigbo and May Ifeoma Nwoye CHINYERE GRACE OKAFOR	81
7	Gender conflict in Flora Nwapa's novels THEODORA AKACHI EZEIGBO	95
8	Culture and gender semantics in Flora Nwapa's poetry OBODODIMMA OHA	105
9	Behind the veil in northern Nigeria: the writing of Zaynab Alkali and Hauwa Ali MARGARET HAUWA KASSAM	117
10	The onus of womanhood: Mariama Ba and Zaynab Alkali IBIYEMI MOJOLA	126
11	Narrative technique and the politics of gender: Ama Ata Aidoo's Our Sister Killjoy and No Sweetness Here CHIOMA OPARA	137
	PART III Popular Culture	147
12	Hausa women as oral storytellers in northern Nigeria SANI ABBA ALIYU	149
13	Gender politics in West African mask performance CHINYERE GRACE OKAFOR	157
14	Anatomy of masculine power: three perspectives on marriage and gender in Nigerian non-fiction STEPHANIE NEWELL	170
15	Gender tempered through metal: women in metal-casting in Benin City, Nigeria ADEPEJU LAYIWOLA	191
	Index	198

Acknowledgements

This book was made possible by generous grants from Stirling University's Internal Research Fund, and the Carnegie Trust for the Universities of Scotland.

The editor wishes to thank Mamie Prentice, Kathleen Murray and Margaret MacMenaman for their secretarial assistance. Special thanks to Susan Sinclair for her invaluable proof-reading skills.

Foreword by Wendy Griswold

In *Writing African Women*, Stephanie Newell began her introduction with a line that still rings true: 'West African societies overflow with local, culturally specific constructions of gender which circulate in literature and popular representations.' Twenty years ago, people who opened Newell's collection of critical essays knew what they were getting: varied reflections on the place of women – as writers, protagonists and readers – in West African novels, stories and poetry. The essays offered sorely needed conceptual tools for understanding the relationship between gender and power in its many forms and the capacity of cultural objects to perpetuate or undermine these power structures.

In the twenty-first century each term in the title has exploded. What is writing? Does texting count? Tweeting, blogging, communicating via Snapchat and websites? Are the power relationships – the ones that forced the late Buchi Emecheta to get up before dawn in order to sneak in some writing before her husband and children's demands took over – at play in the digital age?

And what does African mean? Yewande Omotoso was born in Barbados, grew up in Nigeria and lives in Johannesburg. Her novel *The Woman Next Door* takes place in Cape Town, England and Nigeria. Is she African? Is this a West African novel? A South African one? A global one? And if the latter, does the 'global' bleach out the 'local, culturally specific' constructions of gender?

Finally, what does it mean to be a woman, and what type of woman, indeed what other sexual or gender identity, might one be? The man/woman binary that feminists and womanists and everyone else long assumed has broken down in the new century. Although to my knowledge West African writers have not yet addressed transgendered, bi, genderqueer, and other non-normative sexualities, it can only be a matter of time. Meanwhile Chinelo Okparanta's *Under the Udala Trees*, one of the most talked about novels from the new generation, forthrightly dissects the pains, and celebrates the joys, of lesbian love.

Considered together, these three questions raise a fourth, that of cultural authority. Who gets to decide what is African, what is gender, what is literature, what stories are worth telling? How are they told? Where does the power lie? We might want to rewrite Newell's opening sentence: West African societies overflow with transnational, culturally hybrid, fluid constructions of gender, constructions that circulate globally and digitally, adopting and adapting to issues raised elsewhere while struggling to maintain a voice rooted in the continent's social history. Fair enough. Mariama Bâ didn't have a website, and readers never had to wonder if Flora Nwapa, well-travelled as she was, should be considered Nigerian. Now such questions, and such communicative acts, are inescapable.

Given the yawning gap between then and now, what might these old essays have to tell new readers? It is well understood that localism and globalism are not mutually exclusionary but mutually constructive; to put it more strongly, nobody burrows into the local cultural specificities like a cosmopolitan. Focusing on gender, we must acknowledge that the longstanding African localisms based on the gendered binary – patriarchy, reduction of women to their fertility and even to their production of male progeny, domestic violence, lost property rights, dependency, polygamous rivalry – have not gone away, and the sharp, feminist eyes of these essayists continue to facilitate exploring the conditions of gender.

For African women, things have not so much fallen apart as metastasized, as the new millennium generates new versions of old problems. To cite just one example: if earlier cohorts contended with, and wrote about, domestic violence, the current generation faces domestic, terrorist and military violence. In Chibundu Onuzo's *Welcome to Lagos*, a teenage girl in the Delta faces rape by the very Nigerian soldiers who are supposed to be keeping peace. Boko Haram has made sexual violence a matter of policy.

While posing such questions might suggest that the issues considered in *Writing African Women* are no longer relevant, the exact opposite is the case. In the contemporary climate, to suggest that women – African and otherwise – have somehow moved past the old, binary-based problems, to see gender as a construction, a performance, that can be evaporated with the application of enough theory, to believe we have entered a post-feminist era where power floats free from sex, would be irresponsible, even fatuous. Clear, informed thinking about the gendered nexus of culture and power is needed more than ever. The new publication of Newell's collection is an event to be applauded, and its contents to be pondered.

Wendy Griswold, February 2017

INTRODUCTION
Writing African women: gender, popular culture and literature in West Africa

STEPHANIE NEWELL

West African societies overflow with local, culturally specific constructions of gender which circulate in literature and popular representations. Novels, soap operas, songs and newspapers regularly stage controversial gender debates, creating narratives around issues such as marriage and divorce, polygyny, love, female infertility and prostitution. A great deal of this contemporary West African material, written and published locally, is unknown to researchers outside the country of production. Paradoxically, a silence exists in African studies in the very area where currently noisy local debates are taking place. In spite of efforts by publishers' collectives abroad,[1] global book distribution networks have inhibited the circulation of this material. Local texts, arguments, critiques and knowledge also have been submerged by vocal postcolonial theorists who reside in metropolitan countries. Whether expressed in the themes and characters of novels or located on the level of academic analysis, however, challenging discussions of gender are taking place throughout West African societies.

West African women are born into fluid social worlds, and gender images and ideologies constantly shift to account for their changing status. Contemporary West Africa is filled with a multitude of official and unofficial gender commentators. Of particular interest are the abundance of women writers and woman-centred theorists who offer perspectives which interrogate, reformulate and analyse inherited, popular codes. Concepts such as 'womanism', 'motherism' and 'femalism' have been adopted or coined during this dynamic process in which women write themselves anew, responding as postcolonial subjects to the 'entrapping cycle' specified by Susheila Nasta:

In countries with a history of colonialism, women's quest for emancipation, self-identity and fulfilment can be seen to represent a traitorous act, a betrayal not simply of traditional codes of practice and belief but of the wider struggle for liberation and nationalism. Does to be 'feminist' therefore involve a further displacement or reflect an implicit adherence to another form of cultural imperialism? (Nasta 1991: xv)

The challenge has been to work towards social transformations and construct a women's history while simultaneously avoiding absorption into Western feminist discourses, which have tended to subordinate and speak on behalf of the typical 'third world woman' (Mohanty 1988).

The essays collected in this volume represent a sample of West African gender debates, introducing readers to a wide variety of different, even divergent perspectives that range from Akosua Gyamfuaa-Fofie's raw polemics to Nana Wilson-Tagoe's complex and subtle negotiation with a Western gynocritical model. By linking West African literatures with popular art forms and local woman-centred theories, European and American analytical frameworks have been marginalized deliberately. The aim of this book is to open up a space for the expression of different debates, to provide a forum for a range of African critical perspectives and interpretations.

No specifically 'African feminist' position is agreed upon and the chapters do not express a consensus; instead, a diversity of arguments emerges around the issues of gender, literary theory and the representation of women in West Africa. Such variety is hardly surprising. The societies bounded by the regional label 'West Africa' are not singular, and it would be impossible to homogenize their constructions of gender. It is therefore unfortunate and indicative of regional power relations that the majority of essays collected here have been written by Nigerian and Ghanaian academics; the experiences and expressions of other African women writers and researchers, particularly in francophone countries, are elided by this anglophone emphasis. Discussions of Islamic and francophone literatures are included, however, in an effort to compensate for the bias and to acknowledge that Islamic women writers' protagonists and themes can differ dramatically from non-Muslim texts.

The term 'traditional', frequently wielded in discussions of women's positions and power bases in precolonial societies, is problematized by several writers. While Theodora Akachi Ezeigbo regards it as a crucial discursive pole against which contemporary women's situations can be compared, Sani Abba Aliyu acknowledges that discussions of a precolonial 'golden age' of female equality should be undertaken self-consciously and cautiously. 'In traditional Igbo thought at least,' Ezeigbo writes, 'gender interaction is regarded as being complementary and balanced ... rather than being conflictual or competing for the same positions of social and political power.' For other contributors, such as Chinyere Grace Okafor and Jane Bryce, the binary division between the traditional and modern is rendered redundant by their emphasis on the dynamism and fluidity of contemporary women's identities; their theorizations of gender transcend dichotomies in favour of more manifold models of subjectivity.

Nana Wilson-Tagoe, whose essay opens this volume, brings a recognized feminist framework to primary texts, simultaneously employing and rewriting European and American theories. 'A reading of African women's writing within a feminist framework can bring new energy and vitality to this writing', she explains, going on to offer a gynocritical reading of a range of West African women's texts. Focusing on Flora Nwapa's *Efuru* and Buchi Emecheta's *The Joys of Motherhood*, she explores the ways in which Emecheta inherits and interprets the symbolic figure of the water goddess invoked by Nwapa. Elaine Showalter's gynocritical model changes during its inter-cultural application, however, as Wilson-Tagoe draws attention to West African women's cultural locations and uses gynocriticism to stress the specificity of African women's experience. Focusing on the ways that female subjectivities are reconfigured within literary texts, Bayo Ogunjimi shows how Flora Nwapa and Buchi Emecheta have subverted and rewritten Biafran War novels, which tend to reinforce a masculine 'barrack culture' in Nigeria, perpetuating a patriarchal order and inhibiting women's political empowerment.[2]

The Ghanaian novelist and publisher Akosua Gyamfuaa-Fofie maintains Wilson-Tagoe's tight cultural focus; she moves away from literature, however, to construct a biographical template of Ghanaian women. Gyamfuaa-Fofie specifies the key moves in a socialization process that, she insists, renders women subservient and less ambitious than Ghanaian men.

Newspapers and magazines are an important outlet for African writers, who are confronted currently with a crisis in local publishing as paper prices soar. Both Jane Bryce and Naana Jane Opoku-Agyemang retrieve 'lost' or trivialized female voices from the West African print media. Studying ephemeral sources such as old newspapers and short-lived magazines, women creative writers are located, projecting strong, assertive protagonists that provide role-models for readers. In the process of recovering these submerged manuscripts, Bryce's and Opoku-Agyemang's innovative projects open up under-researched archives to students of gender in West Africa. Little-known writers and texts are explored and theorizations of African women's creative expression are reoriented in the process.

Discussing the transcendence of negative female stereotypes in short stories by two new women writers, Chinyere Grace Okafor focuses on the presentation of professional, political heroines who participate actively in Nigerian public life. She finds that Theodora Adimora-Ezeigbo's and May Ifeoma Nwoye's protagonists experience hardship and rejection but insist on their integrity. Both authors – one of whom, Adimora-Ezeigbo, has written a chapter in this volume – 'rewrite popular myths of female subordination'. They construct a new, assertive femininity, endowing it with a positive power which undermines conventional images of women.

In the next chapter, Theodora Adimora-Ezeigbo (writing under the name she uses for her academic work: Theodora Akachi Ezeigbo) argues that Flora Nwapa writes from a region in which women have a history of economic autonomy and political influence outside male control: this derives from the dual-sex division of labour in Igboland which Ezeigbo, and several other Nigerian writers, believe to have been partially compromised by the colonial encounter.[3] Depicting the conflicts and compromises between married couples in rural and urban areas, Nwapa's writing is said to exhibit a gender model which is fundamentally antagonistic. Images of marital conflict transcend her distinct traditional and modern settings and extend throughout her literary career: for, Ezeigbo finds, marriages are always turbulent and inequitable in Nwapa's writing, always involving massive compromises on the part of women and falling apart when women begin to rebel against subordinate roles.

Obododimma Oha's intricate exploration of Flora Nwapa's *Cassava Song and Rice Song* reveals a similar process. Here, Nwapa's little-known poetry is regarded as a 'gender-oriented counter-rhetoric', which reconstructs the culturally derogated and feminized food-crop, cassava. By investing cassava with a positive significance, Nwapa transforms the

Igbo semiotic system so that women's roles are celebrated and endorsed. 'When the critical lens is shifted and focused on West African women writers,' he argues, adjustments to western feminist theories are required, particularly in relation to the African writers' sense of a specific, non-universal standpoint. Thoroughly located, 'they resist accusations of cultural fraudulence by always situating their rewritings in recognizable African environments'.

Several researchers examine gender debates as they occur within primary material. In her discussion of Zaynab Alkali and Hauwa Ali, Margaret Hauwa Kassam moves respectfully and non-intrusively 'behind the veil' in northern Nigeria to explore a female creativity that is both unharnessed and freedom-loving, both romantic and protesting against discrimination. Both Alkali and Ali share a preoccupation with education, connecting their heroines' attainment of sexual equality, social status and economic freedom with their attainment of educational qualifications. Kassam explores the importance of post-secondary education for women, and her chapter also includes an extensive list of books written by northern Nigerian women.

Adopting an overtly polemical tone, Ibiyemi Mojola utilizes Mariama Bâ's and Zaynab Alkali's novels to emphasize and condemn the impact of polygyny on Islamic women in West Africa. Maintaining the polemical stance, Chioma Opara studies the rebellious, conflictual behaviour of Ama Ata Aidoo's heroines, and demonstrates how alternative female behavioural models are in the process of emerging.

The final section of the book focuses on representations of West African women in popular art forms. Sani Abba Aliyu traces the positive impact of mass communications on uneducated female narrators in northern Nigeria. Transistor radios have altered, but not disempowered, these traditional storytellers. Focusing on Hausa women's historical position as popular oral storytellers, he describes how, in transferring the female voice from the hearth to the air-waves, the potential has been created for secluded Islamic women to become public and vocal without being seen. Thus, if there ever was a 'golden age' of female storytelling, it has been updated and preserved.

In her second chapter, Chinyere Grace Okafor analyses the gender politics of African mask theatres and locates a defensive masculinity in male masking cults. She finds that social power is constructed as masculine by the closed group: it is affirmed during energetic performances to female spectators in which passive, submissive 'feminine' traits are defined. Defensive and deeply insecure, the masking group aims to uphold a sexual status quo by denying all but a select few women's roles. A similar process of exclusion is located by Stephanie Newell in her study of the 'anatomy of masculine power' in the work of three locally published Nigerian theorists. Centring her discussion round Chinweizu's ardent anti-marriage tract *Anatomy of Female Power*, the contradictions and anxieties of contemporary, urban masculinities are revealed, as are the difficulties of formulating a feminist politics. Male writers' and creative artists' repeated, anxious attempts to contain femininity in certain stereotypes is shown to be unsustainable by all of these researchers, however, as texts break down repeatedly from within. If masking cults are dominated by men, Adepeju Layiwola discusses the impact made by women metal-workers upon what had, until their recent entrance, been another male-dominated sphere. Contemporary women metal-workers 'engage fully in the art' she writes, and 'propagate feminist perspectives through their works, casting female figures which are loaded with responses to entrenched patriarchal attitudes in Nigeria'. The craftswomen portray intimate scenes from the separate, neglected sphere of pregnancy and motherhood, casting subversive statements about women's identities into the very forms of their sculptures. Layiwola emphasizes, however, that the lack of a theoretical vocabulary to describe these women's artistic production inhibits discussions of their work and perpetuates a silencing of women's creativity.

Writing for the Nigerian *Daily Times* in 1984, Isoken Sekoni confronted the archives of restrictive popular stereotypes surrounding and constructing women in West Africa. She stated that women 'have been so brainwashed and intimidated that they no longer believe in themselves', having internalized the worst male-supremacist stereotypes. She continued with an urgent appeal to women across Africa: 'Do not let yourself be made a property, a personal possession to be used, exploited and then probably disposed of at will. Step clean out of the ugly, unbefitting and intimidating clothes our ancient colleagues could not refuse wearing' (Sekoni 1984).

Women are rewritten constantly in the popular media, often appearing in negative and stereotyped forms: Mother Africa and her domesticated counterpart the 'good wife' feature as recurrent reference points in films and texts, frequently invoked to signify national and continental regeneration and man's connection to precolonial rural traditions. The youthful 'good-time girl' is also a regular symbol in West African television series and popular texts; as Florence Stratton demonstrated in her analysis of male-authored African literatures, the sexually alluring 'good-time girl' is counterpoised with the mythical mother figure and condemned for her moral corruption (Stratton 1994: 49–52).

Critics have argued that these constructs ensure the stability of a 'masculinist' nationalism which actively excludes women writers from literary spaces and political discourses.[4] Women's texts, on the other hand, are seen to rewrite the female types according to a matrifocal principle. While such formulations occasionally offer a rather rigid, separatist vision of women's writing, a positive and productive critical perspective can be derived from their emphasis on the impact of African women's writing at the level of ideology. West African women's writing tends to focus on specific societies' treatment of the female body. In so doing, women writers might be seen to humanize the female archetypes that signify men's nations, and replace the static Mother Africa symbol with kinetic images of women. As the essays here make clear, African mothers or 'good-time girls' are portrayed in confrontation or arbitration with the gender identities created for them in particular communities. Protagonists' aspirations, and particularly their economic opportunities, are shown to be influenced by the gender rules and expectations of their communities. Elleke Boehmer has emphasized elsewhere that the idealized African Woman of male-authored fiction is removed from her metaphorical role within the dominant nationalist tradition and is pluralized by women writers (Boehmer 1991: 7–11). Authors such as Flora Nwapa expose 'the muddy, grainy underside of nationalism's privileged icon[s]', inserting themselves into history as active, creative subjects (Boehmer 1991: 19).

The researchers in this volume broadly agree that West African women writers challenge, fracture and rewrite the stereotypes and myths that have surrounded and defined them. In this inclusive gesture, the possibility of collective political action is retained, while the multiplicity of female subject positions is preserved. West African women can be seen to share concerns as a strategic community. They do not, however, speak with one voice. This collection of essays demonstrates the variety, bringing together male and female researchers, all of whom are using

West African primary material to explore, to intervene, to write and rewrite the gender theories they encounter.

Notes

1. For general information on publishing in Africa and details of how indigenous publishing is being strengthened, see Altbach (ed.) (1993). The Bellagio Publishing Network Secretariat is located at CODE-Europe, The Jam Factory, 27 Park End Street, Oxford OX1 1HU.

2. Sadly, Dr Ogunjimi died in November 1995 and was unable to make final corrections to his chapter. We include his work both for its own merit and in honour of his memory.

3. For a key text in this ongoing debate about precolonial women's political and economic roles and power bases, see Amadiume (1987). See also WIN (1985) and Oppong (ed.) (1983).

4. See Boehmer (1991); Stratton (1994); Boyce Davies and Adams Graves (eds) (1986).

References

Altbach, P. G. (ed.) (1993) *Readings on Publishing in Africa and the Third World*, Bellagio Publishing Network, New York.

Amadiume, I. (1987) *Male Daughters, Female Husbands: Gender and Sex in an African Society*, Zed Books, London.

Boehmer, E. (1991) 'Stories of Women and Mothers: Gender and Nationalism in the Early Fiction of Flora Nwapa', in Nasta (ed.), *Motherlands*, 3–23.

Boyce Davies, C. and Adams Graves, A. (eds) (1986) *Ngambika: Studies of Women in African Literature*, Africa World Press, Trenton, NJ.

Mohanty, C. T. (1988) 'Under Western Eyes: Feminist Scholarship and Colonial Discourses', *Feminist Review*, Autumn, 65–88.

Nasta, S. (ed.) (1991) 'Introduction', *Motherlands: Black Women's Writing from Africa, the Caribbean and South Asia*, Women's Press, London, xiii–xxx.

Oppong, C. (ed.) (1983) *Female and Male in West Africa*, Unwin, London.

Sekoni, I. (1984) *Daily Times*, Nigeria, 10 August, 18–19.

Stratton, F. (1994) *Contemporary African Literature and the Politics of Gender*, Routledge, London.

WIN (1985) *The WIN Document: Conditions of Women in Nigeria and Policy Recommendations to 2000 AD*, Women in Nigeria, Zaria, Nigeria.

PART I
Theory and Politics

1
Reading towards a theorization of African women's writing: African women writers within feminist gynocriticism

NANA WILSON-TAGOE

The writing of African women has frequently been read within a representational problematic in which the text becomes merely the image of a given reality. In such a context critical evaluation remains trapped in surface descriptions and analyses which tend to elicit only the normative knowledge of the writing.

A reading of African women's writing within a feminist framework can bring new energy and vitality to this writing and actually inspire a theorization within its own specific context and within the larger context of feminist writing. For what a feminist framework does is to introduce gender as a fundamental category in literary analysis, enabling the critic to see representations in texts as mediated by sexual difference and the aesthetic and political assumptions that surround gender. At one level it permits us to contest and revise misconceptions and narrow representations that trap women within a male literary discourse; at another more liberating level it contextualizes women's creative production within a sphere of difference, of a female experience and perception that asks different questions and draws various significances from a woman writer's texts. By concentrating on the particular styles, themes and structures of women's writing, this aspect of feminist criticism, termed gynocritics, moves beyond revisionist interpretations towards a sustained investigation of women's literary production. The focus on female literary difference can provide only a general theoretical framework, however, since the inscription of a woman's sphere and the meaning of female difference may deviate from culture to culture. Thus, although gynocritics identifies four models of difference – biological, linguistic, psychoanalytical and cultural – the emphasis placed on each model may depend on feminine priorities within cultures.

French feminist criticism may, for instance, emphasize '*écriture féminine*, the inscription of the female body and female difference in language and text'; but African feminist critics, while acknowledging biology as a sphere of difference, recognize the possible limitations and stereotyping that it can generate in an African context (Ogundipe-Leslie 1987: 5). French and American feminist critics may assert women's difference within a framework of sexual politics, while African feminists would argue that power relations between African men and women should be reconsidered in the context of an African world made vulnerable by the 'great cataclysmic faults of the ages' (Aidoo 1977: 118).

This chapter works within the framework of gynocritics, especially the 'women's culture' model, which has the capacity to break a monolithic concept of feminism by presenting women's writing as different from the point of view of gender and specific cultural contexts:

> The ways in which women conceptualize their bodies and their sexual and reproductive functions are intricately linked to their cultural environments. The female psyche can be studied as the product or construction of cultural forces. Language, too, comes back into the picture, as we consider the social dimensions and determinants of language use, the shaping of linguistic behaviour and cultural ideals (Showalter 1988: 345).

The women's culture model moves beyond the kind of feminist emphasis that polarizes male and female writing in sexual politics. By presenting a wider framework within which a woman's writing can be defined in terms of cultural contexts and priorities, it acknowledges the variables of nationality, race, ethnicity, history and class as literary determinants which are as significant as gender in a woman's writing. Such a model inevitably invites perspectives on history, anthropology and sociology within the wider sphere of female cultural experience and difference, and generates several other questions. What, for instance, is the relationship between gender and history? How are representations of the same historical experience mediated by gender or class? How are ideas of manhood and womanhood destabilized within a changing world? How do men and women reconstitute new identities in a post-colonial era? How do men and women relate to the same cultural myths? These are all interrogations which, when satisfactorily pursued, should not only revise our notions of artistic representation, but also inspire a rethinking of the conceptual ground of African literary theory and its assumptions about writing and reading. They are questions that would undermine our view of the African literary tradition and force a reconception of its central canon.

The other advantage of such a model is that it does not remove a female sphere from the general culture shared by men, but presents a woman-centred world within the wider political, economic and cultural world, contextualizing it within two traditions at the same time. It is such a sphere that becomes the site of criticism and theory, unearthing the full implications of female consciousness and giving it vitality and voice.

It is only within such a framework that the complex motivations and impulses around the category of gender may be fruitfully engaged in the analysis of a woman writer's works. Such a framework would definitely move us beyond what Katherine Frank sees as the single-minded sexual politics of African women's writing which, 'embraces the solutions of a world without men [since ...] man is the enemy, the exploiter and oppressor' (Frank 1987: 15). Frank's view of the woman writer's outright repudiation of men is only the polemical aspect of a writing which in practice intersects with several other needs and contexts, with the more intimate realities of women as women and with the larger historical facts of existence in a world mediated by other worlds. Ogundipe-Leslie clarifies these other dimensions in her seminal paper on the female writer and her commitment: 'Being aware of oneself as a Third World person implies being politically conscious, offering readers perspectives on and perceptions of colonialism and neo-colonialism as they affect and shape our lives and historical destinies' (Ogundipe-Leslie 1987: 11). Valerie Smith, writing in the context of African–American women's theory, suggests a reading method that would 'hold all these intersecting aspects in a woman's work in mutually interrogative ... relation' (Smith 1989: 48).

Within the framework of such a model, a reading strategy can be formulated to enable us to move beyond the normative knowledge of the woman's text, towards identifying structures and significations and their social import. The reading strategy I have adopted suggests that critical reading can actually construct new meanings from a text by distancing itself from its assumed coherence and discovering the process of its production; it can create meanings from the contradictions which, perhaps unknown to the author, the text continually reveals. This strategy is also based on certain assumptions I have made about the writing of African women: namely, that it is marked by gender perspectives that are mediated by history, culture and class; that it operates within a male discourse and is in constant interaction and dialogue with it through its double-edged perspectives and its revisionist and other interrogations; that women writers themselves engage in dialogue with each other's writing as a way of linking to or differentiating themselves from a continuum of women's writing in a continuously changing female discourse.

The first observation that surfaces in an analysis of African women's writing relates to the writer's reconstruction of the wider society and her exploration of women's lives and experiences within it. Here, the first departure from male traditions of inscription and representation occurs, through the very centrality given to women as characters, the reflection of their sensibilities, the opening up of their consciousness, in effect, the privileging of the female voice and world. Mari McCarty has argued that in voluntarily entering this sphere of female experience, a woman writer can write her way out of the cramped confines of patriarchal space (McCarty 1981: 368); it can be argued that Grace Ogot and Flora Nwapa, very early African women writers, began a tradition of appropriating and valorizing female experience and in the process managed to subvert certain fixed definitions of the female subject.

While in earlier reconstructions of colonial society in the works of male writers, women characters often appeared fixed in roles that remained unproblematized, the works of the early women writers countered fixed images of women through narrative strategies in which their women characters appeared in shifting and seemingly contradicting poses, giving the writers leeway to present them as complex and subtle. Grace Ogot's protagonist in *The Promised Land* (1966) is in one respect a traditional wife, and in another an alert observer and critic both of her husband and of her society. The motif of migration and the juxtaposed perceptions of husband and wife present a framework for Ogot's revisionist subversions of women's defined roles in patriarchal society. In the novel's reconstruction of the colonial world of the 1930s the subject of migration is still traumatic enough to present Ogot with a context for moral and cultural delineations of character. The two perspectives on the subject revealed by both husband and wife may appear to be the dominant conflict of the novel, but there is a sub-text located in the inner thoughts of Ogot's female protagonist. In contemplating her opposition to migration and her impotence in preventing an action that may yet change her life, Ogot's female subject recognizes that the claims of marriage as defined by her community are themselves forms of displacement and imprisonment and an abnegation of choice and will. Such an interrogative perspective may appear contradictory in a character who also appears, on the face of it, to embrace her community and all it stands for.

Flora Nwapa's woman-centred world presents similar juxtapositions of perspectives and perceptions. What such shifting representations do is to counter a fixed and static definition of woman and invite a more problematic awareness of women as individual characters. Indeed, the entire construction of *Efuru* (1966) embodies certain deliberate strategies for unearthing and privileging women's submerged worlds and consciousness. Though the novel appears to unroll in a loose cinematic and unstructured way, it embodies a deliberate strategy to enact the pattern of interactions and relationships which represent the world in which the protagonist defines herself. Thus, if the deliberate realism represents the slow-paced rhythm of life in the protagonist's woman-centred community, it also enacts the flow of feeling from woman to woman, demonstrating what Nwapa sees as a major characteristic of women and the source of bonding and sisterhood between them.

To represent reality in such starkly realistic terms as enactments of interactions may appear to affirm the authority of the community and to hold no paradoxes for either the author or the reader. Yet, *Efuru* is a subversive novel which speaks on the surface of women's powerlessness yet celebrates their power. The women characters themselves continually verbalize their insignificance and impotence in the world of men. Yet the novel itself demonstrates the varied strengths and competence of women. Nwapa's rhetoric of realism therefore conceals certain ironies and is a strategy of narration which presents women in shifting, changeable positions as a way of countering their static definitions in patriarchal society. As a character, Efuru herself embodies some of these shifting and apparently contradictory representations. For she is both within and outside the norms and prescriptions of her patriarchal world, and her reactions to some of its requirements often shift in relation to a pragmatic sense of her own needs as a person and a woman.

Thus, at one point Efuru might disobey tradition, showing an independent will and a personal ethic, while at other times she might embrace traditions and values within the community's definition of women's roles. For instance, her disappointment and internalization of what the community defines as womanly failures may appear to be a total acceptance of the community's values and prescriptions. In line with Nwapa's strategies of narration, however, Efuru does make a second choice when she commits herself to the worship of the water deity. It is a choice that may appear to remain inscribed within the tradition, but it is not totally within it. For the deity is presented as embodying a contradictory element in the community's traditional values: on the one hand, she is goddess and therefore of the community; yet, on the other hand, she does not embody the community's most cherished values of fertility and motherhood, choosing the best and the most unsullied of the community's women as worshippers. The fact that she appears to Efuru in a dream, that she is linked to her in an unconscious, spiritual and metaphysical sense, exposes this contradictory element and brings into focus other choices for women within the traditional community. Does the relationship then create an alternative or additional definition of womanhood, something spiritual and creative within the community, yet apart from it in its particular vision? A reading that relates this choice to the various implications of the deity may throw out several illuminations since Nwapa herself is ambiguous about the goddess's implications as a symbol. Although Maggie Phillips (1994) has seen the deity rightly as embodying a possible contradiction between wealth and fertility, her symbolic ambiguity is such that she could well represent an equally viable and creative alternative to the 'joys of motherhood'.

It is this manipulation of the imponderable forces represented by the supernatural which provides Nwapa with both a context and a narrative with which to write a woman's text from outside the confines of patriarchal prescription. Her representation inscribes a different texture of imagination, voice and style from a contemporary male writer such as Elechi Amadi who has treated a similar context and theme in a strikingly different way. Amadi's *The Concubine* (1966), like Nwapa's *Efuru*, explores the tenuous often inexplicable relationship between men and gods in traditional Igbo society, but presents this relationship almost as something given: in Amadi's world men may expiate, appease and somehow get around the vengeance and capriciousness of gods but may never wrestle with them and win. The fate of individuals caught up in such tragic meshes may arouse pity and fear but is finally no more than what is given. Ihuoma's curiosity about the material world is answered in her earthly incarnation as a mortal woman. Yet she is punished by a jealous supernatural husband. The powerful sea god denies her matrimonial bliss on earth, thus limiting fulfilment of the very qualities that idealize her as a desirable woman and wife (Amadi 1966: 195). Ihuoma's story may be made poignant but it remains unproblematized. There is none of *Efuru*'s urgency to create a different climate of imagination, a different narrative or language which would expose and challenge the patriarchal assumptions that underlie her spiritual and material bondage to the male sea god.

It is in this context of rearranging and rewriting a given reality that African women writers search for new voices, narratives and languages to structure the problematic nature of female experience in a changing African world. Their writing can be seen, then, as a constantly shifting discourse in which writers continually enter into dialogue with each other's writing within a continuum.

It is significant that in her interrogation of Nwapa's perspectives in her novel *The Joys of Motherhood* (1980), Buchi Emecheta should transform the symbolic implications of the sea goddess and do away with the veiled understatements and ambiguities that surround her figure in Nwapa's novel. In *The Joys of Motherhood* the connection between goddess and human worshipper is put to a more powerful and assertive use. The slave woman linked to the goddess destabilizes not only traditional assumptions about fecundity and motherhood, but also old notions of slavery and elitism in a changing world. The slave woman buried alive with her mistress returns to earth to become the 'chi' of Nnu Ego, the privileged daughter of a nobleman. Yet the correlation of slave girl (worshipper of the sea goddess Uhamiri) and Nnu Ego signifies so much in Emecheta's novel that the symbolic import of Uhamiri is rendered much more elaborate and complex. The slave girl/Uhamiri returns as Nnu Ego's 'chi' supposedly out of gratitude to her father for his 'kindness' and sympathy during her ordeal. But the gratitude she offers is more a chastisement, a moral enlightenment and a lesson in social vision.

The symbolism invites several undisguised implications: first, the sea goddess, Uhamiri, is in Emecheta's novel linked not to a wealthy and prosperous woman but to a slave woman at the very bottom of the social ladder. Her lowly status rubs on the privileged status of Nnu Ego's father, pricking a conscience that pushes him to free his slaves as he sacrifices continually to appease the spirit of the slave woman on behalf of his daughter. Secondly, her refusal to give Nnu Ego children and her decision later to saddle her with a succession of children enables Emecheta to create situations that open up several dimensions of the woman's problematic position in traditional society and in a world changed by colonialism.

The world of women, often treated in male fiction merely as a given reality, thus becomes the site of some of Emecheta's most biting and devastating ironies. Whether as a woman without children or as a woman with children, Nnu Ego comes face to face with the constrictions and degradations that plague women in both worlds. As a woman without a child, she is a failed woman, a non-being. Yet 'blessed' with children in the cramped city conditions of colonial Lagos, she is a harassed and enslaved woman whose energies and personality are consumed by perpetually being tied to her children's needs. In both cases the novel's ironies multiply. At one level they are directed against the insensitivity of a patriarchal world that measures a woman's worth merely by her fertility. At another level the community's own expectation about the so-called 'joys of motherhood' are ironically flayed and given a more realistic qualification in the sensitively explored vicissitudes of Nnu Ego as a mother. Maggie Phillips is therefore correct when she argues that Nnu Ego not only 'displays an obstinate dignity and an ever increasing ability to understand the pressures and the small measure of joy incurred in her imprisonment to her children but also learns to appreciate the moral rather than the monetary rewards of her children's advancement' (Phillips 1994: 93).

At yet another crucial level, however, the novel's ironies are directed towards Nnu Ego herself for so internalizing the values that had condemned her as to continue to judge manhood and womanhood in a changed world by the standards of the rural world. Even in the midst of what she can recognize as a disintegrating 'old' world in which old ideas about 'manhood', 'womanhood' and 'senior wife' status are being continually reinterpreted in the lived experiences of men and women, Nnu Ego can still visualize manhood merely in terms of the old rural standards. The ironies against her raise larger issues which in the end remain side-tracked and unexplored because of the often revisionist and polemical thrust of Emecheta's delineations. The larger social issues are suggested in the very context of her delineations. The novel's span from 1900 to the 1930s is not just an indication of a specific linear time but also of the social changes it takes in, particularly the changes generated by a colonial presence and its effect on old ideas about manhood, womanhood and relationships between men and women.

Within this framework certain questions suggest themselves: what are the power relations between men and women in a context in which men themselves have lost their power to new masters? How does manhood disintegrate within such a context? How do men and women reconstitute new roles and redefine old concepts of manhood and womanhood? These seem to be the larger questions suggested by the totality of the world Emecheta evokes. Yet the polemical thrust and the relentless flaying of old attitudes are so dominant in the novel that they tend to limit further delineations of these issues. For instance, Nnu Ego is a character of limited perception who has internalized most of the Igbo values about manhood and womanhood and is therefore, in spite of her author's partiality to her point of view, an object of irony. Her ideas of manhood and masculinity take their cue from her knowledge of the men in her rural village whom she continually contrasts with the urban men in Lagos. These men, 'servants' and 'slaves' of white men and women, are no longer men in Nnu Ego's view, and the Igbo woman in urban Lagos is therefore the slave of a slave.

These may be excellent perceptions, but the basis of the comparison is faulty: for the rural world whose men Nnu Ego idealizes, in contrast to the urban men, has itself been exposed as merciless on barren women and insensitive to their feelings. Are Nnu Ego's perceptions then still part of the author's ironic onslaught on her? Can such large questions and delineations about the disintegration of 'manhood' and the redefinition of gender relations be fruitfully explored through a character who is herself an object of irony? Indeed, the author's partiality to her point of view contradicts the ironic thrust of the text itself, creating tensions between the polemic of sexual politics and the intersecting issues of social formation in a changing world. Even within the scope and excellent delineations presented by *The Joys of Motherhood* we are still at a revisionist stage of African women's writing where the 'woman's sphere' becomes an almost exclusive zone of revision, rewriting and definition.

Women's writing is not outside a dominant male zone. It is inside two traditions simultaneously, and the female territory, as Myra Jehlen (1981) has suggested, 'might well be envisioned as one long border, and independence for women not as a separate country but as open access to the sea' (Jehlen 1981: 592). Thus the truly tough aesthetic of women's writing, especially in those regions beset by legacies of colonization, is an aesthetic which interrogates the totality of the society and claims it as a context for the redefinition of women.

In this sense Mariama Bâ's *So Long a Letter* (1980) may be viewed with Emecheta's *The Joys of Motherhood* as a novel in which the woman's sphere intersects with a larger transitional world within which women grope towards new definitions and roles. Katherine Frank has seen Ramatoulaye's letter as a kind of internal monologue charting the painful process of her liberation from the imposition of tradition and religion towards the kind of self embodied by her friend Aïssatou (Frank 1987: 18). But the process Frank talks of cannot be a liberation from tradition when the letter begins (almost after the events of the story) with Ramatoulaye solidly involved in custom and ritual, and when her own letter is contextualized in a 'mirass', the religious ritual that strips a dead man of his most intimate secrets. The novel is, to my mind, a much more interrogating presentation of the dilemmas, contradictions and compromises of women's redefinition in a changing world. Its recapitulations of the past represent not only a stripping of the inner confusion of Modou Fall but also the entire era of social transition which had promised redefinitions of relationships between men and women in a 'new' world. The epistolary form allows us to witness Ramatoulaye's rearranging and reshaping of the experiences so that what she emphasizes, deflates or conceals sheds light on her own attitudes and contradictions. The text thus works on two subtle levels of irony: Ramatoulaye strips Modou Fall and his world bare of their intimate secrets, and the textual organization of her own letters strips her bare, showing similar confusions and compromises.

Commentators have often interpreted the novel within a representational problematic which misses several textual ironies. Bâ's decision to privilege Ramatoulaye's story, and distance Aïssatou's story, gives us the chance not only to evaluate two different choices but also to assess the protagonist's own reactions to these. If in Ramatoulaye's presentation, Aïssatou's story appears similar to her own, it is because of the muted silences with which Ramatoulaye presents it. For though on the face of it the two women both appear to have reacted against the idea of polygyny, there is a slant to the Aïssatou story, a bias of caste and class which remains muted throughout the narrative.

Aïssatou reacts not only against a betrayal of faith and the idea of polygyny but also against the degradation and oppression of class and caste. Her letter to Mawdo highlights this fact as the first of her grievances: 'Others bend their heads and in silence, accept a destiny that oppresses them. That, briefly put, is the internal ordering of our society with its absurd divisions' (Bâ 1980: 31). Although this is a clear reference to the class divide that propels the plot against Aïssatou's 'low' blood, it is revealingly eliminated in Ramatoulaye's appraisal of the Aïssatou story later on in the text: 'I was irritated. He was asking me to understand. But to understand what? The supremacy of instinct? The right to betray? The justification of the desire to variety?' (p. 34). The subtle silence about class and caste is the text's way of signalling Ramatoulaye's own evasions and her unwillingness to confront fully the spectre of class as an aspect in the redefinition of women in a changing world.

It is not only in such silences that Ramatoulaye's text deflates the impact of class and caste. The deflation is present even in the way it disperses its sympathies within the presentations; in the way it continues to tolerate Aunty Nabu's obsessions about 'blood' as if these were benign foibles, and as if the break-up of Aïssatou's marriage was the result only of polygyny and not of caste.

Although, on the face of it, Ramatoulaye represents the two relationships within the context of nationalist thinking in francophone Africa and the new social ordering it claimed to have envisioned, her muted attitudes to the implications of class, indeed the entire distancing of the ramifications of the Aïssatou story, reveal her unwillingness to confront the social world in its totality. The entire ideological base from which she makes the correlation between the new social force and the new envisaged relationships between men and women is undermined later on in the novel when she herself faces a crisis of betrayal in her husband's rejection of her. Ramatoulaye's responses to this rejection take their cue not from the ideological commitment that had inspired her relationship, but from values outside this commitment. She sees herself suddenly as a woman without a man, and she reasons that happiness and fulfilment are impossible for such a woman (Bâ 1980:

40). Regarding her ageing body with disappointment she begins now to envision marriage in purely physical terms, showing virtually no awareness of that radical ideological commitment which she had elaborated earlier on as the inspiration of intimate relationships between men and women in a 'new' world. And since these silences and inconsistencies are laid bare in Ramatoulaye's own text, we can assume that they are the novelist's ironic pointers to the confusing state of women's definition and to the woman writer's need to interrogate gender, class and society in her interpretation and redefinition of women in a changing world.

Ramatoulaye does achieve some measure of 'liberation', however. After thirty years of silence she can challenge tradition in her own way. She can assert her individuality and personal choices as she does when she offers Daouda Dieng friendship instead of partnership in marriage, thus defining other areas in which men and women can relate fruitfully outside marriage. She retrieves the voice that has been buried under a veneer of custom and accepts the challenges of a single life within a visibly patriarchal world. These expansions enable her to deal with new situations and particularly to appreciate the merits of a female bonding which demonstrates sharing and caring without the sexual politics that surround gender relations in the custom-bound area of marriage. Yet this measure of liberation is still contained within silences, evasions and contradictions which denote Ramatoulaye's uncertain relations to the wider world and her unwillingness (or shyness) to confront it in its totality.

The value of Bâ's novel is this measure of struggle, however faltering, which lays bare the uncertainties and confusions of the woman's attempt to redefine herself within the wider world. The ironies directed at Ramatoulaye reveal what is to be desired and what could have been gained, and it is in this sense that Bâ moves the African woman's redefinition beyond sexual politics.

The suggestions that are implied indirectly in Bâ's ironic presentation of Ramatoulaye's text are explicitly woven into the writing of Ama Ata Aidoo, where the woman writer's creative difference reveals itself in texts in which gender intersects with several aspects of the larger world, and the redefinition of woman becomes part of a general redefinition of men and society. Like all the other women writers discussed, Aidoo's works privilege a woman's sphere of experience instead of representing it as something given. Aidoo's privileging process extends beyond revision and polemic to encompass the domain not only of men but of the entire social world. Her play *Anowa* (1965) is in this sense not about the modern woman, individualistic and rebellious (as commentators have surmised), but about a woman whose understanding of self and redefinition of a woman's place includes a larger redefinition of man and the community. Her construction of a parallel story to the familiar tale of the rebellious daughter who rejects all marriage offers, is therefore a subtle deconstruction and enlargement of the moralistic and punitive traditional tale. By linking Anowa with a priestly potentiality and giving her a prophetic vision[1] Aidoo reverses the traditional tale, making rebellion a projection of possibilities in the relationship between men and women in the community of the play. Certainly, the kind of marriage Anowa envisages in which a man and a woman would share work, share life, share ideas and history, is in contradistinction to the existing reality where 'in order for her man to be a man [a woman] must not think or talk' (Aidoo 1980: 41).

The conflict between husband and wife is similarly extended beyond gender confrontation into a large political and moral issue, as a way of suggesting the intersection between them and of transcending a merely revisionist delineation. The argument over the enslavement of others, which is the source of the confrontation, becomes then the larger sociopolitical base from which Aidoo argues the definition of women in the nineteenth-century Ghanaian community. Her view of slavery as an aberration against life connects the self-annihilation and dismemberment involved in enslavement with the barrenness of her marriage. Her thoughts bring to the fore a childhood dream portending the Atlantic slave trade and the large-scale disintegration and dismemberment it occasioned (Aidoo 1980: 46–7). Indeed, the dream casts her almost synonymously with the land itself as the symbolic victim of the perverted births and the dismemberment (p. 46). At this point, Anowa's consciousness and fate become not the consciousness and fate of an individual woman, but the discerning insight of a priestess whose prophetic vision of a coming disorder can be glimpsed in the circumstances of her own life. Gender relations then intersect with politics and morality, so that even her husband's loss of manhood, which precipitates the disintegration of their marriage, becomes a moral and political issue linked in no small way to the major disequilibrium that Anowa predicts for her community. Anowa's own madness and suicide can then also be explained in terms of the multiple forces at work in Aidoo's delineations. The madness and suicide which seem, on the face of it, to be precipitated by the suggestion of her husband's loss of manhood have larger connotations in the political and moral issues associated with manhood itself; issues that combine marriage, politics, history, culture and morality in a broad redefinition of relations between men and women in Africa.

Aidoo's first novel, *Our Sister Killjoy* (1977), extends the politics of gender relations in even more complex and subtle ways. Here, relations between men and women are not only mediated by history, culture and morality but are also presented in a wider context so that the redefinition of woman becomes simultaneously a redefinition of man. By placing love and sexual relations solidly within the domain of politics, Aidoo widens the woman's sphere and makes it the site of interrogation and debate. Love, she insists, cannot be meaningful for an African man or woman unless it can also acknowledge and contend with that monumental power and lure of Europe, which continually threaten the very survival of African identity (Aidoo 1977: 114).

The premise from which Aidoo writes has several implications for her exploration of gender relations in the novel. First, it necessitates a reconsideration of the power relations between the African man and woman in a world made vulnerable by the 'great cataclysmic faults of the ages' (Aidoo 1977: 118). Here, the imperatives of intangible realities, the need to live life relevantly, to maintain a sense of wholeness and to keep a grip on a sense of community and value render the defined power relations between men and women almost irrelevant in Aidoo's world. Indeed, the novel challenges that very conception of womanliness which posits a woman as a docile and meek other. It is not only in Sissie's words that the challenge is forcefully presented; the very structure of the novel defies this conception by celebrating the powerful presence of a woman's dynamic consciousness as it manifests itself in artistic representation. For *Our Sister Killjoy* is a novel within a novel which invites us to witness the art of creation and the processes of the artistic imagination as a way of convincing us to accept the novelist's *raison d'être*, which is that maleness and femaleness in an African context must be defined in relation to time and history; that even in the old world a woman's situation was much more complicated than it is made to be in the context of the present.

Sissie's plea for a shared life, shared history, shared fears and fantasies with the African male is thus strongly validated in the very perceptive understanding of Africa's place in history, demonstrated in the earlier sections of the novel. Indeed, in some sense, *Our Sister Killjoy* can be seen as Sissie's 'novel'. For it presents her delineation of the 'bad dream' of Africa's contact with the Western world, an adventure which, as she argues, has left the African dazed, lost and denuded of his sense of self (Aidoo 1977: 88–9). Writing is, after all, at some basic level, an attempt to connect the reality of our lives with the kinds of reflections we make on it, and Sissie's novel is structured to make precisely this connection. Its narrative enacts two levels of representation: the surface reality narrated by Sissie, and the insights into its historical referents and deeper undercurrents contained in her subconscious reflections. Thus, whether the narrative is the story of a moderate regurgitating his master's words, or of Sissie basking in plenitude at a German castle, or of deluded Indian and African migrants in Europe, the underlying insights bring us face to face with the fundamental historical facts of a crippling colonial heritage.

It is within such a context that Sissie envisages the possibilities of male–female relationships in a postcolonial Africa. As she sees it, such a relationship would have to encompass not just the surface bonding implied by the idea of love, but also be able to create a language that will overcome destructive history and move through time, savouring what is valuable in the old world, a language, free and independent but also secret and impenetrable enough to sidetrack the power and lure of Europe. In *Our Sister Killjoy*, it is this imperative that comes between Sissie and her lover. It is a political and ideological barrier which by implication reflects a colonial conception of a woman as incapable of political expression and conviction. Sissie's 'unwise' and 'unwomanly' decision to continue to hold opinions and political convictions and to accept her lover's abandonment of her, rather than compromise the nature and quality of what she defines as love (Aidoo 1977: 127, 133), presents a bolder, more courageous response to conflict than the choice made by Anowa whose suicide in Aidoo's play appears contrived and anti-climactic.

A near-parallel representation is Sissie's story of Marija's lonely married life, which represents a contrasting evocation of male–female relationships in a context where the barrier against fulfilment is not a colonial heritage that shackles thought and destroys meaningful communication, but a new materialism. Sissie sees this sickness of the soul spread against 'the background of the thick smoke that was like a rain cloud over the chimneys of Europe' (Aidoo 1977: 65); it is a malaise which historically threw up the bullying slaver and slave trader, the speculator in gold and diamonds, the swamp-crosser and lion-hunter, even the missionary. Thus, two different texts, two different relationships, nevertheless generate a common loneliness in women, a loneliness which in Marija's case remains 'forever falling like a tear out of a woman's eye' (p. 65), and which in Sissie's case is overcome somewhat by political commitment and a love for the crazy old continent, Africa.

The two stories create a double-edged representation in which the politics of history, race and gender intersect to reveal the very complex ways in which the African woman writer can relate both to a woman's sphere and to the wider world around. In the double vision of Marija as a product of a supremacist and oppressive civilization (Aidoo 1977: 48) and at the same time as a victim of its materialist culture and gender relations, Aidoo's protagonist intuitively grasps an aspect of a general female vulnerability with which she can empathize. Those moments in their relationship when she fantasizes about being male and enjoying a delicious but doomed love affair with Marija are also the moments when she assumes a masculine power over Marija, enacting a fantasy of male domination which she not only censures but links to the dominating thrust of the colonial enterprise (pp. 65-6) and, by implication, to the colonial history that has traumatized her continent. That such an awareness should be subtly woven into a delineation which privileges a political perspective demonstrates how the problematic of gender (usually deflated in male writing) can complicate the political and cultural context of African literature and challenge the purely political agenda of its anti-colonial discourse.

The work of all the women writers explored here strives to destabilize the African woman's fixed position in the larger society by redefining and valorizing a woman's sphere which often appears in male writing as unproblematized, as something merely given. Because these redefinitions are explored from woman-centred perspectives, the woman's text (as Showalter has argued) generates its own experiences and symbols which are not merely the obverse of the male tradition or simply an imitation or revision of the writing of her male predecessors but a multi-dimensional discourse embedded in both female and male traditions. It is imperative, then, that the African woman's text be read not as a polarization of male and female traditions, but as a complex discourse with several intersecting points, criss-crossing and interrogating each other continuously: 'the first task of a gynocentric criticism must be to plot the precise cultural locus of female literary identity and to describe the forces that intersect an individual woman writer's cultural field' (Showalter 1988: 349). This analysis of African women's writing stems from such a premise and from the belief that the theoretical concepts of gynocritics are more meaningful in relation to what women writers actually write.

Note

1. Indeed, the old man whose perspective is frequently upheld in Aidoo's play confirms this possibility in his rhetorical question: 'But certainly, it is not too much to think that the heavens might show something to children of a latter day which was hidden from them of old?' (Aidoo 1965: 41).

References

Aidoo, A. A. (1977) *Our Sister Killjoy or Reflections from a Black Eyed Squint*, Longman, Harlow.

Aidoo, A. A. (1965) *Anowa*, Longman, Harlow.

Amadi, E. (1966) *The Concubine*, Heinemann, London.

Bâ, M. (1980) *So Long a Letter*. Trans. M. Bode-Thomas. Heinemann, London.

Emecheta, B. (1980) *The Joys of Motherhood*, Heinemann, London.

Frank, K. (1987) 'Women Without Men: The Feminist Novel in Africa', in E. Durosimi Jones, E. Palmer and M. Jones (eds), *Women in African Literature Today*, Africa World Press, Trenton, NJ, 14–34.

Jehlen, M. (1981) 'Archimedes and the Paradox of Feminist Criticism', *Signs: Journal of Women in Culture and Society* 6, 575–601.

McCarty, M. (1981) 'Possessing Female Space: The Tender Shoot', *Women's Studies* 8, 367–74.

Nwapa, F. (1966) *Efuru*, Heinemann, London.

Ogot, G. (1966) *The Promised Land*, East African Publishing House, Nairobi.

Ogundipe-Leslie, M. (1987) 'The Female Writer and Her Commitment', in E. Durosimi Jones, E. Palmer and M. Jones (eds), *Women in African Literature Today*, Africa World Press, Trenton, NJ, 5–13.

Phillips, M. (1994) 'Engaging Dreams: Alternative Perspectives on Flora Nwapa,

Buchi Emecheta, Ama Ata Aidoo, Bessie Head and Tsitsi Dangarembga's Writing', *Research in African Literatures* 5 (4), 89-103.

Showalter, E. (1988) 'Feminist Criticism in the Wilderness', in D. Lodge (ed.), *Modern Criticism And Theory*, Longman, Harlow.

Smith, V. (1989) 'Black Feminist Theory and the Representation of the "Other"', in C. A. Wall, (ed.), *Changing Our Own Words*, Rutgers University Press, New Brunswick, 38-57.

2
Masculinity: the military, women and cultural politics in Nigeria

BAYO OGUNJIMI

The current discourse on gender and feminist politics in Nigeria has not articulated coherently the role of the 'barrack culture' in the creation of demeaning images of women. The dominant patriarchal presence of the military, and the masculine society created in its wake, must be central to the discourse. This patriarchy is linked, both directly and indirectly, with the conventional, non-military family setting: the relationships between husband and wife, father and children, mother and children are distorted by the looming image of the authoritarian father, the central personality of Nigerian politics, dominating the mental, social, cultural, political and economic activities of the family.

Modern professions, organized and overseen by a male-dominated state, facilitate the construction of masculinity. Jeff Hearn suggests that the state is the 'most fully developed complex patriarchal and fratriarchal [sic] power within modern societies and nations' (Hearn 1987: 93). He argues further that: 'those parts of the state that are more concerned with repression and violence are more fully male-dominated and male-membered than those parts which are concerned with caring, welfare, and reproduction, which are usually male-dominated and female-membered' (p. 94). As 'the great collective father-figure', Hearn continues, the state takes 'the place of all those absent fathers' (p. 115). He identifies an interface between traditional patriarchy and its semblance in modern political dispensation: 'political performance has been the most obvious way for men to show masculinity and "machismo" ... the father-figure is becoming transubstantiated into the body of the state, the professions and law' (p. 115).

Social and cultural alienation relating to mothering, childcaring and childrearing is engendered by the imposition of the military on the family and the state. The masculinization of the state apparatus, and the violence which is the stock-in-trade of the military machine, cause this alienation. Adrienne Rich discusses the effects of such a patriarchal domination of the female sex when she writes about:

> the efforts of women in labour, giving birth to stillborn children, children who must die of plague or infanticide; the efforts of women to keep filth and decay at bay, children decently clean, to produce the clean shirt in which the man walks out daily into the common world of men, the effort to raise children against the attritions of racist and sexist schooling, drugs, killing, exploitation, and the brutalization and killing of barely grown boys in war (Rich 1980: 206).

In order to address the various issues and crises generated by military patriarchy in Nigeria, two levels of discourse will be employed. First, two Nigerian Civil War texts will be examined to expose the hegemony of the phallus and its destruction of the humanity of women. Flora Nwapa's *Never Again* (1975) and Buchi Emecheta's *Destination Biafra* (1986) are relevant for examining the issues at stake; the second discursive level probes the ideological integrity of elite women's agendas for the cultural, political and economic emancipation of oppressed women in Nigeria, focusing on the Better Life Programme (BLP) for rural women initiated by Maryam Babangida, which has metamorphosed into Maryam Abacha's Family Support Programme (FSP). These two levels are placed in the context of dialectical materialism, which furnishes 'the key to the leaps, to the break in continuity, to the transformation into the opposite, to the destruction of the old and emergence of the new' (Lenin 1961: 359–60).

Though a short novel, Flora Nwapa's *Never Again* exudes a complexity of action and purpose. Apart from being written by a woman, the towering narrative voice of an involved female character is heard throughout the novel. The narrator's experience from the beginning depicts the tension and insecurity imposed by war, a Manichean and masculine institution. The narrator, whom we later recognize as Kate says:

> After fleeing from Enugu, Onitsha, Port Harcourt and Elele, I was thoroughly tired of life. Yet how tenaciously could one hold on to life when death was around the corner! Death was too near for comfort in Biafra. And for us who had known no danger of this land before, it was hell on earth ... It meant to be at war – a civil war at that, a war that was to end all wars. I wanted to tell

them that reading it in books was nothing at all; they just would not understand it (Nwapa 1975: 1).

This looks like the ratiocination of an existentialist, but it is not devoid of optimism and humanism.

The war disrupts the family setting: the endless nights of bombing and shelling cause the psychological breakdown of the family; the budding generation of children undergo the most excruciating experience of the war; and women bear the burden of the violence, aggression and family welfare crises. The narrator is tortured and she envisages the tragedy coming to her children:

> If the war lasted another year, they would begin to suffer, first from hunger, discomfort and then ill health. I was determined not to see my children suffer. I would sell all I had to feed them if I had to. They were not going to be hungry. They would not suffer from kwashiokor ... Kwashiokor was a deadly disease of children, more deadly in Biafra than leprosy (p. 25)

Her husband, Chudi, is concerned about neither her anxiety nor the future of the children, manifesting his oppressive masculinity throughout the novel.

Women are used as cannon-fodder on the battlefront: they also make uniforms, cook for soldiers and give expensive presents to officers, including their daughters, who are asked to sleep with the high-ranking men. More revealing of the war situation is the role some women play in the subjugation of their own sex: one female politician is a hypocritical political propaganda machine for the war, dreaming the masculinization of her self, a process which might be perceived as a mutilation of her sex and independence. The woman politician muses: 'Why am I a woman? God you should have made me a man. I would have said to the youths whose blood I know is boiling now in their veins, following me. I'll lead you. I'll fight the vandals. They will not be allowed to pollute our fatherland' (p. 9). This is a negation of the maternal affection and concern that Kate, the narrator, has for the besieged, budding generation. The woman politician possesses the psychology of a political elite that lacks creative energy and consciousness. (This attitude of elitist women will be shown to dominate in the second level of discourse.)

During evacuation, we note the plight of the children making for Mgbidi, a distance of six miles, in the heat of the sun. The narrator paints a pathetic portrait of the evacuation:

Old and young, men and women and children. Goats and sheep. They were walking, walking out of Ugwuata to an unknown destination ... They wept as they went. Where were they going? None of them knew. They knew only that they were going to a place of safety, away from the rockets, away from guns, away from this madness, this fearful insanity (pp. 55-6).

The tragic scene has been attributed from the opening of the novel to the masculine hegemony of the military and the violation of democratic rights of the citizenry: 'Nothing was private any more. We had lost our freedom and democracy. We lost them the day that the Army took over. January 15 1966, was the day when we lost our hard-earned freedom. There was nothing we could do about it. Everyone distrusted everyone else' (p. 35).

In Buchi Emecheta's *Destination Biafra*, the imperialist machine is shown flexing its muscles, forming a patriarchy that permeates the core and periphery of a war-torn society. Apart from the contribution of colonialism to creating the crises that led to *coups d'état* and military rule, imperialism enhances the 'masculine psychosis' suffered by the warlords of the Nigerian Civil War. The Nigerian situation demonstrates Hearn's position that nationalistic wars take place between 'local patriarchies, and are a means of allocating patriarchal rights' (Hearn 1987). Alan Grey's relationship with Debbie, the protagonist in Emecheta's novel, is based on a sexist and class bias, for she is a member of the *petit bourgeoisie*. Grey is afraid of her intellectual stamina and what he regards as her arrogance and independence, but he needs her for his sexual lust and the execution of his imperialist project. The struggle to control the wealth of the nation by the Nigerian and Biafran warlords, combined with the inherent patriarchal formations of ethnicity, tribe, law and religion create a platform for the denigration of the female sex.

Debbie's decision to join the army provokes all forms of anti-feminist insinuations. But 'she knew it was a masculine preserve and did not underestimate the ridicule her announcement would engender once she dared make it public' (Emecheta 1986: 56). Her mother, Stella Ogendengbe, believing in the traditional role of women, detests her daughter's action. The old woman's vision of women's freedom is not one 'where women smoke and carry guns instead of looking after husbands and nursing babies' (p. 97). Mrs Teteku also endorses the biological role of women as reproductive machines: 'I wish that girl hadn't gone to England to learn all this talk of women behaving like men' (p. 119).

Debbie negates this atavistic and biological notion of womanhood, insisting that the expensive education was not just acquired 'to prepare them for life with the first dull Nigerian man'. She detests marriage as a mere activity for breeding until menopause. Believing that there is enough time for domesticity and motherhood, Debbie's friend Babs emphasizes the urgent patriotic need to take care of their bleeding motherland, insisting on responsibilities outside the domestic family setting.

Patriarchy detests this new dynamic developing in women like Debbie and Babs. As if to demoralize Debbie, Chijoke enumerates the problems of the military profession. According to him, men can handle guns better than women, and there are no quarters for female soldiers. All these are biosocial and ideological indices that Juliet Mitchell says must first be eradicated if the female sex is to be liberated at all (Mitchell 1975).

Debbie is subsequently given an intermediary role to perform, persuading Abosi, the Biafran warlord, to halt his actions: she ponders the sexual insinuations of her delicate mission: 'So now these men thought she could use her sexuality to make Abosi change his stand. She was to use her body, because Saka Momoh did not want to get into a war with the Easterners, because no one knew what such a move would precipitate' (Emecheta 1986: 126). True to her fears, Debbie and other female characters are sexually humiliated in the course of the mission, raped and battered by soldiers. The scene is vivid and violent:

> The pregnant woman now began to wail as she was dragged from the main road to the side bush, pushed mercilessly with the butt of a gun; the woman was falling and getting up again, and calling her husband Dede to help her. Debbie wondered what had happened to the child. She heard the tired, strangled voice of the woman calling out in Ibo, begging for mercy as they took her to a different part of the bush (pp. 133–4).

The reader is overwhelmed by sympathy and horror at the way the pregnant Igbo woman is battered: she is cut open, the unborn baby's head cut off and the older child kicked to death. In this scene of elaborate sadism, Debbie admires the maternal affection of her own mother who can use her 'tongue to move the hardest of men'.

Susan Brownmiller (1975) writes that 'forcible rape is a conscious act of intimidation and the secret of patriarchy. Both the possibility and actuality of rape are the main agents of male domination over women' (cited by Humm 1987: 14). Debbie's independent mind aspires towards autonomy and self-actualization in response to her rape. She becomes even more desperate to forge ahead on her nationalistic mission. Consciously or unconsciously, Emecheta is therefore re-creating a revolutionary dynamic in this image of the female sex.

A feminist quest motif develops around Debbie and the other women in the entourage to Asaba, who are confronted with several instances of sexual abuse by male soldiers. Tortured by experience, Debbie has developed an energetic resilience: and Salihu, an officer who attempts to rape her, is confronted by a new kind of womanhood: 'she was going to face a war, a personal war for her womanhood. As she moved she became aware of herself as a woman, a body, different from the mass of all other passengers in the lorry' (Emecheta 1986: 174).

War is a patriarchal and masculine institution bringing havoc to the family structure, for children are mutilated and youths are conscripted into the army. The responsibilities of childcare and general survival rest with women, who are not recognized. In Emecheta's novel, a chapter entitled 'Women at War' reveals that women have to operate guerrilla tactics in order to survive, forging ahead in despair and uncertainty, moving like nocturnal creatures in the jungle. Hunger, starvation and sexual assault typify their experience. The tragic collapse and death of the child named Biafra exemplifies the perpetual state of fear in which women live during the war period. But more symbolically, the death of the child depicts the success of the patriarchal instinct for empire-building, which has fomented the war.

What Eldridge Cleaver regards as 'Ultrafemininity' (Cleaver 1968: 181), emerges in Nigerian war literature. In the society wedding between Julianah and Chijoke, we see the consolidation of a new breed of elite Nigerian women. Emecheta depicts the same elitist female psychology in the ostentatious wedding between Elizabeth and Saka Momoh. Chijoke and Momoh are both warlords embracing bourgeois positions amidst the holocaust of the war.

This new crop of elite women are not concerned with the hardship of other underprivileged mothers and children. The setting of Momoh's house is contrasted with that of the jungles and battlefields where men, women and children languish in the rage of war. Instead, the novelist shows 'pink' children living in affluence. The most nauseating comments about the war come from Elizabeth, Momoh's wife. Like Lady Macbeth, she lacks 'the milk of human kindness', saying: 'those that will die in Biafra are only babies, Captain. Think of the sixteen and seventeen-year-olds we Nigerian mothers are losing. Anyway, don't you know that those people breed like rats? They will soon be replaced' (Emecheta 1986: 200). Albeit an excessive, stereotypical portrait, this aridity in humanistic and ethical values exposes the African elite's class psychology.

Elizabeth is given special medical attention and publicity by the media during the delivery of her child. This is quite antithetical to the situation where young girls and women give birth in agony in the thick jungle, without even surviving to nurse their babies. It is a moment of euphoria for Momoh because he is to become a general and 'the First Lady was going to have a child on that day as well'. Momoh's moral complacency is revealed: 'The thought that each child who had died in Biafra may have cost its parents that much or even more did not cross Momoh's mind. All he wanted was the safety of his own wife and child' (p. 202). The tragedy of a class that lacks a humanistic moral culture is embodied in the monster produced by Elizabeth after her caesarean section: 'It resembled a giant frog more than any human he had ever seen ... It must be a curse' (p. 203). Such symbols recur throughout the novel.

A causal and dialectical relationship links the patriarchy of the military on the one hand and, on the other hand, a social class of affluent, elitist women. The latter exhibits the class psychology and cultural vocation of what Cleaver regards as the Ultrafeminine:

> To enhance her image and to increase her femininity, the domestic component of her nature is projected onto the women in the classes beneath her, and the femininity of the women below is correspondingly decreased. In effect, a switch is made: the woman of the elite absorbs into her being the femininity of the woman below her, and she extirpates her domestic component; the woman below absorbs the elite woman's cast-off domestic component and relinquishes her own femininity. The elite woman thus becomes *Ultrafeminine* while the woman below becomes *Subfeminine* (Cleaver 1968: 181).

Paradoxically, the transubstantiation of the Ultrafeminine from the domestic to the state level imbues her with a masculine energy. It is within this class psychology that we can situate the reactionary role played by the 'First Ladies' produced by military dictatorship in Nigeria.

Before the appearance of General Babangida in the State House, 'First Ladies' used to perform ceremonial and domestic roles such as catering for guests, and visiting the sick in the hospitals and the needy in welfare institutions (Amuta 1992: 52). Inherent in these traditional roles is the psychology of male domination over the female sex. Amuta's position is supported by the fictional world of *Destination Biafra*, where Mrs Stella Ogendengbe and Mrs Teteku, wives of prominent politicians, do not loom large in national politics. On the other hand, Mrs Elizabeth Momoh and Mrs Julianah Chijoke, the wives of war patriarchs, exert some prominence of status. The institutionalization of the First Lady is a direct product of the Nigerian Civil War situation.

The 'First Lady Syndrome' trickles down from the apex of the national polity, through the regional states to the local grassroots level. Wives of military administrators and local government chairmen parade themselves in the manner of First Ladies. The First Lady Syndrome and the elite's newly acquired political and class status do not, however, radically transform the image of women. It is true that Maryam Babangida 'had developed the office of the First Lady as an effective institutional extension of the Presidency' (Amuta 1992: 52). This does not project a liberating theology for womanhood; it only enhances the power of patriarchy. It is also claimed that 'Babangida's imperial presidency may have provided a context in which the First Lady's activist role was perhaps inevitable'. Instead of boosting an active role for women, however, this imperial power only enhances Babangida's custodian theory.[1]

Military governance is an aberration and antithesis of democracy. As an agent of repression, the military 'misrepresents itself and intervenes disastrously in the polity and economy in a futile attempt to conceal its onerous dysfunctionality' (Ake 1993: 3). Scholars like Bade Onimode, Toyin Falola, Ben Turok and Samir Amin perceive military governance in Africa as part of the globalization project of imperialism and capitalism.

Maryam Babangida's Better Life Programme (BLP) was a problematic offspring of the masculinized military political economy in Nigeria. Not much can be found in Maryam Babangida's biography to suggest a dogged commitment to the betterment of downtrodden women in rural settings (Amuta 1992: 53). It would have been impossible for her to commit class suicide by identifying with those Cleaver refers to as 'Subfeminine', making it difficult, in consequence, for her to have achieved the objectives of the Better Life Programme which include:

'raising the consciousness of Nigeria's rural women; forging commonality of purpose among the rural women through highlighting the commonality of circumstances among Nigerian rural women across the conventional barriers of ethnicity and religion, as well as empowering the womenfolk, politically, in the process' (Amuta 1992: 54). The programme became an encompassing network through which the military rationalized the psyches of women in rural areas.

The crisis of confidence created by Babangida's administration still haunts the national psyche. Democracy becomes more elusive and strategies of totalitarianism and brute force have been consolidated under Sani Abacha's regime. It is into this scene that Maryam Abacha has emerged with the Family Support Programme (FSP). The objectives of the new programme include:

- the promotion of a decent health care delivery system
- eradication of the negative social and cultural factors affecting women and children
- assisting rural and urban families agriculturally and economically towards generation of income
- provision of welfare for the vulnerable and disabled (Abdullah 1995: 11).

Elite women's politics have become entrenched in Nigeria through the establishment of the Ministry of Women's Affairs. The First Lady, Maryam Abacha, was lauded for being the architect of this revolution. Iyabo Fagbolu cynically comments on such a feminist revolution:

> How very disquieting that so close to the beginning of the 21st century, this is what Nigerian women have come to! We have become second-class citizens in our country, refugees who are in need of rehabilitation into a system that really belongs to us. So the benevolent military government of Nigeria must create a Ministry to rehabilitate us – Nigerian women – and perhaps our children too, especially the female children who get hooked to suitors before the age of ten.
>
> Let me ask the creators of the Ministry of Women's Affairs a question: Who owns or for whose benefit are ALL the Ministries in the Federal Republic of Nigeria? Are they for Nigerian men and boys only? ... What is this mess called Ministry of Women's Affairs all about? Is it about behaviour or misbehaviour in the home and kitchen? Is it about fashion parades or beauty pageants? What is it all about? It definitely cannot be about governance or policy making (Fagbolu 1995: 5).

Fagbolu perceives the establishment of the Ministry as aberrant, not calculated for the positive development of womanhood in the Nigeria of today or tomorrow.

The crises of motherhood, childcare and childrearing in Nigeria cannot be alleviated by these programmes, which are products of patriarchal institutions. The Ministry and its programmes provide fora for self-aggrandizement by the so-called 'First Ladies' themselves, perpetuating military rule in Nigeria without offering a feminist challenge. We can thus set the commitment and altruism of Debbie in *Destination Biafra* against the hollow nationalism of Nigerian First Ladies. Types like the wives of the military warlords Momoh and Chijoke have appropriated and transformed feminist struggle in Nigeria.

Our two levels of discourse can now be brought together through the discourse of feminism: as an ideology of liberation, it has generated heated debates, particularly between Marxist and Socialist feminists. Socialist feminists berate the gender-blind character of Marxists for prioritizing workers' oppression above women's oppression: it is argued that 'socialist as well as capitalist women remain in the grip of patriarchy' (Tong 1989: 174). Neither the intellectual awareness of the narrator in Nwapa's *Never Again*, nor the *petit bourgeois*, educational and professional status of Debbie in *Destination Biafra*, liberates them from the psychic frame and yoke of patriarchy. The violence and brutality against women in *Destination Biafra* transcend a simple Marxist framework. Socialist feminists emphasize the biosocial and ideological factors, arguing that 'even under socialism, women will remain somewhat oppressed unless the defeat of capitalism is accompanied by the defeat of patriarchy' (Tong 1989: 176).

Critics argue that the First Lady Syndrome is a part of the global execution of imperialism and capitalism. Biney argues that 'First Ladies' use projects such as the Better Life Programme and Family Support Programme to 'attract foreign aid to their countries' (Biney 1992: 31). She concludes that 'the effect has been the promotion of capitalist competition and exploitation' (p. 31). If women's predicament – in literature and society at large – is interpreted from the perspective of production, reproduction, socialization, children and sexuality, we can see that 'First Ladies' are not free from patriarchy. As Biney has argued, wives of heads of state and other prominent men are essentially their husbands' appendages, aiding the dictatorial and anti-democratic governance of their men. The violence of the military and the gender expectations of male-dominated professions in Nigeria demand more than a materialist explanation: and perhaps, for now, it is only in the realm of literary representation that we can hope to find examples of a truly liberated womanhood.

Note

1. The custodian theory, propounded by Babangida, imposes on the armed forces of any nation the authority to enforce the constitution and other decrees. This necessitates a code of professional ethics based on cohesion, hierarchical command structures, discipline and nationalism. The theory paradoxically produces a masculine practice of brute force, violence and anti-nationalist ethics.

References

Abdullah, D. (1995) 'A Refuge for the Family', *A.M. News*, 26 April, 10–11.

Ake, C. (1993) 'Is Africa Democratizing?', *Guardian Sunday*, 12 December, 7–9.

Amuta, C. (1992) *Prince of the Niger: The Babaginda Years*, Tanus Communications and Zomax Publications, Lagos.

Biney, A. (1992) 'First Lady Syndrome', *Africa World Review*, May–October.

Brownmiller, S. (1975) *Against Our Will: Men, Women and Rape*, Simon & Schuster, New York.

Cleaver, E. (1968) *Soul on Ice*, McGraw Hill, New York.

Emecheta, B. (1986) *Destination Biafra*, Fontana/Collins, London.

Fagbolu, I. (1995) 'Ministry of Whose Affairs', *Nigerian Tribune*, 23 May, 5.

Hearn, J. (1987) *The Gender of Oppression: Men, Masculinity and the Critique of Marxism*, Wheatsheaf, Sussex.

Humm, M. (1987) *An Annotated Critical Bibliography of Feminist Criticism*, Harvester, Sussex.

Jaggar M. A. (1983) *Feminist Politics and Human Nature*, Harvester, Sussex.

Lenin, V. I. (1961) 'On the Question of Dialectics', *Collected Works*, Vol. 38. Foreign Language Publishing House, Moscow, and Lawrence & Wishart, London.

Mitchell, J. (1975) *Psychoanalysis and Feminism*, Penguin, London.

Nwapa, F. (1975) *Never Again*, Tana Press, Enugu, Nigeria.

Rich, A. (1980) *On Lies, Secrets and Silence: Selected Prose Works 1966–1978*, Virago, London.

Tong, R. (1989) *Feminist Thought*, Westview Press, San Francisco.

3
Women's role in Ghana's social development

AKOSUA GYAMFUAA-FOFIE

For many years, women in Ghana have been excluded from the decision-making processes affecting their lives, their families and their communities, accepting social attitudes and expectations with resignation, even surrender. In spite of Ghana's renowned status as a broadly 'matrilineal' society, men have been the main architects and beneficiaries of family and inheritance laws. The matrilineal system merely guarantees that nephews will inherit from their uncles through the female line: wealth continues to be confined to males. Not all ethnic groups in Ghana follow the matrilineal system. The northerners, in the Northern Regions, the Gas in the Greater Accra Region and even the Akan system, part of the Akuapims and part of the Fantes do not follow this matrilineal system. Even the Asante inheritance law for individuals who die intestate does not favour women and their children, who deserve a proportion of the husband's wealth after a lifetime spent toiling beside him.

Women have been socialized to accept these laws. Indeed, women have sometimes been the primary agents enforcing restrictive gender rules: in some northern Ghanaian communities, females are circumcised by men in the name of such 'traditional' values, while the women play supervisory roles. Similarly, older women supervise the bereavement rites that a wife passes through, ensuring that the ceremonies are performed to the letter. It is a rule in the Asante system that the woman must mourn her dead husband for one year before remarrying: during this period, custom demands that she wears only black cloth; however, the widower is subjected to no time barrier to stop him remarrying or wearing what he likes after the funeral.

As mothers, women bear the greater responsibility for childrearing and the early socialization of infants. Gendered roles and behaviours are introduced at this important stage of a child's development. If the woman is knowledgeable and well-educated, the children stand to gain from her rich experience. Many mothers employ their status as children's primary educators to suggest to girls that marriage is the essence of a woman's life; daughters are trained to seek money, consumer objects and material gain from suitors, and encouraged to marry wealthy men irrespective of age differences. Girls are socialized into the knowledge that success in life is achieved by marrying successful men: the idea that a woman can become successful through self-confidence and hard work is rarely credited.

In order to maintain the psychological suppression of women, a whole host of Akan sayings instruct women to respect the man's counsel in all aspects of life: *Obaa to tuo a etwene barima dan mu* (If a woman buys a gun, she must keep it in the room of a man); *Obaa tón nyaadewa na óntón atuduro* (A woman sells vegetables but not gunpowder); *se Obaa yen odwan a barima na oton* (When a woman rears a sheep, the man must sell it). All of these proverbs reveal how women have been treated for generations as lacking the capability for reasoning and decision-making.

It is against this background that Nana Yaa Asantewaa, the Queen Mother of Edweso near Kumasi, will ever be remembered by Ghanaian women as a rare role-model: she took action against the British who wanted to take the Golden Stool, which was believed to hold the soul of the Asante nation. Defying the British, this brave individual initiated the 1900 Yaa Asantewaa War. Instead of following this precedent for West African women's organizations to stand up and fight for their rights, however, women in Ghana have continued to live shrouded in silence.

The Asante Queen Mother continues to play an important role in the affairs of women, but her power is limited when it comes to the practical administration of the particular area she oversees: in town affairs, the king or chief has the final word. The queen mother's authority reaches its peak during the nomination and installation of a new king or chief: even then, the all-male coterie of king-makers can reject her candidate. Having her chosen candidate installed ensures her no special privileges either, as the king takes absolute control of affairs concerning the town, and the queen mother serves under him.

The traditional courts, which function in Ghana alongside national courts, are composed solely of male sub-chiefs; in towns serving under the *Asantehene*'s authority (King of the Asantes), the queen mother is the only woman to sit in the court, and there are no 'sub-queens' in Asante to balance the gender equation. One might suppose that a parallel, all-female court operates alongside the *Asantehene*'s sessions, but 'tradition' has not permitted female legislative power on this level. Even the *Asantehemaa* (the Queen of the Asantes) is the only queen mother who has her own traditional court. Her decision is final in any case but she presides over a court that is dominated by men. After gaining independence, Ghanaian kings and chiefs formed into the National House of Chiefs, which gained official governmental recognition in 1971: no such association was accorded to the queen mothers, however, and women's associations remained at the level of unrecognized, unofficial power.

In recent years, the 'First Lady' of Ghana, Nana Konadu Agyemang Rawlings, has helped the queen mother to form a national association of women, in which high-powered figures can add their voices to debates on national issues. The impact of such an association remains to be felt: a channel has been opened by the group, however, into male-dominated political institutions.

Ghanaian traditional religion does not discriminate against women priests, who are able to perform any rite in the same capacity as a man, except during menstruation, when they are banished from religious rituals. Fetish priests and priestesses are believed to be neutral vessels through which the gods operate. Similarly, prophetesses frequently own and lead the local, independent African churches which intertwine Christianity and traditional spiritual ceremonies.

Orthodox religion in Ghana offers fewer opportunities to women: Christianity pulls its own cart-load of discriminatory attitudes towards women, although both the Methodists and Presbyterians now accept women to be trained as ministers. Pentecostal churches are very outspoken when it comes to women being trained as pastors. Although more than 60 per cent of their members are women, a woman is forbidden to be trained as a minister no matter how spiritually mature she is: Pentecostal churches even insist that women address husbands as 'my lord'. The Bible is always cited in support of arguments promoting male authority and female submission and humility. Likewise, and in contrast to inherited, precolonial religious traditions, Islamic practices in West Africa discriminate against women, debarring them from leadership roles.

Crucially, boys have been privileged over girls in the Ghanaian education system. Since schooling became widely available, mothers and fathers alike have backed the idea of educating boys first; many of them believed that the vital resources spent on educating a female child would be wasted when she married.

Even now, many mothers believe that, in tight financial circumstances, boys should be prioritized educationally. Girls are encouraged to take up trading and farming and to marry rather than to seek academic laurels. A common saying emphasizes that an unmarried woman who attains the highest possible educational standard will not be accorded the respect attaching to an illiterate married woman; and no matter how many academic qualifications a woman attains, she has to work for money to earn respect. There have been several campaigns aiming to reduce this discrimination against women: Dr Kwaggir Aggrey diagnosed the problem accurately when he said, 'If you educate a woman you educate a nation but if you educate a man you educate an individual.'[1]

Attitudes towards female education, religious participation and political authority in Ghana are changing. Gradually, Ghanaian women are becoming aware of their talents, adapting their minds to take up positions of authority, instating themselves as role-models for their female inheritors. Women fortunate enough to have attained higher education must see themselves as teachers of their illiterate and semi-literate sisters, treating the knowledge they have acquired with responsibility. FIDA, an association of women lawyers, has come together to defend ordinary, poor women who are being cheated but have no money to engage the services of lawyers. They defend their clients free of charge, asking those with incomes for a token fee. In particular, they intervene on behalf of raped women and in cases relating to inheritance rights.

Suffering no discrimination in national, non-customary law, many women still lack confidence in themselves and shy away from leadership roles for fear of criticism. Women rarely offer themselves as candidates in political elections: in the Ghanaian parliament there are only 16 women among 184 men. Bills presented to parliament which favour women and threaten men's vested interests will be defeated automatically.

In many contemporary Ghanaian homes, women are financially the heads of household. What is lacking in most women is the courage and foresight to invest their capital in property and businesses. Women must identify their priorities and work hard to transform their dreams into realities. Instead of presenting themselves as physical beauties to be appreciated by men in power, women must search for something deeper: for a woman's worth is judged by her talents. It is disappointing to see women parading themselves in 'Miss Ghana' or 'Miss Africa' contests. Our cultural heritage and identity have no place for this bodily exposure. Why women allow themselves to be used as objects for entertainment defeats reason. Rumour-mongering, petty jealousies, back-biting and sexual envy weaken the morals of women and hinder their progress into positions of political authority where they can become part of the decision-making processes, influencing legislation by inserting a gender dimension. Stumbling blocks should be turned into stepping stones, failures turned into successes.

Ghana as a nation has opened fresh pages of a book in which women can write their names. While many men sympathize with the struggle of women towards recognition and fulfilment, others perceive a threat to their leadership positions. They will try to impede the progress of women, and it is up to women to bury every difference and form a united front with shared goals, transforming an unpleasant and exploitative past into a productive and meaningful future.

Note

1. This saying has been credited to Dr Aggrey for a long time.

PART II
Literatures

4
A life on the women's page: *Treena Kwenta's Diary*

JANE BRYCE

> Hi readers! This column is ten years old right now, and that makes the columnist forty-three. Hm, how time flies when you're gainfully and pleasurably occupied! The column has survived under three editors and has gathered fans from all the nooks and corners of the country irrespective of social status, religion or ethnic group ... Clearly it's a success, don't you think? Enough to make the columnist stick out her chest, beat it with pride, and then go shout from the rooftop how important she is in making our lives more relaxed and enjoyable (*Vanguard*, 29 August 1994).[1]

This is how Treena Kwenta's best friend Tayo greeted ten years of the popular column, 'Life with Treena Kwenta – diary of the fun-loving but hard-working single parent'. Since 1984, it has appeared weekly on the women's page of the Lagos-based daily paper *Vanguard*, documenting the routines and melodramas of Treena, her friends and family. Anonymously authored, the column takes advantage of the newspaper vehicle as a purveyor of 'fact', and of the 'soft' slot afforded by the women's page – associated with fashion, domesticity and other such 'trivial' and 'feminine' concerns – to create for itself a space somewhere between 'fact' and 'triviality'. In the process, it accomplishes something unique on the Nigerian journalistic and wider literary scene: loudly and brashly it gives voice to a perspective at once unambiguously feminine and uncompromisingly individualistic, independent, non-conformist and pragmatic. It lacks, in other words, the squeamishness about sexuality, the sense of moral burden and the self-effacement of so much of Africa's more formally presented women's writing.

This alone would make it an interesting object of research, but my motives for writing about it exceed the academic. The commencement of the column coincided, within a few months, with my own arrival in Nigeria to research women's writing, the column's protagonist being, like me, a freelance writer, of exactly the same age. For a while we even rubbed shoulders as columnists in the pages of the *Vanguard*. Though I am not Nigerian, there were many resonances for me in Treena's life and preoccupations as she struggled to balance the demands of family, work and parenthood, with her relentless drive for 'fun'. By presenting Treena Kwenta to a wider public and placing her in the context of women's writing on the continent, I am also offering the personal response of an enthusiastic and committed reader, a gesture no different from many made by those who write to Treena Kwenta, offering advice and encouragement or disagreeing with a particular line of action.

Through this persona, the author of the column subtly and unassumingly succeeds in doing something which many more sophisticated, pretentious or self-consciously 'literary' writers seek to do – that is, to destabilize the reader's sense of where 'truth' ends and 'fiction' begins, crossing the boundary between reality and fantasy, and upsetting the hierarchy of writer and reader. Taiye of Ijebu-Ode writes in to say: 'I have over the years been admiring your style of writing. I mean real life extracts of your diary that could easily be passed for fiction at times, because of the juicy presentation' (*Vanguard*, 'Your Turn', 1993). The author, in effect, sets up a dialogue between herself and her readers, which at times amounts to collusion, for example when she enlists their support against the criticism of her friends: when Tayo berates her for being too romantic, Treena declares, 'My readers understand me and they approve of me, yes?' (*Vanguard*, 29 August 1994).

It is obvious that a great deal of the column's appeal lies in the strong identification it invokes between the persona and the reader, and the verisimilitude of Treena's rendering of events. In Nigeria, the cliché that truth is stranger than fiction is borne out in the drama, sensationalism and extremism of everyday events as reported in the news. In this context, Treena's life, like the lives of many of her readers, is remarkable for its ordinariness. Parties, family meetings, domestic issues, work, lovers, friends, children and her ex-husband form the principal fare of the narrative. Of politics, directly, there is nothing, and only passing references are made to national events. Yet, in a wider sense, the column is profoundly political in its insistence on Treena's right to a 'life' which is not narrowly determined by economic exigencies or powers beyond the individual's control. Treena, like everybody else, struggles to survive in the face of a crumbling infrastructure and corrupt administration, rampant inflation, violence, back-biting and moral hypocrisy. What she represents is the possibility of retaining humanity and a sense of humour in spite of adverse social conditions, claiming a space to be herself according to her own definition. Readers' comments testify to this: 'I love the way you write. You are simply gorgeous' (Mrs C.A.S., Abeokuta); 'I have come to admire the person in you ... I pray for an onward progression of you as a person' (Faith, Onitsha); 'It is certainly no overstatement to confess that I love the woman in you' (Taiye, Ijebu-Ode) (*Vanguard*, 'Your Turn', 1993). In the light of this, some more general issues relating to the perceived role and function of women's writing will be addressed.

In the debate about 'good' and 'bad' writing in Africa, or 'elite' versus 'popular', or, in Bakhtin's formulation, 'official' versus 'unofficial', what emerges is a vertical scale of value in which writing by women occupies a space below male-authored or masculine-oriented texts.[2] This induces in many women writers an anxiety about how their texts will be critically received in the public domain of publishing and academia, the main organs of value attribution. The adoption of 'popular' (unofficial or non-elite) forms by women can be seen as a self-conscious strategy to evade official critical strictures, and predominant among these forms is the romance (see Bryce and Dako 1993).

Another arena for women writers seeking a discursive space which has not been colonized by hegemonic critical values is that of women's magazines, and the women's pages of newspapers. The Ghanaian journal *Obaa Sima* (Ideal Woman) is a good example of the way popular writing by women (largely romantic fiction or didactic pieces), while being incorporated into a wider developmental project for the betterment of women, signals its own reformist agenda. According to Kate Abbam, publisher of *Obaa Sima*, her purpose in starting the journal was 'to educate Ghanaian women about their rights and responsibilities' (interview, 1991). The Nigerian Pacesetter[3] novelist and *Vanguard* women's page editor, Helen Ovbiagele, says of herself, 'I just string words together to entertain and instruct a bit' (letter, November 1993). The author of 'Treena Kwenta' has her persona declare, 'I don't call myself a writer. I merely entertain with the pen' (*Vanguard*, 29 August 1994). The consensus for these women writers appears to be that while pleasure, or entertainment, is their primary objective, it is inextricably linked with women's traditional role of educator.

I am trying to draw attention here to the underlying seriousness of the project of popular writing in the hands of women, in spite of a literary establishment which, over-determined by elitist, ideological, nationalist and masculinist preoccupations, routinely vilifies it as trivial and marginalizes it as trash (see Martini 1989). However simplistic and non-progressive the overt content of popular writing may appear to be, we need to pay attention to its sub-textual messages, to the ways in which formula and genre are manipulated and reshaped to accommodate alternative points of view, and to the whole issue of women's pleasure – why women require Utopian (non-realist) revisionings of their current reality.

The Nigerian feminist writer and critic Molara Ogundipe-Leslie was practically involved at grassroots level with women's issues in Nigeria, as director of the national agency concerned with women's development in the 1980s (MAMSER). She criticizes both the media and the literary establishment for their promotion of female stereotypes, arguing that, 'The press will only be positive when glamorous and powerful women are concerned and that change has only been recent', whereas women's groups representing the interests of less privileged women remain embattled (Ogundipe-Leslie 1994: 171). She speaks of a 'politics of exclusion', whereby 'what women say or think is not considered material for news', and exhorts women journalists themselves to lead the way in 'the positive recreation of the women's image in our society' (p. 175). Specifically, she critiques, 'a situation where approximately 60 per cent of women's articles and programmes are about women in the context of love and marriage. Women readers consume much of the pulp and gossip literature and soft media programmes', and in her list of offenders she includes *Vanguard*. Finally, she issues a prescription to middle-class women (Treena Kwenta and her readers) to 'overcome their false consciousness, demystify their minds, and take an interest to understand their societies. That is, get political, get interested in things around them. Don't just read fashion magazines. Don't read only the soft part of the newspapers, the "human angle" stories, the gossip, the scandal' (p. 231).

Her assessment of what Nigerian women read may well be accurate, but she has already suggested a reason for this: the exclusion or stereotyping of women by the media. Women's pages, 'gossip' and 'soft' news may well be the only places women see themselves and their concerns addressed. Therese Nweke, a leading broadcaster, draws attention to the way the media establishment itself categorizes women as workers and consumers: 'Yet another constraint is that of the straitjacket created by programmes and pages of media material directed towards women which the male-dominated media organisations feel should only be produced by women. Hence female journalists have for a long time fed female audiences with articles on love, gossip, fashion, decorating and food' (Nweke 1985: 206). She places this in the context of women's status in Nigeria in general, where 'most women have no place in the social structure, not even at the bottom ... regardless of their education, their birth, their wealth, their class or even individual achievements' (p. 202). This invisibility or relegation is reflected in women's position in the media professions where, she maintains, 'their progress is marginal and tokenistic', demonstrating this with figures of women in management in various Nigerian media houses (p. 203).

In the light of this depressing picture, Helen Ovbiagele's longevity as *Vanguard*'s women's page editor and 'Treena Kwenta's' survival as a column are remarkable. They represent tenacity, the insistence on women being heard and seen on their own terms in the pages of a major daily paper. They have between them rejuvenated the despised women's page to present an uncompromising airing of a perspective which is gender specific, oppositional and revisionary; and they will not go away. That the column's longevity is appreciated by readers and a source of pride to the author is testified to by Tayo's anniversary column: 'She was a young lady with a spring in her step and a song on her lips, with the social scene in Lagos and Ibadan clamouring for her presence, when she started the column, while, ten years later she's edging towards middle-age and slipping into premature senility' (*Vanguard*, 29 August 1994).

Taiye's letter gives the reader's perspective: 'I have again marvelled at your consistency with the *Vanguard* newspaper, because other columnists (mostly female) that had been on this crusade with you had long switched custom ... I should appreciate the endurance and tolerance you have put in' (*Vanguard*, 'Your Turn', 1993). Though Treena is a 'single parent' by her own choice and preference, Taiye insists that her faithfulness and constancy as a columnist would stand her in good stead in a marriage: 'That you have kept this age-long marriage with this my favourite newspaper, managing a man ... should not ... be too hot for you to handle' (*Vanguard*, 'Your Turn', 1993). Treena's 'marriage' to the paper is a personal relationship which her readers are privileged to view from the inside and to be a part of, their loyalty matching hers. The author repeatedly addresses the reader, moving from the cosy elitism of 'As regular readers will know', to involving them in her private debates with herself, appealing for an opinion and thereby enlisting them in the process of creating the narrative. In the episode 'Brother Joe's Sister' (*Vanguard*, 9 March 1987), she forestalls criticism of her treatment of Joe's wife, Ify, by asking candidly, 'Did I sound like a dragon of a sister-in-law? Pardon me, then', and goes on to explain that she feels Ify disapproves of her being divorced: 'Nasty feminine thoughts, don't you think? Well, I am only being human' (*Vanguard*, 9 March 1987). Five years later, she is referring to a reader by name who has written in to warn her about her new lover:

> At this point I must express my gratitude to Felix, a regular reader of this column who wrote in from Lagos, advising me that I make sure that I do know the nature of Vic's ailment so that I know what marrying him would involve. Kind Felix is very much concerned about my welfare and he says I need to think carefully. I was really touched that he cares so much for me that he took the trouble to sit down and write to me (*Vanguard*, 28 December 1992).

The dialogue continues, with Faith of Onitsha taking up Felix's point:

> I couldn't suppress the urge of adding my own advice to that of Felix. This is because I can't understand why you should marry somebody who professes love for you but will not be able to open his medication box in your presence ... I admire your love for him in spite of all discouragements ... so I suggest that you sit him down and talk to him (*Vanguard*, 'Your Turn', 1993).

This in turn gives Treena a chance to explain something she has already addressed in an episode with Auntie Josephine: why she, normally so outspoken, appears reticent with Vic. On that occasion, Auntie had challenged her, saying, 'I get the impression that you are in awe of him. Is it his age or his wealth that makes you feel inadequate? You're by no means timid or cowardly, but in this relationship you seem a bit weak' (*Vanguard*, 'Back to Sender', 1993). In reply to Faith's letter, Treena explains: 'The problem is because Vic is so much older than I, I cannot be as forceful as I would have been with a younger man. Then, he is so nice and polite and loving that it is difficult to argue or be angry with him. I shall be vigilant though' (*Vanguard*, 'Your Turn', 1993). What these examples show is the degree to which readers are actively involved in the narrative, not simply as consumers, but as participants, and this in turn testifies to the fact that 'Treena Kwenta' speaks to their reality at the same time as it reconstructs that reality, entertains and provides them with escape.

Ogundipe-Leslie expresses an opinion that may seem extreme, but with which other women concur:

> It would be amazing, or perhaps not so, to reveal the existence of crudely sexist gender attitudes in seemingly educated, progressive and sophisticated Nigerians ... Even on the most basic level of conversation, many men are incapable of dialogue with women as equals. The immediate, spontaneous and ingrained attitude is to patronize the women; not to talk as equals, as person to person, but as a superior and wiser intelligence (Ogundipe-Leslie 1994: 155).

Therese Nweke agrees, commenting, 'when all is said and done, Nigerian males regard females as "only a woman",' and this applies in both the public and domestic spheres: 'Cross swords with any male colleague at work, or even husband at home, and the basic consensus among well-meaning friends and relatives alike ... is to humour, to tolerate, not to take seriously, not to behave as if both parties have equal rights, since one is inherently inferior' (Nweke 1985: 202).

In the course of research undertaken between 1983 and 1988, I conducted extensive interviews with women journalists on the *Guardian*, *Vanguard* and other publications, both in Lagos and Kano, and most agreed that social attitudes were an inhibiting factor in their job. It is most important to stress, however, that nowhere among these women – who included editors, columnists and a defence correspondent who went every day to Dodan Barracks to check on what the military rulers were up to – did I encounter anything resembling a victim mentality. Quite the reverse. They were uniformly proud of their profession and of themselves for meeting the challenges posed daily by society's expectations of appropriate feminine behaviour. For middle-class women, 'conformity' does not include the hours kept by women journalists, who can be found on the street, or moving around the city alone at night, when respectable women would be at home looking after their husbands. The inevitable tensions which result meant that women journalists were predominantly young and unmarried; if married, they had sensibly chosen husbands who had some insight into their professional world. Marriage is still *de rigueur* for Nigerian women, and very few would choose to sacrifice the social endorsement it brings on a permanent basis. This does not mean, however, that Nigerian women are necessarily worse off than women in the West, for the single reason that they are never isolated in the home in a nuclear family situation. The sustaining power of women's networks, friendships, professional associations and family groupings is not to be underestimated. To overlook this is inevitably to produce a distortion in perceptions of women's lives and roles in Nigeria, for it is to be blind to the whole 'parallel economy' of women's activities which exists alongside that of men, albeit more muted and accorded less recognition in the public domain.

In the light of all this, 'Treena Kwenta' may be seen as important not only in the more obvious way of giving voice and visibility to a feminine perspective which challenges many of the assumptions of 'appropriate' behaviour, but also for its sub-textual statement of the subversive potential of feminine solidarity. Speaking in the voice of unrepentant individualism, Treena nevertheless operates at the centre of a network of women – mothers, aunts, sisters, workmates, friends – and simultaneously reaches out to women who, while occupying similar networks, may lack her confidence and outspokenness. The column therefore functions on two levels: one, of cosy identification and shared intimacies, the other, more oblique but equally central to its success, of exposure of convenient social hypocrisies, especially the demythologizing of conventional notions of 'femininity'. The paradox suggested by this – of reassurance and challenge, conformity and subversion, collectivity and individualism – gives the narrative both its dramatic tension and its verisimilitude. It not only recognizes life's ambivalence, but wholeheartedly embraces it, revelling in its contradictions and exploiting them for alternative solutions to the problem of being a woman in urban, middle-class, capitalist, late twentieth-century Nigeria. And the key to this essential paradox is in the subtitle: 'Diary of the fun-loving but hard-working single parent'.

The diary format in which the column is presented parallels the newspaper vehicle in its daily reporting of events; at the same time it appropriates a 'public' space for 'private' concerns. The tone is unabashedly personal, confessional and confidential. The episodic nature of Treena's bulletins on her life meanwhile creates the illusion of things happening in time, as in 'real' life. As with a 'real' person, there is a gradual process of familiarization, through which the reader is admitted to the inner circle of those in the know, the 'regular readers'. Unsettling any stable sense of permanent identity, however, is Treena's relentless self-questioning and ruthless honesty. This in turn is part of the pleasure of reading the column, since it permits the reader an enjoyable sense of transgression. Without taking responsibility, the reader can be a voyeur, privy to secrets usually circulated only among intimates, and permitted to listen to 'gossip' without the discomfort of self-censorship. Treena, in other words, says aloud what other people don't even admit to thinking. Hence the paradox: the brashness of the first-person voice obscures the fact that the column is anonymously authored; the ephemerality of the medium and the perceived frivolity of the women's page enable the persona to comment extensively on delicate areas of the collective psyche, without being held accountable; and, finally, through the diary format, what would otherwise be designated gossip is recuperated as heartfelt personal confession, close, indeed, to 'truth'.

'Treena Kwenta' accomplishes all this without the need for alienating ideological labels – such as 'feminist' or 'radical'. In some respects she is deeply conservative, respecting her elders, her role in the family and her role as a parent, and she certainly is a snob. Her favourite adjective for herself is 'classy', which signals a rigid code of behaviour, especially with respect to men and how she expects to be treated by them. Her limited unconventionality, summed up in the designation 'single parent', and her insistence on being happy that way, is predicated on her social class, her independent income and the fact that she has fulfilled society's chief requirement of a woman in that she has had children. This in no way diminishes the column's subversiveness, since divorce is generally taken to be an undesirable state, like widowhood, and one which 'ordinary' women would not seek to advertise. The idea of 'single parenthood' is Western; although a minority of women do function effectively both as mothers and members of the community outside of marriage, 'single parenthood' is not endorsed by Nigerian social mores, and Treena is therefore perpetually in the position of defending herself against family pressure to remarry, in league with the men who would like to make her a wife. The very fact that she resists, and is still resisting more than a decade on, is enough to make her an anomaly.

One of the ways she defuses the tension inherent in her position is through style. 'Treena Kwenta's' complete lack of pretence at literariness is one way of evading judgement, since women's utterances in print are subject to moral censure when they appear to deviate from a standard femininity. By eschewing 'grammar' and adopting a racy, down-to-earth, plain-speaking mode of address, Treena constructs herself as less of a threat. Her colloquialisms, furthermore, are cosmopolitan, not necessarily current, but sufficiently coloured with foreignness to provide an alibi for her naughtiness: she studied in Britain, so she is a 'been-to', and her failure to do things the 'right' way becomes understandable. The column is peppered with expressions like 'sizzling fun', 'hell-raiser', 'ogle', 'put a sock on your drift', 'drivelling', 'nutty old boy', 'lousy Christmas present' and 'dig that dame'. Cumulative references to books she reads, opinions she holds, and other people's attitudes to her, help in the construction of a scale of values and provide clues as to how she should be read. Thus, from her references to Sherlock Holmes (*Vanguard*, 23 February 1987), detective novels (*Vanguard*, 26 January 1987) and Jackie Collins (*Vanguard*, 16 March 1987), there emerges the impression of a lively but determinedly anti-intellectual intelligence. She likes to congratulate herself on her 'natural curiosity' (*Vanguard*, 4 May 1987), which is frequently at war with her pride, and which dictates how she feels other people should behave towards her. Typically, she is perfectly frank about this double standard. When there is trouble between the two wives who occupy the downstairs flat, she complains: 'The trouble with Nanny is that she is not curious enough. Hers is a sleepy mind ... Whoever heard of a nanny who is not a good gossip? It is an essential part of their duties to be able to fill the boss in on happenings around' (*Vanguard*, 4 May 1987). When her children, Heather and Milwan, reveal that they know what is going on, however, she reacts according to her perception of a responsible parent, saying, 'All this was news to me and quite interesting, but I began to scold my kids for discussing Dotun's intimate family matters with her' (*Vanguard*, 4 May 1987). The same contradiction is evident when a friend asks her to keep an eye on a couple who eat at her favourite lunch-time restaurant: 'Curiosity is second skin to me and I love detective stories, but when it comes to sleuthing in real life, particularly that involving love affairs, I bow out. I consider it beneath my dignity to go nosing around to find out who a boyfriend is dating, where they are meeting, etc.' (*Vanguard*, 7 December 1987).

A further contradiction is the coupling of Treena's honesty with her susceptibility to flattery. When Tayo describes 'the ecstasy of reading her and knowing what goes on in her world', Treena responds with 'Thanks Tayo. I do love that word "ecstasy". It makes happiness well up in me', but immediately undercuts it with, 'Now, what do you really want to say? It's taking you a long time to get round to it' (*Vanguard*, 29 August 1994). When (she claims) her editor encourages her with, 'Your life is so full and exciting and your report so entertaining. You keep right on', she purrs, 'You know me and flattery. The above remark shot me several kilometres in the air for some minutes' (*Vanguard*, 'Your Turn', 1993). Treena loves flattery, but unlike most of us, she owns right up; moreover, a well developed sense of irony is always at hand to puncture her own inflated egotism. She does not hesitate to show herself in a bad light, as when reacting to the news that a lover is accompanying his ex-wife to functions: 'Of course, I am not bothered by what I have just heard. Or am I? Is that jealousy or anger welling up in my chest?' (*Vanguard*, 30 March 1987).

An interesting feature of Treena's self-construction is the extent to which she acknowledges and invites the participation of others, particularly her friends, known as 'the gals'. This group, which has remained unchanged throughout the ten years under consideration, consists, apart from Tayo, of Boma, Becky and Liz. These women are all, like Treena, middle-class, professional and (nowadays) forty-something: they provide a counterpoint and touchstone for the way she views herself. Though Becky is married, the others, like Treena, have lost or discarded husbands, and have gone through a succession of men over the years. Tayo, whose 'toyboy', Ade, first makes an appearance in 1987, is still with him in 1993, in spite of the discovery that he has a wife and four children in his home state of Kwara (now Kogi); Boma is a widow; and Liz, alternately known as a 'hell-raiser' or 'conwoman', has a steady relationship with Uka. Like the village women in Flora Nwapa's *Efuru*, 'the gals' form a chorus, commenting on and contextualizing Treena's life. Tayo, the most vociferous, actually takes over the column on more than one occasion, as in 'Analyzing Treena' (*Vanguard*, 31 August 1993) when, tongue-in-cheek, she accuses Treena of being too jealous to let her in on the column and too anxious to appear 'prim and proper' to give her readers the 'really juicy things' she, Tayo, could provide. This time, however, she promises that Treena cannot escape: 'Yes, she is on show this week. Your beloved Treena is on display! She's up for scrutiny' (*Vanguard*, 31 August 1993).

Indeed, every aspect of Treena's life is addressed: her lackadaisical attitude towards getting rich, her dreamy romanticism, her thoroughly ridiculed liaison with Vic, her much older lover, and her failure to manipulate her doting ex-husband, Seb, into improving her standard of living. Tayo systematically debunks all Treena's fondest ideas about herself: 'She thinks she's hardworking and pushy, huh? Hardworking, yes. Who isn't these days when it comes to survival? Pushy? Definitely not!' (*Vanguard*, 31 August 1993). Having got together years before 'to form a sort of emancipated union ... to get more grip on life ... do legitimate things to get rich. Go grab the good life' (*Vanguard*, 31 August 1993), Treena is the only one who has sat back and vegetated, cushioned by the support of Seb. She thinks she's 'no-nonsense', but according to Tayo, 'She's too gooey-eyed and mush-mush to survive', and the evidence for this is that she failed to force Vic to live up to his promise of buying her a house in a fashionable area: 'Where really smart dames got fat cheques on a regular basis, our darling Treena got flowers. Where they got nice flats or posh cars, she got flowers' (*Vanguard*, 31 August 1993). Tayo concludes with the advice that her friend should go back to her ex-husband, who is 'the only one who really understands her and can deal with her' (*Vanguard*, 31 August 1993).

Far from taking offence, Treena appeals to another of her friends, Boma, to adjudicate, conceding that, 'I still love the good life very much, but since I've failed to hit the big times when the opportunity and the zest were there, I sort of sank into a state of lethargy. Tayo's *exposé* on me has woken me up' (*Vanguard*, 6 September 1993). True to form, Boma is as honest with Treena as she is with herself, taking her through all the implications of her dependence on Seb, where his remarriage would leave her, and what she owes herself as a woman to achieve for herself. As a result of this conversation, Treena is empowered to approach Seb for better housing, and for a loan from his company (in which she is a director) to put in a fixed deposit. Boma advises: 'You can always stall on the paybacks. Tell dear old Seb whatever you like ... He won't bite you' (*Vanguard*, 6 September 1993). In this way, Treena is forced by her friends to look out for her own interests in a social context where wives (let alone ex-wives) have no right to property, and a woman is judged by her foresight and entrepreneurial ability. Treena the renegade, the lover of nice things with nothing 'substantial to fall back on. No landed property, no large fixed deposits put aside, nor investments made' (*Vanguard*, 6 September 1993), is brought back in line by collective pressure.

This episode illustrates an important aspect of 'femininity' as defined by Treena and her circle: independence. Though they freely exploit men for material gain, their priority is firmly that of looking after themselves. Meanwhile, they act for each other in the role of family at all the significant events, attending weddings, burial ceremonies, fortieth birthday parties, and so on. After their participation in the burial ceremonies for Vic's brother and sister, they are rewarded with gifts of expensive perfume (a precious and scarce luxury, requiring large amounts of foreign exchange to acquire). Receiving Treena's thanks, Vic comments on how different 'the gals' are from the usual groups of women friends, characterized by 'backbiting, disloyalty and er, er, bitchiness' (*Vanguard*, 30 May 1994). Vic's further remark, that he has never been called on by one of her friends trying to undermine the relationship, reveals the negative side of women's friendships, which the author is evidently critiquing. Pragmatically, Treena considers why 'the gals have so far been able to suppress and control bitchiness' (eschewing political correctness, she does not challenge the use of the word 'bitchiness'), and concludes it is because 'we all got together to analyze our feelings and pinpoint the usual flaws in friendship among women' (*Vanguard*, 30 May 1994). As a result, the group has earned the respect of those outside it. This obviously didactic message suggests another of the column's sub-texts, pointing the way for women to change the status quo by first changing themselves.

By the time the column begins, Treena is already divorced from Seb and living in Aguda with her two children (where she suffers flooding every rainy season, hence her need for a new house). The paradox inherent in 'fun-loving but hard-working' is very much in evidence here, in the rigid demarcation she draws between her responsibility as a parent combined with her consciousness of the need to impress Seb with her ability to cope on her own, and her hectic, 'fun'-seeking social life. All men outside her family and Seb fall into the 'fun-loving' category, except Jerry (1987), who verges on becoming 'serious', and, by 1991, Vic. Even though she complains bitterly when 'hard work' encroaches on 'fun', Treena is always ready to participate in family meetings, look after her father when her mother goes away, put up other family members, and help the children with their homework. Her life is characterized by a struggle to be herself, retain her individuality, independence and freedom of choice, without forfeiting social status, public respect and approval, or her role in the family. An example is Treena's irritable response to her mother's commendation of her for devoting herself to her son's studies: 'The thing is that life is such a drag these days; there is nothing to brighten my day ... I have not danced for ages. I am so weighed down by responsibility that I can choke. And all because I am a mother' (*Vanguard*, 9 February 1987).

Paradoxically, it is motherhood which provides Treena with the licence to indulge her 'fun-loving' side. Her main compensation for her lack of a conventional marriage and all that goes with it are her family, friends and her freedom to determine what sort of relationships she will be involved in and what she is prepared to take from men. A major principle of Treena and 'the gals', amounting almost to an ideological imperative, is a thoroughgoing materialist view of sexual relations. Romance is pleasurable, in fact indispensable, but it is firmly relegated to the realm of 'fun'. When Tayo's 'toyboy' makes his first appearance (1987), Treena's objection is not to his youth, but to the fact that Treena fears he is sponging on Tayo, against the primary rule of the game, by which men pay. An unsentimental distinction is made between 'romance' and 'love': the former is part of the pleasure-seeking bargain between men and women, the latter a technique used by men to mystify and confuse women. Whenever 'the gals' see signs of capitulation to the latter in each other, they are quite ruthless. When Tayo gets back together with Ade after a long separation, Treena comments:

> Tayo is in love. She's so deeply in love that nothing upsets her or makes her angry. I find this attitude very irritating ... It's maddening to have her agree these days to whatever I say ... You cannot have a conversation with her without her dragging in [Ade's] name ... with sickening tenderness stamped all over her, and she would giggle like a lovestruck teenager (*Vanguard*, 'All Over Again', 1993).

Treena herself is not impervious to romantic urges, however, even if she is aware she is indulging in fantasy, as in this episode with her lover Jerry: 'Urged on by the warm and pleasant taste of Cointreau after a lovely dinner, my head lolled on his shoulder and he held me close and nibbled at my ear. He whispered sweet nothings and I whispered sweet nothings to him too. I sat up, looked at him affectionately and tried to roll my eyes dreamily like Tayo' (*Vanguard*, 4 January 1988). When he announces he is unable to spend Christmas with her, her mind clicks back into focus and she instantly allows herself to be persuaded to go and host Seb's Christmas party instead. When it comes to love, Treena is equally clear-sighted, claiming: 'I have always considered myself jealous-proof in romantic relationships ... Why waste your time and precious emotions fighting a boyfriend for paying attention to another dame when you should be getting the best you can out of him?' (*Vanguard*, 6 April 1987). She none the less succumbs to jealousy over Jerry's ex-wife, remaining unimpressed by his talk of love, and thinking, 'What does the average Nigerian man know about love? The word leaves him cold and it does not exist in his lifestyle' (*Vanguard*, 6 April 1987).

Treena ages with her column, and a shift of attitude is detectable by the time she meets Vic, her 'senior citizen', in 1991. At the outset, she is as jaunty and irreverent as ever, defending herself to her friends for being involved with an 'ancient heap', 'creaking bones' and 'Methuselah' (he is twenty-eight years older than she is, and a classmate of her mother's) (*Vanguard*, 'Enters the Senior Citizen', 1991). One suspects the author of again challenging social attitudes in her introduction of the much older lover, but it is also a device to create suspense. Will Treena marry him, in spite of all the disapproval? Should she marry a man with a mystery illness? Why does he keep the nature of it a secret from her? Will she end up nursing and waiting on him? The debate rages, with Treena's parents, friends and readers all having their say. Meanwhile, Treena enjoys the respect she receives, when in Vic's company, from younger men, and, at 'knocking forty', 'Oh! the joy of being treated like a baby!' (*Vanguard*, 'Happy Days', 1991). At the back of her mind, as she freely confesses, 'is the hope that one day he would show me how benevolent he is ... that is, do something tangible for me that would make me grateful to him forever' (*Vanguard*, 'Happy Days', 1991). By December of the following year, however, 'romance' has taken over from economic considerations, and is nudging her towards 'love'. Whereas a few episodes previously she had only reluctantly repeated the words 'I love you' under duress, mentally querying: 'Did I mean those words? I don't know ... I suppose so. However I felt good that the old dear loves and wants me so much' (*Vanguard*, 'Facing Reality', 1992), now when he displays concern for her, 'I simply melted with tenderness in my heart, and tears of joy sprang to my eyes' (*Vanguard*, 21 December 1992). Once again, the columnist is using her privileged position to teach a lesson in sensitivity to her (male) readers. This is made explicit in the following paragraph: 'I mean, how many men would notice that their women have a face, let alone observe that that face does not look happy? ... I know that there are millions of sisters out there whose male companions don't care a hoot about their moods any more' (*Vanguard*, 21 December 1992).

As a result, she assures him 'that as long as there was breath in me no-one can replace him in my heart' (*Vanguard*, 21 December 1992). This is out of character for Treena, who is generally wary of such declarations, but 'the darling deserved such endearing and encouraging words at that moment' (*Vanguard*, 21 December 1992). 'Love' is still, evidently, viewed with a healthy scepticism, doled out as a reward on the appropriate occasion rather than succumbed to. It in no way obscures Treena's vision of the kind of life she wants for herself. Quizzed by Liz on where she sees the relationship going, she looks at her friends and notes that all but Boma have settled down with steady partners (though not necessarily husbands), and asks herself:

> Now, do I still want to play the field at forty-one? Er, not really. Changing partners has suddenly lost its attraction. At the same time one is not really keen on all that wifely bit ... I want a detached companion who would have time for me, yet who I would not have to look after in any way (*Vanguard*, 'A Step Forward', 1991).

This is a preference shared by Liz, who is trying to convince her lover, too, that they are better off keeping separate residences. Tayo rashly moves in with Ade and is then faced with a dilemma when she is promoted and able to afford better accommodation: how does she take advantage of this without Ade coming along? 'The gals' are convened to offer advice, and Treena points out that she can always throw Ade out if he doesn't behave: 'You sling out the fellow whenever you like. I think it would be a jolly good thing to do. Give the men a taste of their own medicine', but that as he has acquitted himself fully within the parameters of the relationship, 'To leave him behind would seem heartless. It wouldn't show love' (*Vanguard*, 'Ade the Traitor', 1992–93). These parameters reveal the extent of the pragmatism with which the whole subject of intimate relationships is viewed by Treena and her friends. There is a conspicuous absence of the long-suffering, self-sacrificing 'feminine' behaviour to be found in some of the more 'literary' narratives.[4] The collectively drawn line between 'love' and 'romance' (repeatedly transgressed, but sanctioned by ridicule) ensures that no member of the group acts on impulse or is blinded by passion or sentiment. As Tayo says, she has 'called [her] confidantes together to deliberate', and they are very clear about the issues (*Vanguard*, 'Ade the Traitor', 1992–93). They are not unfair, however. If the man keeps his part of the bargain, he deserves to be recompensed: 'After all, he's been a companion to her publicly and privately for a couple of years now, married or not married. He's behaved himself so far ... She's not ruining his home since he chose to keep his family in Kwara State' (*Vanguard*, 'Ade the Traitor', 1992–93). Tayo's view, in the light of his wife's recently announced fifth pregnancy, is different:

> Hm, it's a question of monkey dey work, baboon dey chop ... I put money in his pocket, live with him, sleep with him, tolerate his moods, slave for him in short; while she lives a life of ease over there and is relaxed enough to get pregnant. And you're asking me to invite such a traitor to share my home (*Vanguard*, 'Ade the Traitor', 1992–93).

The collective response to this revelation is again ridicule. If she does not want a child, why is she worried? A married lover has a right to sleep with his wife, and Tayo is making a fool of herself. Marriage is not about 'fun'; it is a serious contract involving children. The difference is spelled out by Treena when she is being called on to act as mediator between Tayo and Ade: 'Mind you, when you say "in love", you are not referring to a married couple. To me, no matter how much you and your partner love each other, you stopped being in love when you got married. Marriage takes out the excitement of being in love' (*Vanguard*, 'Peace Moves', 1992).

Consonant with this is her reaction when Vic insists she stop seeing Seb, her ex, which she not only refuses to do, but actually stops seeing Vic himself (*Vanguard*, 'Dark Storm', 1993). While she resents the fact that Vic's first wife accompanies him on trips abroad for treatment, her code does not permit her to express this. But nor will she allow herself to be bullied, in spite of the pain the separation causes.

In conclusion, 'Treena Kwenta' deals realistically and pragmatically with the situation facing many urban, middle-class Nigerian women today, one which could be characterized as 'contemporary polygamy'. Christian morality, with its attendant notions of romantic love and monogamous marriage, is a relatively recent phenomenon in Africa, and its adoption by the middle class and elite has given rise to manifold contradictions. The legacy of colonialism invests Christian marriage with a spurious 'respectability', which, though sought-after, is maintained only at the cost of hypocrisy and mystification. In a cultural context where polygyny is ingrained, it is not uncommon for men to have a public wife, and other 'wives' or girlfriends, who may also have children for them. The price of maintaining the fiction of 'respectability' is borne, needless to say, above all by the women, since it requires acquiescence on their part without the licence to pursue other relationships on an equal footing. This is not so in the world of Treena Kwenta. Here, the columnist has created an alternative reality, based on an actual material social situation, but reshaped to be more equitable and beneficial to women. In this world, stigmatized states such as widowhood and divorce are presented as much-prized autonomy. The women in this world repudiate all pretence at a narrowly defined Christian morality (though they may go to church), and the convenient mystifications through which social control is exercised. Accepting the status quo which decrees that men have multiple partners, they simply assert their right to do the same, overturning the double standard that says there is one rule for men and another for women in affairs of the heart. They do this, moreover, without sacrificing their participation in those aspects of their society necessary for a full and satisfying life: the extended family, motherhood, work, business success, parties, social life and, above all, other women's friendship.

While neither overtly feminist nor dogmatic, the column is, at least to a limited extent, Utopian, offering male and female readers a space for imagining a changed society and a greater balance in gender power relations. Its deliberate silence on the subject of political power in the larger sense should therefore not be read as facile escapism, but rather as an insistence on the right of ordinary people – that is, readers – to pleasure, recreation and, most importantly, agency. The women of Treena Kwenta's world, though confronted with the same ambiguities, contradictions, conflicting interests and economic constraints as everyone in Nigeria, are never passive. The *Diary* is a record of life-in-process, open-ended, fluid and with no fixed outcome. The paradox of the subtitle, 'fun-loving but hard-working', suggests a world-view which is profoundly optimistic, even in the face of the most repressive and life-denying military regime it has been Nigeria's fate to experience. It is not that 'Treena Kwenta' ignores this dimension of the Nigerian scene, so much as takes it for granted. Since it constitutes daily reality for a hundred million people, it hardly needs spelling out. Treena only does what the other 99,999,999 of her compatriots are doing: gets on with her life as best she can. So, in the September following the hi-jacking of the presidential election in June 1993, and the accession of yet another illegal, unconstitutional, undemocratic government, Treena is preoccupied by the 'impasse' in her cousin Sally's marriage. In passing, she mentions how difficult it is to deal with family matters while her parents are away in Ghana, but: 'We felt that the political impasse (that word again) in the country should be over, one way or the other, before they had insisted that their place was where their children were' (*Vanguard*, 'Mending It Up', 1993). The use of the word 'impasse' in these two contexts not only signals consciousness of the wider political scene, but also makes a statement about priorities. Military regimes are notorious for vesting power in 'the boys' rather than 'the gals'. In Treena Kwenta's world, it's the other way around.

Notes

1. The extracts quoted in this chapter fall into two distinct gropus. Extracts in the first group, published from January 1987 to January 1988, were collected by me while in Nigeria, and are therefore followed by complete dates of publication. Those in the second group were sent to me in Barbados by Helen Ovbiagele, via a network of friends and contacts in Nigeria and the UK. Unfortunately, in the process of reducing the *Vanguard* newspaper page for photocopying, all but a few of the dates were lost. I have done my best, using surviving dates and cuttings from the same period sent by Dr Nina Mba from Lagos, to place the extracts chronologically, but this is often no more precise than the year (1991 to 1994). These extracts are therefore referred to by their sub-heading, for example 'Your Turn', published in 1993. To anyone who has done research in West Africa, these problems of technology and communication will come as no surprise. From anyone else, I can only crave indulgence.

2. See Bryce (forthcoming). For a comprehensive overview of the issues surrounding popular culture and its categorization and evaluation, see Barber (1987).

3. Macmillan in Africa publish a series of African popular novels, including romances, thrillers and detective stories, called 'Pacesetters'.

4. I am thinking here of novels such as *Behind the Clouds* by Ifeoma Okoye (1982) and the novels of Funmilayo Fakunle: *The Sacrificial Child* (1978), *Chasing the Shadow* (1980) and *Chance or Destiny* (1983). 'Treena Kwenta' is closer in spirit to the tough-minded, emotionally independent women of Flora Nwapa's and Buchi Emecheta's novels.

References

Barber, K. (1987) 'Popular Arts in Africa', *African Studies Review*, 30 (3), September, 1–78.

Bryce, J. (forthcoming) 'Women and Modern African Fiction', in K. Barber (ed.), *Readings in Popular Culture*, James Currey, London.

Bryce, J. and K. Dako (1993) 'Romantic Fiction as a Subversive Strain in Black Women's Writing', *WASAFIRI* 17, Spring, 10–14.

Fakunle, F. (1978) *The Sacrificial Child*, Fakunle Major Press, Oshogbo, Nigeria,

— (1980) *Chasing the Shadow*, Fakunle Major Press, Oshogbo, Nigeria.

— (1983) *Chance or Destiny*, Fakunle Major Press, Oshogbo, Nigeria.

Martini, J. (1989) 'Sex, Class and Power: the Emergence of a Capitalist Youth Culture in Nigeria', *Journal of African Children's Literature*, 1, 43–59.

Nweke, T. (1985) 'The Role of Women in Nigerian Society: The Media', in Women in Nigeria Editorial Committee, *Women in Nigeria Today*, Zed Books, London, 201–7.

Ogundipe-Leslie, M. (1994) 'The Image of Women and the Role of the Media', in M. Ogundipe-Leslie, *Re-creating Ourselves: African Women and Critical Transformations*, Africa World Press, Trenton, NJ, 168–77.

Okoye, I. (1982) *Behind the Clouds*, Longman, Harlow.

5
Recovering lost voices: the short stories of Mabel Dove-Danquah

NAANA JANE OPOKU-AGYEMANG

It would be fair to begin with the proposition that the reputations of even the best writers generally describe a perpetual rise and fall in the public eye. Rarely do a writer's name and work remain constantly fixed on the critical horizon. The writer's appeal fluctuates from age to age, depending on how well his or her style, tone and total achievement reflect current concerns and tastes. The thrust of the whole Renaissance, for example, regenerated interest in ancient learning. Consequently, such dormant literary voices as those of Cicero, Plato and Virgil were raised and drawn to the centre of English literary interests.

Sometimes, a critic's view can adversely affect the popularity of a writer. Here we may cite the example of D. H. Lawrence. This English novelist enjoyed a high reputation in academe until the appearance of Kate Millet's *Sexual Politics* in 1969. Millet's is one of the first books to articulate a broad theoretical base for the discourse on sexuality in literature. She uses literary and historical models, including D. H. Lawrence, to argue that sexual relations between men and women have been grounded in misogyny, that they express themselves in a view of life which is patriarchal, and that indeed such power arrangements result in the oppression of women both at the institutional and personal levels. The reputation of Lawrence, since Millet's work, has undergone radical revision.

At other times, it is the work of a critic that raises the life and work of a forgotten writer from oblivion to public notice. The work of the metaphysical poet John Donne, for example, regained public recognition when the critic T. S. Eliot placed it at the centre of the English literary map (Eliot 1962: 302–11). To the example of Donne we can add that of the African–American woman folklorist, writer and critic, Zora Neale

Hurston. Intensely famous for a brief spell in the Harlem Renaissance, Hurston died a pauper after she had worked as a domestic servant. She was buried in an unmarked grave, her writing abandoned along with her unclaimed body. The creative writer and critic Alice Walker's unrelenting efforts to reclaim Hurston's work have been very successful. Walker has managed to uncover the writer's invaluable contributions and has today placed them at the centre of African–American literary practice (Walker 1983).

The tide of social and political movements can raise or bury a writer's reputation. The themes of protest and conflict in African literature, for example, were directly related to the political movements of the 1950s and 1960s. Such themes are on the wane, and both the writing and the criticism have become complex and fragmented, if not open-ended. In this context writers associated with protest have been devalued.

In the rise and fall of writers' reputations, perhaps women have recorded the highest casualties. It is therefore not by accident that a major project of feminist scholarship continues to be the recovery of women's lost contributions, and part of the aim of this ongoing project is to retrieve lost literary voices that run the risk of sinking into complete obscurity.

Received wisdom suggests that creative literature by African women did not make its mark until the 1960s with the publication of writing by Efua Sutherland, Flora Nwapa and Ama Ata Aidoo, among others. My search for 'lost' African women writers has unearthed other unheard voices in abandoned newspapers, journals and anthologies that precede these well-known writers. Such literary antecedents include the pioneer African and Ghanaian woman writer, Mabel Dove-Danquah, who started publishing stories in the early 1930s. Focusing on six hitherto understudied and ignored short stories, one can begin to appreciate Dove-Danquah's strong awareness of the complexities of gender discourse.

Author, journalist, legislator and political activist, Dove-Danquah wrote and published the six stories between the 1930s and 1960s. These are 'The Happenings of a Night' (1931), 'Anticipation', 'The Torn Veil' and 'Payment' (all published in 1947), 'Invisible Scar' (1966) and 'Evidence of Passion' (1969). Although a couple of critics mention Dove-Danquah's 'Anticipation' in their essays, as far as is known, no sustained critical attention has been paid to her fiction (Agovi 1990; Brown 1981; Jones-Quartey 1975).

A pioneer writer, Dove-Danquah's first published short story, 'The Happenings of a Night', appeared in serialized form in her own column, 'Ladies Corner' in *The Times of West Africa*, between 14 September and 3 October 1931. This point is important because it shows an African woman writer in the early 1930s having almost complete control over her manner of literary production, contradicting the widely held notion that women began writing in the 1960s.

'The Happenings of a Night' comes to the reader from the interior monologue of Araba Djan, a young woman 'brought up in a very select and refined atmosphere'. Araba is engaged to be married to Afla Tekonsere, 'a young man about town'. She spends an evening out with her fiancé and a group of friends, who all return to Afla's home to extend the good time. Araba strays into a room and falls asleep. The rest of the narration comes from her hiding place where the reader becomes an unwitting eavesdropper. Araba finds the behaviour of the people whom she observes completely unacceptable; she spends a greater part of her time vacillating between gathering the courage to put a stop to the orgy or sneaking out and going home.

This earliest attempt at story-writing by Dove-Danquah shows her potential for analysing the psychology of characters. The group of people is drawn from the emerging upper-middle class and their flat characters merely serve the function of carrying the writer's scorn for indecency and irresponsibility. 'The Happenings of a Night' suggests that the educated elite 'fell apart' much earlier than the post-independence era which provides the context for works by African writers who, some three decades later, focus on this group.[1]

'The Happenings of a Night' fictionalizes the moral degradation into which the men and women have fallen or have been pushed. By isolating herself from the group, Araba plays the role of social critic. The use of the interior monologue is most appropriate in this story. Araba is the only one in the group who expresses disapproval at the excessive drinking, smoking, loud conversation and general debauchery of her peers. As a result she can speak only to herself. Drawn to her hiding place, we observe her anguish over the fate of her class and of her country. We also notice her unsteady, earlier attempts to intervene. The suspense is over-stretched at times, but the writer does not allow it to get out of hand. When Araba finally surprises the group at the climax of the story, she experiences a sense of relief, and the change in circumstance diffuses the tension, propelling the story to a remarkable end.

A significant fact is that, by the end of the story, we observe Araba's transformation from weakness to strength. Instead of eavesdropping and apologizing for her lack of will, she effectively disrupts the activities of the unsuspecting crowd. Although she does not say a word, her presence is enough to extract some measure of guilt and her appearance directs the course of the rest of the evening for the group. Besides, Araba gives herself the time to evaluate her own reasons for marriage; she abandons them, sensing that marriage under conditions such as she had seen would thwart her spirit. Her decision not to get married is important because it shows the development of this female protagonist who now questions 'that form of happiness that is derived from matrimony'. This attitude calls marriage itself into question and we see a repetition of it in three other stories: 'The Torn Veil', 'Invisible Scar' and 'Evidence of Passion'. Dove-Danquah's stories suggest a radical revision of the institution of marriage even in the 1930s. Her characters take decisive steps in redressing their perceptions of unfairness. This repeated behaviour in her stories places the writer at the forefront of the cause of women's struggle for choices in West African society.

The most anthologized of her stories, 'Anticipation',[2] tells of a chief, Nana Adaku II, *Omanhene* of Akwansin. This powerful man falls in love with Effua, a beautiful dancer, during an annual traditional festival *Odwira*. He quickly sends his linguist to woo her for him. Having decided to possess this woman, he vows to pay any amount that her people might demand as dowry. If she is already married, he plans to pay off her husband: 'I must have her as a wife', he declares with childish impatience (Dove-Danquah 1947: 3). The linguist is successful in bringing the woman to him for the night; the chief makes elaborate preparations and displays his wealth in 'anticipation' of the consummation of the marriage. Effua chooses this strategic moment to remind him that she is already one of his forty wives, whom he married barely a year earlier. The structure of this story is particularly effective: the tension builds up until the very end when the punchline is delivered and resolution occurs.

Two major episodes in this narrative undermine the chief: the first occurs during the festival when his status as a chief prohibits him from laughing in public. He has to keep a grim face when the clown deliberately tries to provoke him. This scene holds the chief up to ridicule because the public is not tied to a similar code of behaviour. The second episode occurs as he indulges in foreplay with his 'new bride'. The revelation of the identity of Effua rudely curtails the chief's pleasure. Both Effua and the reading audience witness the discomfiture of the chief. Effua's people are also in the corridor, ready to thank him for giving so much money to their daughter. They know that the chief, the custodian of traditional wisdom, has inadvertently married his wife a second time. Through their accounts of the remarriage the public will have a good subject for gossip and mockery. This will especially poke fun at his fallibility and raise questions about his authority.

The narrative is unsparing in its judgement of the chief. The social and political structures of which he is the head support his greed. The narrative suggests that it is in the interests of the disadvantaged in the community – both women and men – to challenge the internal social and political dynamics that govern society. There is a relationship between the subordination of the woman and a larger pattern of oppression that needs scrutiny; it is not a simple matter of men against women, but a complex case of the powerful against the powerless. Seen in this way Dove-Danquah becomes a forerunner of Sembene Ousmane and Ngugi wa Thiong'o, whose literary works advance the cause of the underprivileged in African society.[3]

The 'new type of modern woman' introduced in 'Anticipation' is, the narrator explains, 'hardhearted and masculine hearted, she insists on the perfect lover as well as the income and other necessaries, or stays forever from the marriage unbliss' (Dove-Danquah 1947: 3–4). The reference is important as a forecast, in the 1940s, of the woman who would emerge to question and even challenge dominant conceptions of womanhood.

The story also raises a number of concerns regarding the depiction of character. For example, the women emerge as inarticulate, passive creatures, and the reader does not have the opportunity to share their thoughts on the subject of polygyny. Furthermore, there is no information on the economic and social underpinnings of their actions. These concerns arise because their point of view is not handled to maximum effect. What is obvious is that, by denying voices to her women characters about subjects that influence their lives, the writer unwittingly denies the story a powerful effect. More than this, her failure to include women's voices reflects the writer's subconscious identification with an essentially male view of marriage.

We have already noted the ridicule to which the chief is subjected in 'Anticipation'. The reader does not share the chief's view about the whole institution of polygyny, either. During such an important festival as *Odwira* the chief does not even address his subjects, for his sole concern is to get a woman into bed. What gains emphasis is his uncontrolled sexuality and unconcern for others and his state. By seeing him solely through character in action, the reader cannot evaluate the chief's reasons for marrying so many women, unless it is sheer appetite. The only person who is ill at ease with the polygynous marriage arrangement is the narrator, who functions as an outsider, directing her anger exclusively at the central male, and representing an ideal audience response to the text.

The political and social circumstances at the time and place of publication of this story are important, for they suggest a rationale for the choice of subject-matter and its handling. The period of nationalism saw British efforts directed, among other areas, at weakening the traditional power base. The silence of the chief and the women represents a tacit allusion to the current political and social upheavals hidden in the text. The traditional symbol of authority in 'Anticipation' lends itself to a subversive attitude towards colonial hegemony. Expressed differently, the images of the chief as a being driven solely by sensual appetites and of women as beings without will combine to describe the crippling effect of colonialism, imposed from without on existing political structures. The chief has become the metaphoric representation of the absence of purpose, control and direction in those who, perhaps, were once powerful, and certain of their destinies. This silence articulates clearly a desire to provoke discussion of the subject of hegemony.

I understand the spirit of the critic K. E. Agovi's charge that Dove-Danquah 'deftly succeeds in portraying the institution of polygyny as bereft of love, affection and romance – a mindless institution in effect' (Agovi 1990: 251). I can also grasp his assertion that the author reveals 'a mind that is still in bondage to European assumptions about African institutions' (p. 251). However, I think it is also possible to read the import of this story on two levels. On one level, 'Anticipation' is an attempt to fictionalize the unquestioning misuse of power against the disadvantaged in society. Existing and imposed structures of power support this abuse. On another level, the story explains, through its characterization, the silence and invisibility that characterize human beings when they are robbed of their known sources of power. It should be noted in this story that women become the underdogs of the underdogs. The subversive element lies more in what we do not see than in what exists overtly in the text. This view would confirm the tenuous position of the writer in a colonial context, writing for an audience 'still in bondage'.

Dove-Danquah's criticism of norms that govern marriage receives further attention in 'The Torn Veil'. This narrative, like 'The Invisible Scar', is suffused with aspects of the ghost story. 'The Torn Veil' tells of a recent member of the new middle class, Kwame Asante, who decides to take a second wife. His current wife, Akosua, with whom he has lived for ten years, the mother of their three children, cannot speak or write English. Refusing to be pacified with money, this wife leaves her matrimonial home along with her three children. Meanwhile, Kwame Asante goes on with his church wedding. In the evening, having had too much of everything, his conscience begins to gnaw at him. As a result he dreams of Akosua, who wears a bridal outfit, and the beauty of this figure attracts him. Trying to get hold of her, Kwame hits his head on a piece of furniture and dies. A scrap of the bridal gown is found in his hand when his body is discovered in the morning, and his second marriage is not consummated.

Of special interest in this narrative is Akosua's strength as central character. She is disappointed and angered by her husband's desire to marry someone he believes to be of a social status superior to hers. Consequently, Akosua decides to leave her marital home, rather than adapt to his intentions. The altercation between wife and husband after his announcement is important in dramatizing the confidence and energy of this strong female character:

> 'I say you can keep your twenty-five pounds, fifty pounds or hundred pounds. I will have nothing to do with it. I will not be paid off.'
> 'What! What! Come! Come! Don't do anything rash.'
> 'If you dare touch me I shall strike your face.'
> 'Strike your master, your husband? Are you mad?'
> 'I shall leave this house.'
> 'If you dare to disgrace me by leaving the house before I am ready for you to go, there will be trouble ... You know our Native Customary Law.'

> 'Yes, I know your Native Customary Law is a grave to bury women alive, whilst you men dance and beat tomtom on top of the mound of earth.' (Dove-Danquah 1947: 9).

This is a strong repudiation of polygyny which compares with Aïssatou's reaction to a similar situation some four decades later in Mariama Bâ's *So Long a Letter* (1980). Dove-Danquah's character lives in a time and place which denies her the options opened to Aïssatou. She does not bloom as Aïssatou does. It looks as if Akosua has so tied her self-worth to her marital status that without that prop she loses the will to live. Akosua dies. Although the narrative does not explain the cause of her death, we can infer that the shabby treatment has something to do with it. These two deaths strongly register the narrative's total rejection of the disruptive effects of polygyny.

Worth noting is that when Akosua finds life unbearable in her marital setting she discovers a 'haven' in her father's house. When her husband attempts to make amends by contacting her people, the narrator tells us that no one takes the slightest notice of him. Clearly, this man's arrogance falls outside the traditional code of marital conduct; there is therefore a way in which the wider society does not uniformly condone his behaviour.

'Two sources support Kwame's action: first, there is the Native Customary Law: which, like some other laws in the Gold Coast, needs disinfecting, for though it aids the man to gain his desire when it is at its fiercest, it in no way safeguards the position of the woman when the man's passion abates' (Dove-Danquah 1947: 6). Secondly, 'Kwame Asante, like many of our men, had floundered in his sense of values; the western impact on his mentality had sent it all askew' (p. 10). His conduct shows a combination of the worst in the traditional system and a maladjustment to the colonial, imposed system. The woman Kwame selects to be his second wife, Martha, is formally educated; she does not question the basis of Kwame's power which enables him so casually to dispense with one woman and marry another.

Akosua on the other hand, confident in herself, is the only one to attempt a method of 'cleansing' by removing herself from a potentially unhappy marriage arrangement. Kwame Asante takes it for granted that she would understand his need for a 'frock woman'. In his discussion of his impending marriage, he does not even once consider her emotions. When we watch her sob in her room after her utter repudiation of polygyny, we can recall similar scenes in later writing that show that women did not uniformly support it.[4] Dove-Danquah's story 'The Torn Veil' also proposes fundamental changes that will truly reflect the interests of society as a whole.

'Payment' tells of a woman who loses a son after consulting several healers. One healer promises to save him. She sees through this 'medicine man' who demands a high price for his 'cure', and the tension reaches its climax when the medicine man stretches out his hand for payment. Instead of the money he is expecting, the woman slaps him in the face. Again Dove-Danquah has depicted a strong woman, this time strong both emotionally and physically. At the beginning of the story we see her closing the eyes of her dead son, the child she had worked so hard to save. Then, upon the realization that the healers have only taken advantage of her, she decides to have her revenge by striking one of them. As in the previous stories, the narrative shows a man who takes advantage of a woman, and of a woman determined to assert her rights.

'Invisible Scar' was serialized in the *Weekly Spectator* between 10 and 24 September 1966. The initial scene is set in a doctor's office. The direct description of the patient portrays him as an average, middle-aged man with a medium build, an 'oval face ... light brown colour ... snow white hair and iron gray eyebrows'. His 'multi-coloured kente cloth and velvet shorts' denote a firm economic standing. The reader is not prepared for the dramatic turn of events which interrupts the brief conversation between patient and doctor. Suddenly, a lurid smile plants itself on the face of Asare, the patient. He doubles over, racked by acute pain, while his whole countenance is distorted 'beyond recognition'. Resorting to biblical language, the omniscient narrator who opens the story tells of the 'unquenchable and relentless flames of hell' which the patient feels in his heart. While the doctor is convinced that he is dealing with a lunatic and prepares to call for help, Asare shouts for his son who presently enters. The boy places his hands on his father's abdomen, just below the navel, and peace is instantly restored to him.

Dove-Danquah's ability to build suspense is displayed once more in this narration, and it is successfully sustained in all three instalments which carry the story. The technique is supported by an adept structuring of various exciting episodes which feed the curiosity of the reader alongside the skilful manner in which the author releases information.

The rest of the story, which carefully unravels the mystery, comes in a combination of the confessional, the autobiographical and the epistolary forms of telling. These techniques, which mark part of the growing artistry of Dove-Danquah, succeed in creating a sense of immediacy, so that events are drawn from the distant past into the immediate past, lending credibility, realism and a sense of urgency to the narration.

The narrative point of view adopted for the greater part of this story differs from the others that we have seen so far, for this one comes from a male perspective. In a letter which Asare addresses to the young doctor and which is read after his death, he tells of a fifteen-year-long marriage to a woman whose charm and sincerity had originally attracted him. He paints the following picture of his married life: 'I did what I liked, kept mistresses and had children ... I criticized her work as a reporter, her frocks, her cooking, her manners, in fact I did what many of my friends do to break the spirit of their wives and so completely destroy their personality.' Asare fails to make a connection between his own negative attitude towards his wife and her psychological alienation from him. Instead he seeks the help of a quack spiritualist, Beard, who simply nurtures the seeds of mistrust about his wife which are sprouting unrestrained in Asare's mind. Only after she dies of neglect and emotional abuse does he realize he could have attempted to win her back 'by playful gentleness, a little sense of humour and a surprise present now and again'. Worthy of note is that even this afterthought excludes a reappraisal of his extra-marital affairs and confidence-sapping attitudes. It does not mention respect, either. Asare who, by his own admission, dishonoured the marriage, sees adultery by his wife as the only probable cause for her withdrawal from him and he proceeds to make real this suspicion by circulating letters he has constructed, full of 'infamous allegations and deliberate falsehoods'. These malicious allegations by her own husband tear her 'reputation into shreds'. Shocked by such a profound betrayal of trust, she decides to leave her husband, who responds by assaulting her. She leaves him anyway, setting up a new home with their child.

This habit of women of removing themselves from unhappy relationships is a distinctive feature of the major characters in Dove-Danquah's stories. Asare reflects on his wife's display of initiative: 'my wife had appeared fragile enough and yet what a fight she had put up and to what lengths I and my friends had gone and sometimes I wondered whether we had won'. The 'lengths' to which Asare refers include his defamatory accusations that caused her own family to condemn her, thereby deepening her alienation.

Asare's brief attempt at reconciliation is backed not by a genuine feeling of regret, but by a deeply selfish motive: he is assailed by a string of ill luck and he believes that a reunion with his estranged wife would halt it. As part of the bargain he agrees to provide support for their son, but he reneges on his promise of financial assistance, notwithstanding the 'strong language' she uses to tell him 'what she thought of him'. The frustrated woman seeks redress from the legal system and gets none, largely due to his illegal and corrupt interference with the lawyers. When one lawyer refuses to be bribed by Asare and suggests in a letter that the wife be provided with monetary support, his response is to send this lawyer an expanded version of the libellous letter as his reason for refusing to comply with his request. It is the final blow which kills the woman; a post-mortem examination attributes the cause of death to 'shock and malnutrition'.

Mrs Asare exacts her vengeance from beyond the tomb when she appears to Asare, charging him, 'You raked up all the old lies, the scandalous allegations, the filth and the mud you had heaped on me'. In the ensuing argument she transfers to him the wound which she had earned during the caesarean operation for the birth of their son, whose parentage he denied as part of the contents of the vicious letter. The 'live' scar, which only Asare can see, is her way of perpetually reminding him of how she felt about his cold-hearted behaviour.

The fact that this woman can, like Akosua of 'The Torn Veil', launch her vengeance from beyond the physical world confirms the absence of such opportunities for women in the social world beyond the stories. Asare has claimed that 'whatever a man does is right; he is above the law and the husband is the dictator of the law'. Extra-textual evidence would not support this claim, however. The power which men wield over women is more effectively supported by an underlying obligatory force – the power of custom – to compel behaviour along the lines of sex and gender.

'Evidence of Passion' challenges and upsets the notion that a husband is the 'dictator of the law' for, in it, Mrs Dacosta obtains justice against her husband from a law court. 'Evidence of Passion' appeared in the February edition of *Drum* (Ghana Edition, 1969). This story is also important for its subject-matter and its manner of presentation, set in the court room where a divorce is taking place. Mrs Dacosta, a wealthy and sophisticated woman, seeks a divorce from her husband, a lawyer. Her case rests on physical abuse, infidelity and misappropriation of her wealth by her husband. He denies the charges and wants his family back. We may note that the subject of divorce hardly features in the African novel.[5] Dove-Danquah's story takes us into the court room where the reader observes the performance of both the prosecution and the defence. The whole narrative works towards a climax in which the plaintiff alleges that she surprised her husband in bed with their ward, now Mrs Paton. The event led to a slap by Mr Dacosta and the loss of a tooth by Mrs Dacosta. Mrs Paton reveals that her own husband died three months after their marriage, because of a fight between him and Mr Dacosta in her bedroom.

The fact that two women and one man are denied a peaceful life by another man is of interest. The struggle moves from the arena of sexual discrimination to one involving the powerful and the disadvantaged. The relationship between Mr Dacosta and Mr Paton recalls the power of the chief in 'Anticipation', who helped himself to other people's wives. Solidarity is forged between Mrs Dacosta and the Patons because Mr Dacosta is the common abuser.

Dove-Danquah's stories offer two broad images of women. On the one hand there is the example of Effua whose behaviour does not appear to upset existing structures. Araba, together with Mrs Dacosta, Akosua and the mother and Mrs Asare, on the other hand, openly question, challenge and offer alternative ways of conceiving of womanhood and of society. By so doing the writer reveals a complex female perspective.

The point of this exercise in retrieval is part of a larger effort to return such writers as Mabel Dove-Danquah to the critical arena. The project focuses on diurnal and journalistic sources where most of these writers' material can be found. In 1975, K. A. B. Jones-Quartey held an interview with Dove-Danquah. At the time she was seventy years old and partially blind, but she was articulate, witty and firm in her convictions. However, she expressed regret that nobody seemed to care about her achievements. Jones-Quartey himself agreed with her by commenting, 'history, indeed seems to be passing this woman by without further notice' (Jones-Quartey 1975: 40). It would be tragic if such writers were to be forgotten and allowed to disappear unnoticed, because they form an important part of the literary history of Ghana and Africa. Indeed, the map would be incomplete without such rich lodes.

Notes

An earlier version of this chapter, 'Mabel Dove-Danquah: A Pioneer African Writer', was presented at the Colloquium of the Pan-African Historical Theatre Festival, Ghana, December 1994. Research was made possible by a fellowship from the Fulbright Senior Scholar Award Program 1993–94, and is hereby gratefully acknowledged.

1. See, among others, Armah (1969); Ousmane (1973); Ngugi wa Thiong'o (1982a).
2. 'Anticipation' has been anthologized in sources including the following: Cullens Young (ed.) (1947: 37–42); Hughes (ed.) (1960: 163–7); Shelton (ed.) (1968: 100–4); Kwakwa (1974; 120–24); Bruner (ed.) (1983). Three of Dove-Danquah's stories – 'Anticipation' (1947), 'The Torn Veil' (1947) and 'Payment' (1947) – are published in *The Torn Veil and Other Stories*. Page references are made to this edition, published in 1975.
3. See for example, Ousmane (1960; 1973); Ngugi wa Thiong'o (1982a; 1982b).
4. See, for example, Bâ (1981); Ousmane (1974: 38–53); Aidoo (1991).
5. The rare examples of texts which focus on divorce include: Aidoo (1970: esp. 66–9; 1991); Bâ, (1981); Dangarembga (1987).

References

Agovi, K. E. (1990) 'A Dual Sensibility: The Short Story in Ghana 1944–80', in E. N. Emenyonu (ed.) *Literature and Black Aesthetics*, Heinemann, Nigeria, 247–71.
Aidoo, A. A. (1970) *No Sweetness Here*, Longman, London.
— (1991) *Changes: A Love Story*, Women's Press, London.
Armah, A. K. (1969) *The Beautyful Ones Are Not Yet Born*, Heinemann, London.
Bâ, M. (1980) *So Long a Letter*. Trans. M. Bode-Thomas. Heinemann, London.
Brown, L. (1981) *Women Writers from Black Africa*, Greenwood Press, Connecticut.
Bruner, C. H. (ed.) (1983) *Unwinding Threads: Writing by Women in Africa*, Heinemann, London.
Cullens Young, T. (ed.) (1947) *African New Writing: Short Stories by African Authors*, Lutterworth, London.
Dangarembga, T. (1987) *She No Longer Weeps*, College Press, Harare.
Dove-Danquah, M. (1931) 'The Happenings of a Night', *The Times of West*

    Africa, 14 September, 2; 15 September, 2; 16 September, 2–3; 17–18 September, 2; 19 September, 2; 21–22 September, 2; 23–24 September, 2–3; 25 September, 2–3; 26 September, 2–3; 30 September, 2–3; 1–2 October, 2; 3 October, 2–3.

— (1947) 'Anticipation', 'The Torn Veil' and 'Payment', in P. Iyatemi and M. Dove-Danquah, *The Torn Veil and Other Stories*, Evans Brothers, London and Ibadan, 1975.

— (1966) 'Invisible Scar', *Weekly Spectator*, 10, 17 and 24 September.

— (1969) 'Evidence of Passion', *Drum* (Ghana Edition), February, 32.

Eliot, T. S. (1962) 'The Metaphysical Poets', in D. J. Enright and E. de Chickera (eds), *English Critical Texts*, Oxford University Press, London.

Hughes, L. (ed.) (1960), *An African Treasury: Essays, Stories, Poems by Black Africans*, Crown Publishers, New York.

Jones-Quartey, K. A. B. (1975) 'First Lady of Pen and Parliament – A Portrait', *International Centenary Evening with Aggrey of Africa*, Ghana Association of Writers, Accra.

Kwakwa, B. S. (1974) *Ghanaian Writing Today*, Ghana Publishing Corporation, Accra.

Ngugi wa Thiong'o (1982a) *Devil on the Cross*, Heinemann, London.

— (1982b) *I Will Marry When I Want*, Heinemann, London.

Ousmane, S. (1970) *God's Bits of Wood*, Heinemann, London.

— (1974) 'Her Three Days', *Tribal Scars and Other Stories*, Heinemann, London.

— (1976) *Xala*, Heinemann, London.

Shelton, A. J. (ed.) (1968) *The African Assertion: A Critical Anthology of African Literature*, Odyssey, New York.

Walker, A. (1983) *In Search of Our Mothers' Gardens and Other Essays*, Harcourt Brace Jovanovitch, New York.

6
Rewriting popular myths of female subordination: selected stories by Theodora Adimora-Ezeigbo and May Ifeoma Nwoye

CHINYERE GRACE OKAFOR

A cursory look at two of the writers acknowledged by the Association of Nigerian Authors (ANA) in 1994[1] indicates a pair as different as literary and mathematical signs: one, Theodora Adimora-Ezeigbo, is a literary academic (writing as Theodora Akachi Ezeigbo), while the other, May Ifeoma Nwoye, is a practising accountant. Since Adimora-Ezeigbo lives in the fast capital city of Lagos and Nwoye lives in the ancient, provincial city of Benin with its traditional outlook, one might expect the divergence to increase. However, their artistic inclinations as writers and particular predilection as women writers overshadow any notions of disparity, for they engage with the wave of 'womanist' assertions sweeping through rural and urban West Africa.

When circumstances during the Nigeria–Biafra War (1967–70) enabled Igbo women to take up roles usually assigned to men, the majority of whom had gone to war, they embraced the change with a force that has made a lasting impact on the social structure. Women who became contractors, breadwinners and household heads as a result of the war are now permanent and accepted features of Nigerian life.[2] The contribution of women to the war, not only in the rear but also in the forefront of battle and across the fighting zones, legitimizes and enhances their assertiveness in the culture. The war situation also enabled women to break into the territory marked out as 'masculine', for they began to organize and create mask performances, a sacred activity hitherto the prerogative of men.[3]

With equal determination, women have invaded the literary domain hitherto dominated by men.[4] As writers, they have brought new angles and insights into fiction, rejecting portrayals of women as self-effacing, docile and passive observers in the world of men (Austen-Peters 1994:

33). Chinua Achebe's and Cyprian Ekwensi's constructions of women's experience as tangential to the 'masculine' world[5] have been challenged in the novels of Flora Nwapa and Buchi Emecheta, whose heroines are vital and viable individuals, engaging in a world shared with men, defining their own spaces and contributing to the social reality of that world. They present the woman-as-insider's experience of the world and are therefore able to portray women's struggles and triumphs as they intersect with the reality of that world, not only through sexual roles but also through other self-actualizing ventures. Dealing with 'the submerged realities of African women's lives' (Boyce Davies 1986: 255), Nwapa and Emecheta thus annunciate womanhood in a manner unknown in fiction written by Igbo men.

Along the same lines as Nwapa and Emecheta are a host of other women writers: Rosemary Uwemedimo, Mabel Segun, Ifeoma Okoye, Rosina Umelo, Karen Aribisala, Adaora Ulasi, Zaynab Alkali, Mary Okoye, Teresa Meniru, Chary Onwu, Helen Ofurun and others, who have brought new insights into fiction read by children, youths and adults (Otokunefor and Nwodo [eds] 1989). These writers are all concerned with accessing and exciting the consciousness of young and adult readers, a necessary step in remoulding psyches that have long been fed with half-truths and untruths about women's lives. According to Ann Adams Graves:

> whether from the Negritude movement with its romanticization of women or from the more recent years in which she is depicted with greater fidelity – the images [of African women] are ... less than whole, incompletely formed, images imposed on women by others, or otherwise unrealistic. All, however, are seen through the eyes of males who are the dominant figures in the literary works as well as in the lives of the women characters in the works (Adams Graves 1986: 25).

Two contemporary women writers, Nwoye and Adimora-Ezeigbo, contribute in distinctive ways to the dismantling of the stereotypes, falling easily within Nwapa's and Emecheta's matri-focal field of vision because many of their short stories explore women's experiences from the insider's position. They are particularly concordant in their attack on stereotypes and misconceptions, writing in order to expose myths of female subordination and to explode inherited negative stereotypes of women. The myths of female subordination include the view that women are inferior, weak and peripheral beings in a world where men are central and superior.

Originally, 'mythos' signified a plot or story, but myth will be viewed here in an extended sense as a fictitious idea or fantasy, an unscientific account, theory or belief. Myth does not exist independently of text and society, but is always buried within a specific form, immersed in the framework of a tale, history, poem or ritual. Myth is not a form but an essential content, 'encased in verbal covering' (Ruthven 1976: 27). Myths of female subordination are often encased in literary forms produced by men. In the works of Wole Soyinka, for example, women are objectified as sex symbols in a world where female experience is confined to their relations with men as foolish virgins, mistresses and matrons (Boyce Davies 1986). They are not given enough room to explore other possibilities for self-fulfilment outside these sexual roles. Similarly, although Ayi Kwei Armah's characterization of women in *Two Thousand Seasons* (1979) is multi-dimensional, his portrayal of women in other novels is largely uni-dimensional: they are usually parasites and liberating prophets who are 'lovers, wives, or blood relatives of the central male figure' (Busia 1986: 89).

Onuora Nzekwu's heroine in *Highlife for Lizards*, Agom, mouths the popular male view about women's weakness and subordination: 'It is natural for a man to be direct in his ways with women and she to be devious; him to be plain, she to be subtle; him to roam the earth as he pleases, she always to be home; him to be strong, she weak' (Nzekwu 1965: 191). Although spoken by a woman, these ideas emanate from the male-oriented psyche nurtured by society; woven into the fictional world, such representations in turn service the social reality, as readers internalize the reinforced or rewritten gender ideals. According to Ogede, 'some women have come to accept the male stereotypical assumptions about themselves' (Ogede 1994: 107). When male-centred views of society are projected on to literature, and imbibed by the readership, the ideas become endemic and can be dented, debunked or erased only through systemic and persistent attack by those who recognize them for what they are – that is, misconceptions of reality. Nwoye and Adimora-Ezeigbo are aware of these ill-conceived notions, which they try to destroy by rewriting popular myths about women.

In their stories, the two writers present a contrary view to popular stereotypes: women are depicted, first, as central characters in the narrative; second, as bold, courageous and determined; third, protagonists possess traits usually ascribed to men, thereby showing that such traits are not gender-specific; fourth, women are shown engaging in life through professional experience; fifth, the characters' lives are not confined to sexual roles; and, finally, they are actors in a world shared by men and not passive reactors in a man's world.

Of the twelve stories in Nwoye's collection, *Tides of Life* (1994), seven have women as protagonists. Of Adimora-Ezeigbo's eight stories in *Echoes in the Mind* (1994), five centre on women. The predominance of female-focused tales certainly represents a gender-centring that is contrary to the form of male-centred literature. And female characters' aspirations are not restricted to sexual roles as wives, mothers, mistresses and other appendages of patriarchy. Instead, professional women are portrayed as politicians, village dancers, village potters, writers and manageresses who experience life in their own right. This is contrary to the stance of novelists such as Cyprian Ekwensi: in *Jagua Nana's Daughter* (1986) the heroine is a lawyer who does not experience life as a lawyer, nor does she make a living by her profession, earning her income instead as a mistress.

Nwoye's 'Unruly Driver' focuses on a manageress struggling to establish her authority over a subordinate, a male driver whose brashness continually threatens to undermine her authority and dent her confidence. Emphasis is placed on the authority of the manageress, who is not named. Presented as an assertive woman who is sure of her capabilities, she is humble in her approach to subordinates. The driver tries to negate the manageress, arriving late at her premises and 'blowing the horn violently at the gate as if he had not time to waste' (Nwoye 1994: 72). Halfway through the journey, he tries to frustrate her by attempting to terminate the trip. Changing tactics, the woman abandons her placatory stance, becoming authoritarian. Surprisingly, this method achieves the desired result and '[b]y the return trip to Benin, he was quite reasonable and behaved like a subordinate and I the officer' (p. 73).

Character and motivation are barely developed in the story, and the plot is sketchy, yet the writer succeeds in using the anecdote to represent the struggles a woman goes through in trying to assert her rights among subordinates who are not used to receiving orders from women. The heroine's anonymity is a device that universalizes the experience: her awareness of the driver's sexism and her rejection of it, as well as her authoritarian (though delayed) assertion of power over her subordinate, reveal a feminist impulse reminding one of Chikwenye Ogunyemi's assertion that 'feminism smacks of rebelliousness, fearlessness, political awareness of sexism and an unpardonable (from the male viewpoint) drive for equality between the sexes' (Ogunyemi 1985: 9). The protagonist experiences her world as an important official, not as a sexual being.

Women's struggle for their rights is a common enough feature of daily life in West Africa. Some women do not enter the world positively, however, abandoning the struggle for progress and achievement; such a woman is Rose, the anti-heroine of Nwoye's 'Blessed Romance', who succumbs to family pressure and dislocates herself from society in order to be available to possible wooers. Through this action, she mars her career potential and the dislocation triggers an unhealthy attitude to work. Rose spends official time seeking excitement by making telephone calls, a practice that earns her the sack. Nwoye is contemptuous of Rose, whom she punishes: for not only does the young woman lose her job, but the 'romantic' prize won through the telephone calls does not meet her expectations. The story ends on a didactic note as Rose swears to leave the town altogether. This story is a moral lesson for women who want to reap without sowing: for the 'prize' is an ugly man beaming a smile at Rose, exposing a yellow and 'incomplete set of teeth ... Rose looked more dizzy than confused. She could not place the beautiful voice of the technician with his short physique, not to mention the thick lips' (Nwoye 1994: 55–6).

In spite of her lack of drive, however, Rose has been bold and daring, qualities she shares with the manageress in 'Unruly Driver' and other heroines of Nwoye's fiction. The confidence of Nwoye's characters is comparable to that of the women maskers in the writer's cultural tradition, displaying vibrant energy in their celebration of female power. In the villages around Aba, women mask cultists defiantly ululate their freedom, declaring their ability to break through the gender boundary that once barred them from dancing with the gods in the mask theatre: *Ono l'ura tehu, Tehu kpodahuya, Egede shuru gede* (Whoever is sleeping, wake up, Try hard and wake up, Something great has happened) (Okafor 1993). Their call to women to rise up and take advantage of the new theatre and enjoy their new structure of female assertion is reminiscent of the *Ebre* women dancers of Calabar who, in an exuberant song about female assertiveness, smoke pipes like men and declare that, 'we shall no longer be mattresses for men' (Okafor 1994).

Nwoye's assertive protagonists recall the feminist import of these traditional women's performances: similarly, Adimora-Ezeigbo's stories have female characters who boldly enter the world. 'Agaracha Must Come Back' is about a young woman, Edoro, who makes a bold choice when she decides independently to marry a Nigerian soldier whom her Igbo people regard as an enemy. Aware of the atrocities committed by Nigerian soldiers during the Biafran war, Edoro believes that 'not all federal soldiers were bad and irresponsible' (Adimora-Ezeigbo 1994: 11). Her action resembles that of the village *belle* of the Igbo traditional tale who refuses eligible bachelors from her community and marries a handsome stranger against her parents' wishes: the stranger turns out to be an evil one in disguise. Such a story is used to make girls conform to parental and societal dictates,[6] submerging the personalities of young women who are compelled to conform to societal pressure, succumbing to the spouse chosen for them.

In Adimora-Ezeigbo's story, the bride, Edoro, refuses to conform to the oral prototype. Her choice is a revolutionary one that has potential for success or failure. Like her counterpart in oral literature, however, she fails, for the soldier husband brutalizes her; but she perseveres, like Buchi Emecheta's heroines, who 'adopt a positivistic view in crisis and do not just fold their arms in tears and self pity' (Chukwuma 1989: 4). She trains as a nurse and falls in love again. Before travelling abroad with her new man, she takes another courageous step by seeking a reconciliation with her people. She fails. Again she does not give up, becoming determined to tackle the reality of a life created by her own personal choices. Only her mother, Ugonma, defies the people and gives her support.

Edoro's experience exemplifies a West African woman's effort to assert her individuality in a world full of obstacles created by her patriarchal background and marital experience. Tackling the problems with courage and determination, she triumphs, fails, and continues with the struggle. The writer reveals a positive feminist impulse in her depiction of the courage and determination necessary for women's struggle in patriarchal environments where a woman is defined through her socio-political standing in relation to her father or her husband.

Beyond the depiction of brave and adventurous women, Adimora-

Ezeigbo and Nwoye reverse and rewrite misconceptions of women's nature. Nwoye's 'The Urhobo Dancing Maiden' is a reversal of the popular image of the shy and reluctant female lover, imprinted on the psyche through its persistence in popular stories. Nwoye creates a situation in which she reverses a well-known myth of the male as the wooer of a fair maiden: the bold dancer is now the wooer of a fair, shy, giggly and 'reluctant' young man – a notion which is brought into sharp focus through its dramatization in a public gathering in which the confused audience 'clapped, cheered and jeered' (Nwoye 1994: 68). In a similar manner, Nwoye reverses the jealous wife stereotype, 'a character which reappears with amazing frequency in African literature' (Boyce Davies 1986: 249). In her belief that jealousy is not gender-specific, she creates a story, 'Men Cry Too', in which a confident and independent woman who is sure of her capabilities has a husband who is threatened by her confidence and is afraid of losing her. Although some women who are subjected to situations of insecurity do employ direct, indirect and sometimes underhand survival techniques, Nwoye seeks to show that such methods are not the special preserve of women. She believes: 'Women are not the only ones who do the things they [men] accuse women of. These include being petty, suspicious, emotional and jealous ... The general idea is that if a woman makes trouble, her husband will dispense of her and get another one ... as if they are three for a penny.'[7]

A realistic situation is created in which a husband, Charles, is plagued by the fear of losing his wife to her ex-boyfriend, Jerry, who appears to be economically stable and confident. Sweating and lugging a jerrycan of petrol, Charles thinks he cuts a poor figure as he encounters the smart and handsome Jerry who has just returned from America 'loaded' with dollars. His feeling of insecurity, suppressed since Jerry left the country, resurfaces and, when members of his family are not at home, he has a 'free period of moaning, lamenting or crying' (Nwoye 1994: 25). Comparing himself with Jerry, he realizes how unkempt and dreary he has become, blaming it all on the harsh economy of the country: 'This stupid country has emasculated me. Has done me in!' (p. 26). He goes to the extent of persuading Rita, his wife, to accept his plan to move the family to another area far from Jerry's neighbourhood, and is only saved from the move by Jerry's return to the United States.

Throughout the period of Charles's acute jealousy, Rita shows understanding, neither flirting with Jerry because of her husband's insinuations, nor becoming unduly restrained in her behaviour just to prove her innocence. Instead, she pampers the man's delicate ego by agreeing to move because he is becoming paranoid. Her strength of character and her husband's weakness leave the reader in no doubt about the answer to the question she asks in the end: 'Tell me Charles, you and I, who is the weaker sex after all?' (p. 37). The answer is demonstrated indirectly by the events and characterization.

In the same spirit of rewriting the woman's angle, which has been distorted by the myths of a male-oriented society, Adimora-Ezeigbo reworks the popular stereotype of women's unwavering support for men. The saying, 'behind every successful man is a woman', is constantly repeated at Nigerian wedding ceremonies and other gatherings to reinforce the traditional, unequal status quo. Adimora-Ezeigbo reverses and questions that notion in 'Inspiration Bug'. The heroine, a writer, makes her career the central focus of her life. She can do so partly because of her understanding husband, whose character is not well developed, for the emphasis is on depicting the force of the 'inspiration bug', the muse compelling the writer to work. The heroine is impatient with the notion that men should always be supported by good, self-sacrificing, understanding women, so she has no apologies for responding to the muse and making it her primary concern: 'my mind dwelt on the selfless sacrifice made by spouses, companions, mistresses, and lovers of past and contemporary writers to foster their career ... women who were contented to remain in the background' (Adimora-Ezeigbo 1994: 111). Clearly aware of the implications, Adimora-Ezeigbo depicts a relationship in which a husband contains his wife's 'excesses' as she develops her career. The 'excesses' include the amount of time she spends on matters not strictly considered wifely and motherly, such as her comic disruption of the conjugal ritual with her husband because she feels the urge to make some notes. Similarly, she abandons a Christian sermon that captivated the congregation in order to rush off and complete a story. Such 'excesses' emanate from her profession as a writer, and she has no apologies to make. Her husband, like the wives and mistresses represented by male writers, understands and accommodates the protagonist's actions.

In Adimora-Ezeigbo's 'The Missing Hammer Head', female 'excesses' include 'wasting time' attending political meetings and planning career strategies. These activities potentially provoke tension and conflict in homes: but there is hardly any tension in the homes created by Adimora-Ezeigbo, because of her characterization of men as husbands who help women to achieve their goals. Men are not subordinated or subdued. Unlike the situation in Aidoo's *Anowa* (1965), where the heroine's moral strength towers above and contrasts with her husband's weakness, Adimora-Ezeigbo rewrites husbands as professionals and partners in the home, whose positions are not threatened by their wives' confidence and political voices. Adimora-Ezeigbo's idea seems to be that '*beside* a successful woman is a man'. This is not a reversal of the popular saying, 'behind every successful man is a woman'; it is a modification that equalizes the gender relation.

African feminism does not subscribe to a monolithic and exclusive empowerment of women, but to a multilateral growth that incorporates the woman, her family and her male relations. Equal partnership and mutual support contribute to a successful relationship. This 'womanist' position explains the only near-tragic story in Adimora-Ezeigbo's collection, 'Agaracha Must Come Home', which centres on a heroine who has stood behind rather than beside her cheating husband, supporting him; this heroine grovels for the support of a rigid and chauvinistic community that is unable to forgive her for expressing her individuality as a human being and a woman with emotions.

In Adimora-Ezeigbo's fiction, interest is sustained by the directness of the narration. The writer does not show the shyness of the 'demure maiden' who is seen and not heard, but thrusts her words forward for impact, in the manner of traditional female satirists. In exposing one man's injustice to a woman politician in 'The Missing Hammer Head', Adimora-Ezeigbo has him stripped of his clothes so that his vital organ, the symbol of his malicious manhood, can be exposed for what it is, an 'armoured car', dangerous, scheming and ruthless (Adimora-Ezeigbo 1994: 50). The enormity of the man's crime is sharply exposed through the vision of his over-sized penis:

> Even at rest the thing was extraordinarily large. Too large to seem to be part of the man's lean frame. It was like a thing apart, a huge black thing nestling at the mouth of a hole. At rest. The persistent prodding from the sergeant's baton activated the latent volcano making an eruption inevitable. It rose powerfully, trembled a little and pointed steadily at the sergeant as though it was a gun aimed at him (Adimora-Ezeigbo 1994: 50).

This illustrates Adimora-Ezeigbo's satirical directness as well as her symbolic use of language. The large penis, usually believed to stand for the essence of maleness and the instrument to make women tremble with excitement, is depicted as an instrument of violence and the bane of humanity. The man's penis is portrayed as an instrument of aggression and destruction not only for the woman, Fola, but for the world as it aims dangerously at the policeman. Violence and male aggression are symbolically depicted, threatening women and social stability.

Another effective stylistic device which Adimora-Ezeigbo uses in 'The Missing Hammer Head' is naming and the withholding of names. The man is not named, symbolizing male chauvinists who believe that no matter what a woman achieves, she is still inferior to the lowest male: 'I be man, you be woman, upon all de money you get, I day important pass you' (Adimora-Ezeigbo 1994: 51). Called simply, 'the man', or given the symbolic name, 'yam seller',[8] the criminal remains anonymous during the planning and execution of his revenge on Fola. Fola is treated as if her achievement as a woman is the reason for his inferiority: his anger at her pride is not based on that trait *per se*, but on the fact of its existence in a woman. For comparative reasons, her pride is shown to be much less than her own husband's arrogance, flagrantly displayed in the police station.

Similarly, Nwoye develops a distinctive naming technique in her stories. It is a major device in 'Dark Shadows', used to portray a widow's struggle with her in-laws. The usual belief that a widow should co-operate and do all her in-laws ask of her is contradicted by Nwoye's story, in which the widow refuses to drink the water used in washing her husband's corpse; she calls on his spirit instead, eliciting a supernatural intervention that deals with her adversaries and rescues her. Nwoye generalizes the widow's plight by withholding her name in the major, realistic part of the story. Towards the end when she employs the device of divine intervention, Nwoye particularizes the experience by providing the widow's name for the first time. Previously she has been called, 'the widow' and 'the wife of the dead man'; during the epiphany, the widow's name is mentioned, indicating Gloria's particular affinity with the event of the epiphany: 'The unidentified shadow covered the body of the dead man where it lay and part of it fell directly on Gloria, the dead man's wife, for that was her name ... a terrible thunder exploded, snatching the cup away from Gloria's hand' (Nwoye 1994:

90). From the moment of supernatural intervention, the author freely uses Gloria's name. While the name 'Gloria' appears up to ten times in the remaining few pages of the story, suggesting exaltation and splendour, its distortion into 'Gurorea' by the old man indicates an aberration of the vulnerable womanhood symbolized by the widow's plight. The widow therefore has to spend time, in spite of the chaotic situation, correcting the old man's mispronunciation of her name. The correction is a symbolic act heralding a new beginning for the widow and the society which must learn, like the old man, not to dehumanize a woman simply because she has lost her husband.

Although Nwoye has personalized the conclusion as a particular experience that pertains to Gloria, the question of a realistic solution to the problem of the widow's plight is still unanswered by the story. Can supernatural intervention solve a widow's problem? Not many readers can accept divine intervention as a realistic option. Nwoye's *deus ex machina* stands out as a trick. Non-acceptance of the technique must automatically excite a reader's mind into seeking realistic alternatives. Questioned about the problem of this story, Nwoye thinks that a realistic solution lies in legislation and fights by women's groups: 'There should be a legal policy against maltreatment of widows. They should be protected by the state through the police and other legal avenues. The violence meted out on widows breeds more violence in the society through the participants and observers and children who therefore see such as normal.'[9]

Unlike Nwoye's unrealistic conclusion to 'Dark Shadows', Adimora-Ezeigbo's rescue of the suffering heroine, Fola, and provision of justice is realistically achieved in 'The Missing Hammer Head'. Human rather than divine intervention occurs in this story. This difference in fictional resolutions should not be mistaken as indicating a major difference in the two writers' attitudes towards the physical and supernatural dimensions of West African society. Like Nwoye in 'Dark Shadows', Ezeigbo manifests a belief in supernatural intervention in stories such as 'Who Said Dead Men Can't Bite?' where the spirit of a dead Akobundu takes revenge; similarly, in 'The Verdict', the spirit of justice vindicates Maduka.

An affinity has emerged between Nwoye and Adimora-Ezeigbo: both writers focus on female characters not as passive reactors in the world of men but as human actors in their world shared by men. Aware of the obstacles in their paths arising from their gender and standpoints, they try to work out ways of solving their problems with courage and determination. In doing this, Nwoye and Adimora-Ezeigbo demonstrate qualities and ideas that are contrary to the popular ideas and misconceptions of womanhood propagated in orature and in the fiction of male-oriented writers. Nwoye and Adimora-Ezeigbo represent women's perception of themselves as individuals questioning the obstacles in their lives. Women are portrayed as vital and viable human beings, not as appendages or peripheral beings in a world dominated by towering male protagonists. The two writers have thus joined other writers, both male and female, in debunking the 'myths and shibboleths' (Ogundipe-Leslie and Boyce Davis 1994: 4) about African cultures. They have added to the growing body of feminist literature started by their predecessors, Nwapa and Emecheta.

Their brand of feminism is not antagonistic towards the opposite sex: both writers seek to show that character traits are not gender-specific and female aspirations are not limited to sexual roles. Without being confrontational, most of Nwoye's women tackle problems without the help of male partners, while Adimora-Ezeigbo's women are usually in sexual partnerships with understanding men. Neither writer subscribes to the exclusion of men from women's world. In fact, the world of their stories is a free world shared by all, in which women strive to define their spaces in spite of all obstacles.

Unlike traditional male maskers and the modern male novelists, all of whom have tended to portray women as uni-dimensional beings who are silent and gentle, Adimora-Ezeigbo and Nwoye have depicted women in their multi-faceted dimensions. Loudly proclaiming dead the myth of African women's voicelessness, their women are bold, co-operative, considerate, authoritarian, obedient and reckless. One can see that, in spite of their differences, the two writers' interests and opinions converge on matters concerning African women. This is hardly surprising for, in their primary professions, both writers operate in male-dominated domains where women struggle to find space, to progress and gain the respect of colleagues and subordinates.[10]

Notes

1. Theodora Adimora-Ezeigbo's *Echoes in the Mind* took the fourth position while May Ifeoma Nwoye's *Endless Search* was honourably mentioned. The event

was the award ceremony organized by the Association of Nigerian Authors (ANA) to release the result of the 1994 national competition.

2. The hardship ushered in by the present economic depression has exacerbated the burden on the womenfolk whose husbands have lost their jobs or whose normal income can no longer sustain the family because of the devaluation of the Naira.

3. The women of Izzi area of northern Igboland started producing and wearing masks in honour of *Uke* oracle for the safety of the community during the Nigeria–Biafra war.

4. See Otokunefor and Nwodo (eds) (1989).

5. Achebe (1958; 1960); Ekwensi (1961; 1986).

6. Among the Luo, such stories are designed to make young girls heed the advice of older women or match-makers (see Ayodo 1994: 122).

7. Personal interview with May Ifeoma Nwoye, 20 February 1995.

8. In Igboland which is Adimora-Ezeigbo's birthplace, yam is men's product and therefore symbolizes the male essence.

9. Personal interview with May Ifeoma Nwoye, 20 February 1995.

10. Personal interview with May Ifeoma Nwoye, 20 February 1995. Recall the heroine's struggle to assert herself in Nwoye's 'Unruly Driver' and the heroine's triumph when she declares that the driver has become reasonable (Nwoye 1994: 73).

References

Achebe, C. (1958) *Things Fall Apart*, Heinemann, London.

— (1960), *No Longer At Ease*, Heinemann, London.

Adams Graves, A. (1986) 'Defining "Woman's Place": Female Portraiture in African Literature', in C. Boyce Davies and A. Adams Graves (eds), *Ngambika: Studies of Women in African Literature*, Africa World Press, Trenton, NJ, 25–6.

Adimora-Ezeigbo, T. (1994) *Echoes in the Mind*, Foundation, Lagos, Nigeria.

Aidoo, A. A. (1965) *Anowa*, Longman, Harlow.

Armah, A. K. (1979) *Two Thousand Seasons*, Heinemann, London.

Austin-Peters, O. (1994) 'Feminism in Post-Independence West African Drama', *JMLAN: A Publication of the Modern Languages Association of Nigeria* 2, 33–38.

Ayodo, A. (1994) 'Definitions of the Self in Luo Women's Orature', *Research in African Literatures*, 25 (3), 121–30.

Boyce Davies, C. (1986) 'Motherhood in the Works of Male and Female Igbo Writers: Achebe, Emecheta, Nwapa and Nzekwu', in C. Boyce Davies and A. Adams Graves (eds), *Ngambika: Studies of Women in African Literature*, Africa World Press, Trenton, NJ, 241–56.

Busia, A. P. A. (1986) 'But Caliban and Ariel are still both Male: On African Colonial Discourse and the Unvoiced Female', Annual Selected papers of the African Literature Association, in K. Harrow, J. Ngate and Clarisse Zimra (eds), *Crisscrossing Boundaries in African Literatures*, Three Continents Press, Washington, DC.

Chukwuma, H. (1989) 'Positivism and the Female Crisis: The Novels of Buchi Emecheta', in H. Otokunefor and O. Nwodo (eds), *Nigerian Female Writers*, 2–18.

Ekwensi, C. (1961) *Jagua Nana*, Heinemann, London.

—— (1986), *Jagua Nana's Daughter*, Spectrum, Ibadan, Nigeria.

Hay, J. and S. Stichter (eds) (1984) *African Women: South of the Sahara*, Longman, London.

Nwoye, M. I. (1994) *Tides of Life*, Uto, Lagos, Nigeria.

Nzekwu, O. (1965) *Highlife for Lizards*, Hutchinson, London.

Ogede, O. O. (1994) 'Counters to Male Domination: Images of Pain in Igede Women's Songs', *Research in African Literatures: Special Issue – Women as Oral Artists* 25 (4), 105–20.

Ogundipe-Leslie, M. and Boyce Davies, C. (1994) 'Introduction', *Research in African Literatures: Special Issue – Women as Oral Artists* 25 (4), 1–6.

Ogunyemi, C. (1985) 'Women and Nigerian Literature', *Guardian*, Lagos, 25 May, 9.

Okafor, C. G. (1993) *Translation of Mask Chant*, Unpublished manuscript.

—— (1994) 'From the Heart of Masculinity: Obodo Uke'so Women's Masking', *Research in African Literatures* 25 (3), 7–18.

Otokunefor, H. and O. Nwodu (eds) (1989) *Nigerian Female Writers: A Critical Perspective*, Malthouse Press, Lagos, Nigeria.

Ruthven, K. K. (1976) *Myth*, Methuen, London.

7
Gender conflict in Flora Nwapa's novels

THEODORA AKACHI EZEIGBO

Gender conflict is a reality in every society: it is a vital aspect of social experience, manifesting a struggle for power that is of increasing interest to researchers and scholars throughout Africa. While generalizations cannot be made about gender relations in West Africa, it is possible to suggest that, in traditional Igbo thought at least, gender interaction is regarded as being complementary and balanced; it is based on a division of labour into separate gender spheres, rather than being conflictual or competing for the same positions of social and political power. The balance is best seen in the co-operation existing in social and political organizations formed by men and women which protect, preserve and enhance the rights of individuals and the welfare of whole communities.

Young males in Igboland are socialized to be aggressive and fearless, while females are brought up to accept self-erasure and subordination. This aspect of the 'complementarity' equation is assumed to create marital harmony in the future home. When women refuse to accept such a status quo, however, and demand a share of male-dominated power, conflict erupts in the marital relationship, and inherited structures of gender and power are destabilized. Unlike family and community politics, the marital relationship manifests high levels of gender stress: Flora Nwapa's novels explore this reality, depicting husbands and wives locked in struggles, displaying an ongoing, 'debilitating warfare in the marital zone' (Ogunyemi 1995: 5).

In Nwapa's depiction of traditional and modern Igbo societies, gender conflict arises from the physical and psychological aggression directed by men against women. Nwapa demonstrates the woman writer's power in West Africa, to explore, redefine and 'write out' conflict from the conjugal relationship. *Efuru* (1966) and *Idu* (1970) both focus on gender relations in 'traditional' Igbo societies and *One is Enough* (1981) is set in the 'modern' period of post-civil war Nigeria.[1] Viewed together, these novels explore the continuities and shifts in marital relationships in different Igbo societies, representing an expanse of Nigerian history from the traditional rural past to an urban, postcolonial present. Nwapa's presentation of women immersed in these diverse contexts bridges the rural–urban divide commonly attributed to West African societies, revealing common situations which empower as well as limit women, reducing or exacerbating gender conflicts. Although she did not declare herself to be a 'feminist' until a few years before she died, Nwapa's narration of gender conflict from the earliest texts manifests a Nigerian feminist orientation.

By limiting the analysis to an ethno-literary study of Igbo society, rather than upholding national (Nigerian) or regional (West African) perspectives, problems shared by African nations and the regions will be situated locally: Obiechina writes, 'in a multi-ethnic nation like Nigeria, it is imperative that the culture and life-ways of the component units should be given full airing so that national sentiments are built upon the foundation of understanding' (Obiechina 1971: 11). An emphasis on dynamic community relationships avoids the temptation of making sweeping universalist statements about 'the African woman'. If Nwapa's representations of gender conflict are relevant to the rest of Nigeria and Africa, it is because elements of Igbo political structures and socialization models are common to the continent, relevant in different social and cultural locations.

The Igbo people are found in all parts of Nigeria, but are most numerous to the east and west of the River Niger: numbering about 20 million, the Igbo ethnic group is one of the largest in Nigeria. It is patrilineal, so property and the political power attaching to property ownership are received by right of birth along the male line. Essentially controlled by men, who are heads of families, clans and communities, these societies formulate common ideas and interpretations, launching them into the world as the community's reality. Imbibing and internalizing these ideas from childhood, boys and girls have their social environments coloured, developed and formed. As T. Uzodinma Nwala observes: 'When systematized, these ideas present a coherent picture of the people's beliefs about the nature of the universe, its origin and end, and their conceptions of the nature of man in such a universe, the nature of the beings that exist in the universe and their relationship' (Nwala 1985: 5).

If colonialism partially ruptured and resettled these beliefs and structures, its impact on marriage was negligible. Marriage remains a highly regarded social institution in Igbo society, and to be an eligible but unmarried woman is considered disastrous. While a single adult man is looked upon with disapproval, perhaps disrespect, an unmarried woman is regarded as unfulfilled and a pariah. In traditional Igbo society, every normal woman had a husband, and marriage was ensured by such practices as polygyny and the levirate arrangement, whereby a widow was inherited by her husband's brother, becoming a wife in his household. A common saying among the Igbo is *Nma Nwayi bu di* (A woman's honour resides in her status as a married woman). Mission Christianity, mass education and Western culture generally have eroded this belief.

The transition away from the Igbo marriage ideal is a central theme in Nwapa's *One is Enough*, where Amaka divorces her husband and consciously chooses to remain single rather than remarry. Amaka's decision challenges the social pressure on Igbo women to secure husbands and remain married even if life becomes brutal and miserable. Nwapa wrote a similar scene into *Efuru*, where the heroine leaves her husband: the major difference, however, is that Efuru's decision is determined not by choice and self-assertion, but by a series of marital misfortunes.

Gender conflict appears to have been limited in traditional communities by socialization and educational practices, which encouraged an acceptance of men as the polygynous heads of families, and the perception of women as the property of husbands; meanwhile, the communal celebration of virility, strength and courage propagated the spirit of subservience and obedience in the average Igbo woman: feminine 'weakness' was institutionalized.[2] Constructed as 'weak' and allocated weaker social positions, women accepted their secondary status, which consolidated their inferior self-images.[3] As long as women accepted inferior positions, marital relationships were relatively free from gender conflict. Women's emancipation and monogamy have impacted on modern women, however;[4] by challenging male domination, new areas of gender conflict have opened up in modern society.

Efuru and *Idu* depict the marital experiences of two rural women: by giving Efuru and Idu 'titles', Nwapa endows them with strength, voice and authority which challenges traditional gender roles. Efuru conforms to the social construction of femininity in the sense that she is an exceptionally beautiful, generous and morally upright woman, distinguishing herself locally as a successful trader. In all aspects an exemplary person, she nevertheless ends up childless and lonely after two unsuccessful marriages. Her strongest points lie in the strength of her character, her generosity and moral probity. This tragedy hinges on a double misfortune that reveals the gender inequalities permeating Igbo marriages: first, Efuru has formed relationships with irresponsible and faithless men, whom she is expected to respect and obey; second, Efuru's only child sickens and dies in a community where, '[i]t was a curse not to have children. Her people did not just take it as one of the numerous accidents of nature. It was regarded as a failure' (Nwapa 1966: 165).

If gender conflict arises from women challenging the established, inherited order, it is mediated in *Efuru* by the heroine's status as an innocent victim of both circumstance and male brutality. She does not challenge directly. While Efuru does disobey her father's wishes by marrying Adizua, who does not pay the customary bride price, she tolerates her two husbands' unfaithfulness, betrayals of trust, exploitation and gender oppression. Efuru's first husband, Adizua, abandons her for a socially and morally inferior woman. History repeats itself when Eneberi, her second husband, betrays her trust, fathers a son by another woman, fails to turn up at her father's funeral and hides the fact of his three-month prison sentence from her. Efuru cannot help being, '[a]ngry because she had again loved in vain. She had deceived herself all these years, as she deceived herself when she was Adizua's wife. She was filled with hate and resentment, qualities that were foreign to her nature' (p. 209). Accused of adultery and repaid for her love with deceit, ingratitude and distrust, Efuru finally elects to leave Eneberi and return to her father's house. In spite of the financial and moral support she has given her two irresponsible husbands, Efuru has met with rejection, abandonment and false accusations.

Paradoxically, although she is an embodiment of the ideal wife, Efuru cannot survive married life in an unfair, male-oriented community. Nwapa highlights the contradictions of a society in which women are considered men's appendages, no matter how successful they are or what they have achieved in life. The authority of women in polygynous marriages is violated by men, who have extra-marital relationships and illegitimate children, refusing the financial commitment and responsibility brought by officially sanctioned second marriages. According to the double standard, women are cast out if they are rumoured to have strayed.

It is Efuru's rejection of Eneberi's oppressive and exploitative behaviour that generates conflict in their relationship: she possesses the qualities of independence, moral fortitude and emotional strength, which enable her to reject gender oppression, leave both husbands and achieve independence. Gender conflict in *Efuru* therefore arises from one woman's struggle to free herself from oppression, refusing to accept domination, marginalization and exploitation.

Unlike Nwapa's heroine, most women in 'traditional' Igbo societies tended to accept the status quo, allowing themselves to be oppressed by the patriarchal ideology; economically dependent on their husbands, women's movements and choices have been limited. Among other exceptional characteristics, Efuru is completely independent financially and, consequently, able to leave Eneberi and live a fulfilled and useful life in her community. Research on traditional Igbo societies reveals that most women were able to evade absolute male domination by embarking on independent income-generating activities, keeping their profits separate from men's income (Amadiume 1987; Ezeigbo 1990).

In Nwapa's second novel, *Idu*, explorations of female financial dependence and the emotional turbulence it generates are juxtaposed with the portrait of a successful, independent trader. Abject poverty and bitter marital conflict exist in the home of Ogbenyanu, a woman who lacks business acumen and relies on her husband and other relations to survive. Industrious and enterprising, in contrast, Idu controls a successful trading business with her husband, giving financial help to Ogbenyanu and her husband Ishiodu. Ogbenyanu is described by a townswoman in derogatory terms that the narrator does not intervene to moderate:

> she does not know how to trade. That is why we say that she has no sense. A woman who does not know how to trade in our town is a senseless woman. She is not a woman at all. You know that when she had just married Ishiodu, Adiewere and Idu gave them some money to start trading. In no time they were in debt, and Idu and Adiewere had to pay off their debts for them. (Nwapa 1970: 29)

Without social value as a trader, Ogbenyanu cannot break free from her marital imprisonment in the same way as Efuru; consequently, when she flees her husband, taking her children, her mother cannot cope with the burden of responsibility and engineers her return, actively supported by Idu and Adiewere. Ogbenyanu's dependence on Ishiodu, Idu and Adiewere is so total that she has no choice except to return to a situation that is intolerable to her.

In Nwapa's novels, marital relationships are saturated with gender conflict: men and women are shown to relate more harmoniously in relationships other than matrimony, particularly as friends, companions and lovers. Matrimony demands a shift in power relations, requiring commitment and devotion from both partners if it is to succeed. One feature of Igbo marriage patterns has not changed over time: a woman is required to have children, especially male children, for her husband. The failure to procreate jeopardizes her position in the family. Women are pressurized to offer devotion and loyalty to husbands, tolerating a man's unfaithfulness and cruelty. If conflict arises as a result of man's failure or inadequacy, it is the woman who gets the blame and subsequently suffers.

Nwapa's novels depict the persistence of this attitude. In *One is Enough*, set in contemporary Nigeria, Amaka experiences severe pressure and trauma because she has not conceived after six years of marriage. Secretly, her husband, Obiora, has abused her status as the senior wife of a potentially polygynous household, and has had two sons with another woman. Devastated by the revelations, Amaka's acceptance of inherited gender rules and roles is thrown into crisis: 'Was a woman nothing because she was unmarried or barren? Was there no other fulfilment for her?' (Nwapa 1981: 25). Refusing to submit, Amaka leaves Obiora after openly condemning his infidelity and insensitivity.

What is interesting about Amaka's experience, compared with the experience of Efuru in 'traditional' society, is that the 'modern' woman is not prepared to tolerate marital infidelity nor to accept her husband's illegitimate children. Efuru gladly welcomes the child resulting from her husband's affair, conforming with her people's belief that, 'it is only a bad woman who wants to have a man all to herself' (Nwapa 1966: 63). On the other hand, Amaka refuses to accommodate Obiora's 'other woman' and the two boys who are the fruit of that relationship.

The majority of modern Nigerian women reject the institution of polygyny, which has become another area of gender conflict in contemporary society. Educated women, in particular, find it intolerable and dehumanizing to have to share a man with another woman. In Nwapa's *Women are Different* (1986), Dora's daughter, Chinwe, moves out when her husband brings in a seventeen-year-old girl as her rival. An educated or emancipated woman who tries to accommodate polygyny may discover its many pitfalls, as Esi does in Ama Ata Aidoo's *Changes* (1991): Esi soon realizes that, while polygyny gives her a certain independence – including the choice to evade 'marital rape' – and time for her career as a data analyst, it also brings feelings of loneliness, neglect, jealousy and depression. Ultimately, polygyny must be identified as an instrument of oppression wielded by men to subjugate and dominate women in Nigeria; it introduces conflict into the home and encourages rivalry among co-wives.

During a writing career spanning nearly thirty years of Nigerian history, Nwapa maintained a consistent attitude towards polygynous men. Depicting women in a variety of roles, operating as priestesses, contractors and traders, peace is always shattered by men's infidelity in relationships, and conflicts engulf polygynous marriages. Amaka is exploited shamelessly by Obiora, just as Efuru is exploited by Adizua and Eneberi; Amaka uses the profit from her business to buy a car for her husband, just as Efuru provides Adizua with the money to pay her bride price, subsequently supplying the capital for their trading activities. Both women work hard for their families to prosper: yet neither woman's effort is appreciated by her lazy, ungrateful and unfaithful husband.

Nwapa is one of the many African women writers to have exposed the inherited cultural practices that inhibit the emancipation of women and delay their empowerment. Although she rarely writes overtly 'feminist' declarations of Nigerian women's independence, Nwapa tacitly encourages women to escape from bad marriages. In most of her work, one woman or another courageously attempts to leave the marital union at the point when it becomes dehumanizing and oppressive, or when personal aspirations remain unfulfilled. Offering role-models to her readership in the form of these heroines, Nwapa constructs a community of hard-working and successful businesswomen and civil servants. In fact, they often fare better than their men, who come to rely on them for financial support.

In *One is Enough*, Amaka leaves Onitsha for Lagos, accumulating enough wealth to buy a car, building houses in the city and at home. Amaka's manner of acquiring wealth, by 'using her bottom power' (Nwapa 1981: 126), compromises her moral integrity: her success in this venture and the absence of authorial condemnation of it implies, however, that Nwapa is making a strong case for female economic independence. Likewise, dignified single parenthood is promoted. In finally proving to the world that she is not barren by giving birth to twins, Amaka also demonstrates that she has chosen independence; and she refuses to marry Reverend Father Mclaid when he renounces the priesthood to become a more literal kind of father. She states:

> I don't want him. I don't want to be his wife ... I don't want to be a wife any more, a mistress yes, with a lover, yes of course, but not a wife. There is something in the word that does not suit me. As a wife, I am never free. I am a shadow of myself. As a wife I am almost impotent. I am in prison, unable to advance in body and soul. Something gets hold of me as a wife and destroys me. When I rid myself of Obiora, things started working for me. I don't want to go back to my 'wifely' days. I am through with husbands. I said farewell to husbands from the first day I came to Lagos. (Nwapa 1981: 132)

Compatible and harmonious relationships do occur in *Idu* and *One is Enough*, founded on love, mutual respect, trust and moral probity. Through them, Nwapa shows that successful marriages are possible. Crucially, the reason that Efuru's marriages fail while Idu's marriage succeeds is simply a question of the type of man each woman marries. Idu's husband is responsible, dependable, loving and considerate: when he dies suddenly from a mysterious sickness, Idu, who is pregnant with their second child, cannot live without him and soon 'followed her husband to the land of the dead' (Nwapa 1970: 218). Nwapa endorses such relationships based on mutual understanding and affection.

In *One is Enough*, both Amaka and her friend Adaobi are strong and independent women, with well-developed materialistic instincts. The difference in their conception of married life arises from their contrasting marital experiences: marriage has caused 'years of frustration for Amaka and years of fulfilment for Adaobi' (Nwapa 1981: 68). Adaobi's monogamous marriage to Mike is depicted sympathetically in order to highlight the positive and harmonious potential of marriages based on trust and reciprocity. Giving another layer of meaning to the title, Nwapa appears to be saying that monogamous marriage is desirable and fulfilling – one wife is enough for a man – and a woman should have the right to leave a failing relationship.

In Nwapa's novels, the increasing levels of gender conflict express married women's reduced tolerance of abusive domestic situations. Challenge and change are therefore built into the conflict situation, for women have stopped accepting inherited socialization models and stepped into new, more assertive roles. Marriage generates gender conflict more than any other relationship in Nwapa's novels. Focusing on areas of gender conflict in 'traditional' and 'modern' Igbo societies and exploring the social factors contributing to conflicts, Nwapa offers strategies to women for escaping conflict-ridden relationships. Economic independence is promoted alongside the forging of monogamous relationships based on love, trust and mutual understanding. Nwapa's vision is therefore feminist-oriented, encouraging women to maintain positions of strength, autonomy and equality in their relationships with men.

Notes

1. 'Traditional' society refers, first, to that period of Igbo history before Igbo areas were colonized by the British; and second, to the late nineteenth and early twentieth centuries, when European influence was being felt, but without any appreciable influence on the local cultures.

2. It was the ambition of every male to be in a position of strength and to acquire wealth. To be equated with a woman was one of the greatest insults an Igbo man could receive. In Achebe's *Things Fall Apart* (1958), Okonkwo suffers intense shame when, as a little boy, a playmate calls his father an 'agbala', meaning 'woman' and, pejoratively, a man who has taken no title.

3. Though there were institutions in traditional society, such as the Association of Daughters and the Association of Wives, which gave women some measure of power and influence, these did not quite protect her from a position of weakness in the Igbo patriarchy.

4. Research carried out by scholars (Amadiume 1987; Ezeigbo 1990) shows that Igbo women engaged in subversive and rebellious acts whenever their rights were infringed upon in precolonial society; their political organizations were eroded by colonial rule and patriarchal postcolonial culture. However, it should be stated clearly that Western influence and colonial rule were not totally negative: trading and educational opportunities were made available to Igbo women, through which they were able partially to empower themselves. Ironically, by means of western education, the Igbo woman has been able to reclaim and repossess the economic and political power she lost in the process of colonization.

References

Achebe, C. (1958) *Things Fall Apart*, Heinemann, London.
Aidoo, A. A. (1991) *Changes: A Love Story*, Women's Press, London.

Amadiume, I. (1987) *Male Daughters, Female Husbands: Gender and Sex in an African Society*, Zed Books, London.

Ezeigbo, T. A. (1990) 'Traditional Women's Institutions in Igbo Society: Implications for the Igbo Female Writer', *African Languages and Cultures* 3 (2), 149–65.

Nwala, T. U. (1985) *Igbo Philosophy*, Ikeja, Lantern Books, Lagos, Nigeria.

Nwapa, F. (1966) *Efuru*, Heinemann, London.

— (1970) *Idu*, Heinemann, London.

— (1981) *One is Enough*, Tana Press, Enugu, Nigeria.

— (1986) *Women are Different*, Tana Press, Enugu, Nigeria.

Obiechina, E. (1971) *The Couch* 3 (2), September.

Ogunyemi, C. O. (1995) 'Introduction: The Invalid, Dea(r)th, and the Author: The Case of Flora Nwapa, *aka* Professor (Mrs.) Flora Nwanzuruahu Nwakuche', *Research in African Literatures*, Special Issue on Flora Nwapa 26 (2), 1–16.

8
Culture and gender semantics in Flora Nwapa's poetry

OBODODIMMA OHA

One of the major contentions in feminist critical linguistics and in Western feminist theory is that language and culture have been greatly masculinized.[1] European and American scholars and writers have insisted on the need for a linguistic revolution in order to reject the masculine symbolic and signification systems which perpetuate the derogation and domination of women by men. Annie Leclerc bitterly expresses this feminist dissatisfaction:

> Nothing exists that has not been made by man – not thought, not language, not words ... We have to invent everything anew. Things made by man are not just stupid, deceitful and oppressive ... More than anything else, they are sad, sad enough to kill us with boredom and despair ... We have to invent a woman's word (Leclerc 1992: 74).

Leclerc's anger signifies a desire to deconstruct the masculine symbolic, and to create a language (or code) that does not debase and subordinate the woman. Indeed, what feminist critics and linguists object to in language and cultural production is man-made *meaning* which reflects, as Cixous maintains, 'dual hierarchical oppositions' (Cixous 1994: 38), with the woman always placed on the negative pole. This masculine structuration has far-reaching consequences, especially as language is a powerful instrument in social and political life. As Spender has asserted persuasively, 'the group which has the power to ordain the structure of language, thought, and reality has the potential to create a world in which they are the central figures, while those who are not of their group are peripheral and therefore may be exploited' (Spender 1992: 106).

The linguistic problems which confront women's writing are ubiquitous and, to a large extent, universal; writers in West Africa also wrestle with masculine languages and meanings. When the critical lens is shifted and focused on West African women writers, at least three adjustments to Western feminist theories are required: first, women writers in West Africa frequently appear to resist absorption into a feminist universalist standpoint, creating characters, scenes and situations which are specific and local to West African contexts; second, women writers often deconstruct androcentric, culturally accepted meanings and attempt instead to generate meanings favourable to African women. They resist accusations of cultural fraudulence by always situating their rewritings in recognizable African environments; and third, women writers tend to be less committed than men to the 'domestication' of language and meaning.

The challenges facing West African women writers are greater than those facing their European and American counterparts. The woman writer has to negotiate with meanings produced and imposed by the masculine order. She also has to deal stylistically with the influence of her African cultural background and European colonialism; for language and culture are interdependent and one of the avenues for the expression of such interdependency is literary production.

To most West African women writers, English is a second language requiring domestication. As an 'intruding' code, the English language must endure some unusual manipulations in the hands of the African writer to whom it has been given as a colonial legacy (Achebe 1975), and the African writer has to write in such a way as to accommodate and convey local non-English meanings, expressing what has been referred to as the 'local colour variety' (Oyeleye 1990: 28). The West African writer might therefore experience first-language 'interference' in her use of English: if this is the case, she has a double score to settle with masculine-ordered semiotics, not only against her local primary linguistic system, but also against her second language. In other words, the issue of 'linguistic interference' requires modification in recognition of the different forms of interference faced by West African women writing in a foreign language: their task is to rework the semantic modes of both the first and second language, both of which favour the masculine order, overtly or covertly. As a 'newly born' type of creativity, postcolonial, questing and questioning, West African women's writing inherits the Cixousian contention that, 'writing is working; being worked; questioning (in) the between (letting oneself be questioned) of same *and* of other without which nothing lives' (Cixous 1994: 43).

To Flora Nwapa, the task of rewriting images of women in the attempt to rupture a masculinized culture indeed involves the notion of writing as 'working' and 'being worked', presenting a woman-centred interpretation of gender relations. Nwapa's critics have accused her of handling language in a manner that imitates the 'localisation' or 'traditional village' trend set by Achebe's generation of male African writers (Taiwo 1986: 137-42). Taiwo in particular fails to recognize the fact that both Achebe and Nwapa are situated as writers in a postcolonial melting pot of Nigerian cultures, likely to be influenced in similar ways by their shared Igbo heritage.

Okpewho writes that, 'the return to the traditions has become something of an intellectual duty which has been performed by various African writers and scholars with varying degrees of credibility and skill' (Okpewho 1988: 23). Nwapa's selection of rural Igbo settings and modes of meaning is not necessarily an indication of Achebe's influence on her writing, however. The application of such normative models manifests a phallocentric critical perspective, in which the male writer is taken as the standard, from which the female can only be deviant. Nor has Nwapa passively applied the English language, but has tried to reinvent it and fill it with 'feminine' voices. Although Nwapa uses modes of meaning supplied by the strongly masculine Igbo culture, she tries to deconstruct the inherited meanings and images, particularly when they attach to images of women. 'To deconstruct' in this case does not necessarily mean the total rejection of modes of meaning. As Butler has explained: 'to deconstruct is not to negate or to dismiss, but to call into question and perhaps, most importantly, to open up a term, like the subject, to reusage or redeployment that previously has not been authorized' (Butler 1990: 18).

In her poetry, Nwapa's major concern is with gender and, most importantly, with women's subjectivity in a male-controlled milieu. *Cassava Song and Rice Song* (1986) is Nwapa's only collection of poems: throughout the collection, she redeploys language, shifting the boundaries of recognizable, local metaphors and similes to emphasize gender as a positive factor in Igbo culture. Nwapa's gender-oriented counter-rhetoric revolves round food and agriculture, a significant choice of focus since West African women are the primary participants in food production and supply networks (Ardayfio-Schandorf 1993). Through food and farming images, Nwapa seeks to signify a socially productive

Igbo womanhood; not simply 'feeding into' the Mother Earth or 'good housewife' stereotypes that pervade West African cultures, Nwapa portrays women undertaking culturally specific 'female' tasks.

The notion that there is, in Igbo areas of Nigeria, a *'dual-sex hierarchy* in which men and women exist in parallel and complementary positions and roles within the society' (Acholonu 1995: 6), does not erase the dominant Igbo perception, being interrogated in Nwapa's writing, of the male as a superordinate and the female as a subordinate. Proof of patriarchy's reign in Igboland can be seen in the process of surnaming: unlike Ghana, no man or woman takes the mother's or grandmother's name as a surname. In fact, an Igbo aphorism clarifies the point: *Ajo nwa na-aza aha nne ya* (A bad child answers his/her mother's name).

Nigerian commentators such as Acholonu, who seek to construct a history of precolonial gender equality, claim that the colonialists introduced the concept of women's subordination to Africa (Acholonu 1995: 78). Perhaps it is safer to say that different degrees of female subordination exist in European and African cultures. Male power and control in Igboland find expression in a range of cultural practices, including crop-production where cassava, labelled a staple and 'common' foodstuff, is associated with women, who are, tradition holds, its rightful cultivators.[2] The woman–cassava association devalues woman by attaching the negative attributes of cassava to her: she becomes common, low in value and odoriferous like her crop. The cultivator and the crop are conflated as 'same': and the derogation of one becomes the derogation of the other in the male-dominated economic system.

It was – and still is in some parts of Igboland – a cultural given that women take responsibility for the cultivation, marketing and cooking of cassava. In the agricultural district of Uli, for instance, gender differences and discriminations are signified clearly by the crops: yam signifies maleness and cassava, the subordinate crop, signifies femaleness. While Structural Adjustment and economic changes have forced most rural husbands to change their attitude to cassava,[3] some husbands in Uli still do not allow their wives to plant cassava alongside yam; cassava cannot be planted until the yam crop has gained richly from the soil. Of course, there is no question of planting cassava before planting yam. A domestic parallel of this situation can be found in those homes where a woman serves food to her husband before going to her kitchen to eat with the children.

Just as man is in control of the human society, yam is empowered to control the farm, which might be regarded analogically as a crop version of society: conversely, human society is a kind of farmland where prejudice and gender conflict are cultivated.

The cultivation of cassava is therefore inextricable from gender roles; cassava is assumed to be such a 'low' crop that it would be demeaning for a man to cultivate it. In Igboland, male farmers would wish to be referred to as *di ji* (husband of yams), and never *di akpu* (husband of cassava): to be addressed as *di akpu* is to be greatly insulted,[4] and indeed, the term is never used in Igbo discourse. As Spender states, 'All naming is of necessity biased and the process of naming is one of encoding that bias, of making a selection of what to emphasize and what to overlook on the basis of a "strict use of already patterned materials"' (Spender 1992: 107–8). The suppression of *di akpu* is a suppression of meanings that challenge maleness and male supremacy.

There is also a class–gender interface in the cassava–woman association. One of the weapons used by men in maintaining their gender supremacy is the economic exploitation or financial deprivation of women: since cassava is seen as the foodstuff of the poor, it could well be associated with woman whose position parallels that of the Marxian 'common man' in capitalist systems. The discrimination extends into traditional Igbo nutritional culture, where titled men belonging to the 'upper class' (the *nze na ozo*) used to refuse any foodstuff processed from cassava tubers, insisting that utensils used in cooking cassava should not be used to cook their own meals. There might be fair health grounds for this refusal, as some species of cassava, such as *manihot utilissima* (bitter cassava), contain hydrocyanic acid, which must be removed before the cassava can be eaten safely. Other species, such as *manihot palmata* (sweet cassava) however, do not have the acid (Komolafe et al. 1985: 94). All types of cassava are always well processed by rural dwellers before they are eaten. The point is that cassava has come to be associated with the poor: it is a social signifier of poverty and femininity in Igbo cultures, suggesting both subordination and muteness.

By demeaning cassava as a poor person's foodstuff and preferring to buy imported rice, Igbo purchasers exhibit class-consciousness, since the ability to buy rice indicates membership of a moneyed class. Situated in this context, it becomes understandable why Nwapa, a poet with an intricate awareness of Igbo gender politics, chooses to use the woman–

cassava association as a literary paradigm: by glorifying cassava, the muted crop, she glorifies the woman, the muted social being. The destinies of cassava and woman are linked by a poetic imagination in which masculine language is deliberately distorted. In rewriting women's cultural roles, Nwapa implicitly questions masculine logic. The 'frame' of cassava as woman and M/other is not part of an original poetic restructuring of language, for it has been available as a given association in a culture dominated by masculine cognition. By translating the frame, or form, into her subject-matter, however, Nwapa responds to masculine presuppositions, attempting to transform prejudice into glorification, hate into love, dishonour into honour, and disadvantaged weakness into privileged strength.

Women's image is constructed indirectly in *Cassava Song and Rice Song* by feminizing cassava and investing it with positive significance. Inheriting the negative association of cassava and women, Nwapa re-evaluates cassava in order to rewrite and re-evaluate women. Using figures of association – particularly simile, metaphor and personification – she alters the cassava–gender interface, subtly disrupting its familiar, recognizable cultural associations. Addressing and praising cassava, she re-evaluates its producers:

> As children, you fed as
> You were like a mother
> You fed us fat
> But we easily forget
>
> You must pardon us
> Great Mother Cassava
> Great Mother Cassava
> You must pardon us
>
> (Nwapa 1986: 2)

Cassava is personified, likened to a mother and finally referred to directly as 'Mother'. This process deliberately dislocates what is culturally accepted as *normal* or *natural*. In Chomskyan transformational grammar, such a dislocation would be understood as a violation of 'selection restriction rules', explained by Radford as 'semantic/pragmatic restrictions on the choice of expressions within a given category which can occupy a given sentence-position' (Radford 1990: 370). In natural language, if we are to follow this concept of selection restriction, we would not say, 'Cassava must *pardon* us', since the act of pardoning can only (naturally) be performed by conscious entities. In asking for pardon from cassava, Nwapa suggests that it has consciousness, elevating and empowering it to the position occupied by human and spiritual beings in Igbo culture.

Personification enables Nwapa to construct cassava as female. Cassava is not just '*like* a mother', for this simile facilitates the subsequent metaphorization, making the relationship closer and stronger. Cassava *is* 'Mother'. As figures of association, metaphors perform crucial 'paralogical' functions in discourse.[5] Verbrugge argues that metaphoric language activates a 'transformational process', in the sense that one event is transformed into 'another event that was previously experienced as very different in kind' (Verbrugge 1984: 168). He also argues that this transformational process is:

> *fanciful* in quality, since it alters conventional identities. It is *directional*, in that one event (the topic) is transformed by a second (the vehicle). It is *partial*, in that the topic is not completely reidentified as the vehicle ... it is *fusional*, because there is a plastic remodelling of the topic by the vehicle, rather than a preservation of separate identities (Verbrugge 1984: 168).

Moving from one frame to another and back again, the cassava–mother relationship is fused into one 'Great Mother Cassava' (Nwapa 1986: 2). Inseparability is emphasized, not merely as a covert bonding, but as overt event:

> Who will wash the pot?
> Who will wash the mortar?
> Not me.
> Not me.
>
> 'Never mind'
> Mother says quietly
> 'I'll wash the pot
> *Mother and Cassava are one.*'
>
> *Yes they are one*
> One loves her children
> The other
> Also loves her children.
>
> Both you and Mother

>   You are long suffering
>   You love your children
>   You are wonderful.
>
>   (Nwapa 1986: 11; emphasis added)

Motherhood and its admirable qualities therefore constitute the semantic core to the metaphorization of cassava as woman. Existing in a positive relationship to culture, *Cassava Song and Rice Song* subverts the patriarchal Igbo interpretive tradition in which the link between women and cassava is derogatory.

Other gendered names for cassava in *Cassava Song and Rice Song* include Great Mother, Great Woman, Lover of Children and Mother Cassava. This variability in naming opens up and pluralizes cassava, which is singular and resistant to other interpretations in the masculine-ordered culture. The multiple references triggered by Nwapa's rewriting of cassava conforms with Spender's assertion that: 'if more than one set of names were available, users of the language could elect to use those names which best reflected their interests ... But because it has been males who have named the world, no such choice exists and the falseness of the partial names they have supplied goes unchecked' (Spender 1992: 109). The otherness of mothers and female cassava-producers in Igbo societies is thus not regarded by Nwapa as an inferior otherness; it is presented instead as an empowering difference that places M/other (cassava) in a relationship of equality – even superiority – to Father (Yam):

>   Don't be angry
>   Great Mother
>   You were our Saviour
>   During the war.
>   You have been our Saviour
>   Long before the war.
>   *When the yam disappeared*
>   *Great Mother was with us.*
>
>   We sing for the yam
>   We have yam festivals
>   Why, oh why are
>   These denied you?
>
>   (Nwapa 1986: 9; emphasis added)

The disappearance of yam during the Nigeria-Biafra war reflects not just a literal scarcity, but also the irresponsible disappearance of the father from the home and farm, shirking his responsibility, leaving the m/other saddled with the role of primary provider. Ironically, rural Igbo societies recognize and celebrate the father, just as the father's symbol, yam, is celebrated annually.

Nwapa's presentation of female strength is ambiguous. The pounding process implies that, while women's self-sacrifice, suffering and endurance might sustain others, they are, like the cassava, pounded down and consumed by the process.

> We pound you
> We pound you
> We continue to pound
> We pound and pound
>
> You endure the pounding
> For our sake
> For the sake of your children
> You endure.
>
> (Nwapa 1986: 8–9)

'We pound you' could also mean 'we beat you' or 'we torture you', suggesting the hardship and brutality some women suffer in the compound.

The feminization and personification of cassava as 'Dear Mother' (p. 34) expresses the reverence for motherhood manifested throughout African societies. The idealization of the mother figure is psychologically and culturally ingrained, permeating literature and music at all levels.[6] Nwapa's use of cassava to express reverence for motherhood implies that the importation of rice, to compete with and displace cassava, is a treacherous gesture on the part of men in authority. By turning to imported rice, the masculine economy becomes like a promiscuous husband who prefers the non-wife in order to humiliate the actual wife and mother. 'Cassava alone can sustain us', Nwapa insists (p. 69): The feminine economy is sufficient, hinging on selflessness. The voice in *Cassava Song and Rice Song* expresses the request to be recognized by a society where the economy of female pounding and giving has been silenced. This voice describes the 'positive face' of women,[7] actively praising, thanking and acknowledging:

Praising:

> We thank the almighty God,
> For giving us cassava.
> We hail thee, Cassava
> The great cassava.
>
> (Nwapa 1986: 1)

Thanking:

> The young ones eat
> The old ones eat
> The father eats
> The mother eats ...
>
> Then everybody
> Is happy
> As happy as can be
> Thank you, Mother Cassava.
>
> (p. 13)

Acknowledging:

> You, Mother Cassava
> You deserve recognition
> You are no cash crop
> But you deserve recognition.
>
> (p. 43)

These sentiments are not necessarily directed towards the food-crop called cassava, but towards women and mothers whose social and domestic roles are made visible through the crop. *Cassava Song and Rice Song* is a mediating text, indirectly addressing female interests by praising the feminine foodstuff. Nwapa's concern with gender in *Cassava Song and Rice Song* has drawn attention to a neglected aspect of cultural life in Igboland; by focusing on food culture, she has highlighted the silence of women, making their derogated daily activities visible and socially valuable.

Notes

1. See Woolf (1992: 33–40); Cixous (1994:37–45); Irigaray (1985); Kristeva (1980); Cameron (1985).

2. Male discrimination against women in Igbo cultural life was demonstrated during a kolanut ritual at Flora Nwapa's maternal home when participants at the 1994 WAACLALS conference went to pay their last respects to the late writer at Oguta. Traditionally, kolanut should be 'shown' round (to visitors) before it is finally broken. The person who was mandated to perform that duty carried the kola dish to a female German conferee, but was sharply called to order by our host, Flora Nwapa's younger brother, who explained that it was wrong and untraditional to 'show' kolanut to a woman before it is broken. I quickly noted that down in my diary.

3. SAP has now forced some men to cultivate, process and cook cassava in Igboland.

4. This perception of association with cassava as insulting is not limited to Igbo culture. In *Anowa* (1965), the Ghanaian writer Ama Ata Aidoo presents the derogatory view of cassava in a speech by one of her characters, Badua: 'Anowa, why Kofi Ako? Of all the mothers that are here in Yebi, should I be the one whose daughter would want to marry this fool, this good-for-nothing *cassava-man*, this watery male of all watery males?' (Aidoo 1965: 15; emphasis added).

5. See Schon (1979); Verbrugge (1984); and Hoffman (1984).

6. I am referring in particular to Nico Mbarga's popular song 'Sweet Mother', which indeed evokes natural emotion for motherhood.

7. 'Positive face' is explained by Brown and Levinson as the desire to be treated or seen as a desirable member of society (Brown and Levinson 1978: 67). Lim and Bowers have further sub-categorized positive face into 'fellowship face' (the desire to be treated as a desirable member of an in-group) and 'competence face' (the desire that one's abilities be recognized and/or respected) (Lim and Bowers 1991: 420).

References

Achebe, C. (1975) *Morning Yet on Creation Day*, Heinemann, London.

Acholonu, C. O. (1995) *Motherism: The Afrocentric Alternative to Feminism*, Afa Publications/Let's Help Humanitarian Project, Owerri, Nigeria.

Aidoo, A. A. (1965) *Anowa*, Longman, Harlow.

Ardayfio-Schandorf, E. (1993) 'Household Energy Supply and Rural Women's Work in Ghana', in J. H. Momsen and V. Kinnaird (eds), *Different Places, Different Voices: Gender and Development in Africa, Asia and Latin America*, Routledge, London, 15–29.

Brown, P. and S. Levinson (1978) 'Universals in Language Usage: Politeness Phenomena', in E. N. Goody (ed.), *Questions and Politeness: Strategies in Social Interaction*, Cambridge University Press, Cambridge, 56–289.

Butler, J. (1990) 'Feminism and the Question of Postmodernism', unpublished paper, presented at the Greater Philadelphia Philosophy Consortium, USA.

Cameron, D. (1985) *Feminism and Linguistic Theory*, Macmillan, London.

— (ed.) (1992) *The Feminist Critique of Language: A Reader*, Routledge, London.

Cixous, H. (1994) 'The Newly Born Woman', in S. Sellers (ed.), *The Hélène Cixous Reader*, Routledge, London, 37–45.

Hoffman, R. R. (1984) 'Recent Psycholinguistic Research on Figurative Language', in S. J. White and V. Teller (eds), *Discourses in Reading and Linguistics*, New York Academy of Sciences, New York, 137–66.

Irigaray, L. (1985) *This Sex Which is Not One*, trans. C. Porter, Cornell University Press, New York.

Komolafe, M. F. et al. (1985) *Agricultural Science for West African Schools and Colleges* (2nd edn), University Press, Ibadan, Nigeria.

Kristeva, J. (1980) *Desire in Language: A Semiotic Approach to Literature and Art*, Trans. L. S. Roudiez, Columbia University Press, New York.

Leclerc, A. (1992) 'Woman's Word', in D. Cameron (ed.), *The Feminist Critique of Language*, 74–9.

Lim, T. S. and Bowers, J. W. (1991) 'Facework: Solidarity, Approbation and Tact', *Human Communication Research* 17 (3), 415–50.

Nwapa, F. (1986) *Cassava Song and Rice Song*, Tana Press, Enugu, Nigeria.

Okpewho, I. (1988) 'African Poetry: The Modern Writer and Oral Tradition', *Oral Tradition and Written Poetry in African Literature Today* 16, 3–25.

Oyeleye, L. (1990) 'Domesticating the English Language in Nigeria: The Example of Achebe's Local Colour Variety', *Journal of the Nigeria English Studies Association* 10 (1), 28–45.

Radford, A. (1990) *Transformational Grammar: A First Course*, Cambridge, Cambridge University Press.

Schon, D. A. (1979) 'Generative Metaphor: A Perspective on Problem-Setting in Social Policy', in A. Ortony (ed.), *Metaphor and Thought*, Cambridge University Press, Cambridge.

Sellers, S. (ed.) (1994), *The Hélène Cixous Reader*, Routledge, London.

Spender, D. (1992) 'Extracts from *Man Made Language*', in D. Cameron (ed.) *The Feminist Critique of Language*, Routledge, London, 102–10.

Taiwo, O. (1986) *Social Experience in African Literature: Essays*, Fourth Dimension, Enugu, Nigeria.

Verbrugge, R. R. (1984) 'The Role of Metaphor in our Perception of Language', in S. J. White and V. Teller (eds), *Discourses in Reading and Linguistics*, New York Academy of Sciences, New York, 167–183.

Woolf, V. (1992) 'Women and Fiction', in D. Cameron, (ed.) (1992), *The Feminist Critique of Language*, 33–40.

9
Behind the veil in northern Nigeria: the writing of Zaynab Alkali and Hauwa Ali

MARGARET HAUWA KASSAM

Until recently, not much was known about the female aesthetics and cultural experiences from which northern Nigerian women writers derive inspiration; nor was the depth of their contribution to the African literary tradition adequately recognized. Some of the silenced voices, subsumed by the male-dominated literary society, include artists such as Zaynab Alkali, Hauwa Ali, Hauwa Gwaram, Hajiya 'Yar Shehu in addition to the new female writers such as Talatu Wada Ahmed, Hadiza Sidi Aliyu, Karima Abdu Dawakin Tofa, to mention only a few.[1] Marginalized or excluded from the mainstream literary tradition, these women have been trying to break through the barriers which hitherto relegated them to the background and continue even in contemporary literature on Hausaland. Coles and Mack observe that: 'up until the 1970s, much of the published literature touched only peripherally, if at all, upon women. In fact, much of the early scholarship on "Hausa society" actually documented and analyzed the activities, perceptions, and ideals of Hausa males' (Coles and Mack [eds] 1991: 4). Coles and Mack can locate only one 'significant exception' to this trend: Mary Smith's biography, *Baba of Karo: A Woman of the Muslim Hausa* (1954).

The patriarchal society in which they exist has excluded northern Nigerian women from full participation in the creative arts. This is ironic, considering women's symbolic status as 'custodians' of culture and tradition. Ada Adeghe affirms that 'in Nigeria and other African societies, it has often been the primary duty of female members to pass down traditional wisdom, cultural mores and value systems to future generations ... through the use of folklores, proverbs, riddles and songs, which convey moral lessons to the younger generation' (Adeghe 1993: 118). Operating outside the parameters of Western education, female relatives have been vital to the education a child is supposed to acquire;

mothers in particular are regarded as a crucial part of a child's upbringing, to such an extent that, 'a failure on the part of the child to grasp and adhere to cultural norms is generally considered a failure on the part of his mother' (p. 118).

Women's relegation to secondary positions in society seems to affect the quality and quantity of their artistic output: for instance, women are discouraged from participating in the performing arts, considered to be a male sphere, so when they dare to embrace it as a profession, they risk being stigmatized. Nevertheless, women such as Barmani Coge, Hajiya Fati Pampo and other Hausa women poets have crossed social and cultural barriers (Mack 1981). Even in the official 'silence', women can find their voices and express themselves through creativity. Beverly Mack testifies to the fact that, even in seclusion, Hausa women were producing literary works as far back as the nineteenth century (Mack 1991: 181). According to her findings: 'female praise-singers have in earlier times been highly regarded as the guardians of social mores and historical traditions, and Nana Asma'u, who lived in northern Nigeria in the nineteenth century, is still known for her contributions to the Islamic cause through her inspirational written religious verse. She is remembered as an exemplary traditional Muslim woman' (Mack 1991: 181).[2]

Literary history in the West shows how famous women writers such as Jane Austen, Emily and Charlotte Brontë and George Eliot, writing from their 'little corners' (Woolf 1929), defied patriarchy in order to express their talents and contribute to what is regarded today as European literary culture. Translated into the 'little compounds' of a Hausa context, it is difficult to make a cross-cultural comparison between the number and availability of artistic opportunities. The gender problematic in northern Nigeria revolves round the combination of physical seclusion and psychological marginalization, a situation made worse where the women are not educated. To an extent, this culturally specific double-bind of patriarchy explains the dearth of written works by women from the northern areas. Behind the veil, however, lies an untapped source of female creativity.

According to Habiba Sabi'u-Baba, before the advent of Western education in northern Nigeria, literature 'had existed for centuries in the forms of Arabic and Arabic-based languages such as *Ajami*' (Sabi'u-Baba 1994: 2). She attributes this to the influence of Islam, which spread to Nigeria from northern African countries. Apart from the influence of religion on creative writing, authors are influenced considerably by folklore and orature, which, as Sabi'u-Baba says, 'shows itself in the writers' choice of subject-matter, characterization and narrative technique' (p. 2). Other factors influencing women's writing in the region include gender inequality, restrictive behavioural and expressive codes for women, limitations in the acquisition of education and gender discrimination in the distribution of resources.

Zaynab Alkali and Hauwa Ali come from north-eastern Nigeria. They are highly educated women and both of them are university lecturers, belonging to the small class of writers in northern Nigeria who write in English as a result of their exposure to Western education and culture.[3] In *The Stillborn* (1984) and *The Virtuous Woman* (1987), Alkali's preoccupation is with the plight of young girls in a society where their only viable option for long-term emotional survival is to strive and achieve a meaningful education.

The various conflicts in *The Stillborn* are portrayed through the lives of the central family: Li embodies the dynamics of social change – albeit moderate change – and her vivacity often leads her into 'conflict with the traditionalists and the over-zealous Christians, both represented by her father and grandfather' (Sabi'u-Baba 1994: 9); her father, Baba, holds uncompromising Christian principles which fuel the crisis in his own home; and her grandfather, Kaka, represents a dying tradition at the birth of modernity. Li is not against 'tradition' *per se*, but rebels against those aspects of tradition which her father wields high-handedly in his efforts to confine her to the house and restrict her movements in the village. Ironically, Li appears to be on better terms with 'the ancient one' than with her father, who seems to be afraid of her 'spookiness' (Alkali 1984: 9–12). By condensing different cultural tensions into one family, Alkali highlights the issue of social change and its contribution to inter-generational conflict; in this way, she emphasizes the religious and cultural dilemmas facing multi-ethnic communities alongside challenges to established familial structures, for Li represents 'the latest generation of Africans eager for a measure of social freedom' (Bamikunle 1986: 12). Refusing to respect his authority, in a gesture not condoned by Alkali, Li sneaks out of the house to attend night-time village dances and meets her boyfriend, Habu Adams, in the woods (Alkali 1984: 20; 30).

As a whole, *The Stillborn* is an episodic rendition of several interwoven stories. At the centre of these stories is Li's life-story, which acts as a gravitational force pulling the complex threads of the societal relationships together. On one hand, the novel can be regarded as the story of 'the village', which remains nameless throughout; on the other hand, the story is about the life of a particular, named young woman, who returns with altered attitudes to the village after completing her primary education (p. 1).

In her dreams of the city, Li constructs it as a female-gendered version of 'paradise' where women can make use of their education and earn independent incomes (p. 55); attempting to embark on a route towards the realization of these dreams, she marries Habu Adams, who betrays her love, marries a 'city wife' and abandons Li in the village. The ideal of attaining 'paradise' through marriage is further shattered when Li finally joins Habu in the city, for he maltreats her.

Running parallel to Li's rebellion, offering a potential counterpoint to her failure, are the stories of her more conformist sister Awa, and of Faku, her childhood friend. Awa's coping strategy is to conform to tradition, and she suffers like her sister at the hands of men, being maltreated by the Headmaster whom she eventually marries. Her acquiesence with traditional norms makes her a victim of the patriarchal society to which she sacrifices her life. In spite of fleeing to the city for refuge, Li's friend Faku also becomes a victim of the ubiquitous patriarchy, tormented by her husband and co-wife because she has only one child.

Unlike some city women who go into prostitution for commercial reasons, Alkali emphasizes that Faku engages in the trade as a survival strategy to ease her life of misery (p. 100). Like other African women writers who depict women in the city, Alkali makes the point that women who engage in prostitution are not intrinsically bad: instead, more often than not, they are victims of their vicious societies. Faku manages to transcend her situation – again by education – by acquiring the necessary skills to get a job as a social welfare worker in the city. In spite of having different personalities, lifestyles and ambitions, all three young women have their dreams shattered by the restrictive gender codes permeating society. Oppression and confinement do not affect Li alone. Articulating concern about the generally low status of women, Alkali portrays the poor socio-economic conditions and the frustrated potential of these three different young women in northern Nigeria.

Alkali emphasizes Li's ultimate success in attaining an education and economic independence, 'making it in life' without requiring male connections to facilitate her progress (p. 102). By virtue of her economic status and higher education, and in the absence of male leadership, Li becomes 'the man of the house' (p. 101), a position she assumes in an official and public capacity when mourners pay their last respects to Kaka. The ambivalence of this act of 'social acceptance' is obvious, for Li has been re-gendered and accommodated officially as a man, neutralized as a rebellious and exceptional woman. Willing to revive her marriage, she seeks out Habu for an equal partnership, restored on her own terms. *The Stillborn* does not resolve these contradictions, leaving the feminist reader with a sense of discomfort and ambivalence, unsure of whether to condone Li's successful negotiation of the status quo: readers might see it as a subversion or as the self-silencing of assertive womanhood.

Similar issues of female education, empowerment and virtue preoccupy Alkali in *The Virtuous Woman* (1987). Presenting these issues through the story of a young 'cripple' called Nana A'i, Alkali takes a doubly didactic position, commenting on what constitutes female virtue in society and rewriting physical disability as inner moral strength, offering her heroine as a role-model worthy of emulation by young female readers. Nana A'i is described as beautiful, considerate and intelligent, 'an embodiment of virtue in the village ... neither conceited nor arrogant because of her beauty' (Alkali 1987: 12). Nana is also said to be very patient and obedient to her grandfather's teachings, absorbing his wisdom and refusing to accept lifts or gifts from strangers, opportunities that other girls in the novel do not like to miss. Lovable and loving, the heroine nevertheless will act out of character and fight to defend her grandfather's integrity (p. 17).

The journey motif is employed in the form of a socially conscious travelogue which describes what life is like in the rural areas of northern Nigeria; readers are shown the deplorable government services, particularly resulting in untarred roads, which are full of pot-holes, becoming death-traps during the rainy season (p. 38). Depicting a serious road accident, Alkali voices a national outcry against the sheer negligence of the authorities. Corruption in Nigeria is also condemned. Alkali depicts the abuse of power at various levels: a male secretary victimizes the young girls for refusing a ride from him and, later, a policeman bribes a lorry driver after accusing him of overloading the vehicle. The theme of corruption is a familiar one among many Nigerian writers today.[4] A committed writer like her contemporaries, Alkali is concerned about the ills of her society, seeing writing as a means of morally correcting such ills.

Hauwa Ali shows more clearly than Alkali the effect of transformations in culture and religion on the lives of young women. *Destiny* (1988) is a love story of the Mills and Boon 'forbidden love' variety, tracing the attempt of a girl named Farida to be educated and become a career woman. The romantic connection that develops between Farouk and Farida links two teenagers from different cultural and social backgrounds, for Farouk is Senegalese, the son of an ambassador, and Farida is the daughter of a Nigerian policeman. Both of them are Muslims, however, and the narrator emphasizes that 'they belong to the same linguistic group, the Hausa' (Ali 1988: 4). Fate strikes their love in the form of Farouk's father, who sends him abroad to study; and Farida is forced by her guardians, Uncle Abba and Aunt Nana, to marry a rich, middle-aged man, Wali el-Yakub; she remains with him, pining for her love and obsessed with furthering her education in spite of Wali's opposition. Reunited by fate, Farouk and Farida become husband and wife at last (p. 90).

Throughout the novel, Farouk and Farida's love is symbolized by the red rose, making the text intertwine with other love stories, especially Western romantic fiction. The flower garden we encounter in Ali's novel signifies an urban culture: and Aunt Nana sees it negatively as manifesting the influence of Western education and values on Farida.

A parallel, non-romantic 'gift-giving' economy operates in the novel. It is common practice among the Hausa for a man to woo a woman with gifts, encouraging competition among her suitors from whom the girl will choose the man she prefers. Sometimes a young woman is given to the man with the most gifts – to the highest bidder, as it were. According to this parallel economy, and in contrast to the roses of the young couple's romantic, mutual desire, Farida is given to Wali because of his wealth, subverting love as a criterion for marriage.

There is a strong connection between fate and Islam in the novel: for predicaments and misfortunes are generally attributed to Allah in the story. Again, the Islamic explanatory frame exists in competition with the language of romantic love: the marriage between Wali and Farida is interpreted as predestined by Allah, and Farida eventually accepts the situation as her 'fate' since 'it is God's will for her' (Ali 1988: 48–9). In this way Ali reveals the extent to which religious discourse has been used to mask the manipulation of young women to suit people's selfish interests in society. Farida's guardians force her into marriage with Wali because, according to them, they want to be secure financially in their old age (pp. 45–7).

When Farida's acceptance of her fate wanes, education returns to the forefront of the novel. Farida's desire for post-secondary schooling is opposed strongly by her relatives (p. 32): in a patriarchal situation, marriage takes its place as the more valuable destiny for women. Wali echoes the dominant voice of society when he says, 'a girl should be married before she is eighteen' (p. 32). Inter-generational conflict emerges over the need for education; only the young people seem to see higher education as a necessary step towards a better life. The necessity for female higher education and the economic empowerment it provides seem to be the central messages of the novel. In contrast to female education and emancipation, Ali stages a discussion of forced marriage, condemning a cultural practice that defies all reasoning. The imposition of early marriage on girls is presented as a way of denying them equal opportunities with boys to realize their full potential in life: the heroine is shown protesting against the choice of husband made by her guardians, and her rebellion almost makes her commit suicide (p. 38).

Although Alkali published her first novel in 1984, while Ali started writing only in the late 1980s, both writers can be placed together at the forefront of female writing from northern Nigeria; and they share several novelistic preoccupations, especially a concern for education and the status of women in society. Both writers benefited from higher education in the Muslim north, where Western education for girls has not been considered a priority. In spite of Alkali's more ambivalent engagement with feminist politics, female education is promoted in both women's novels as a necessary tool for social change and modernization.

Women from northern Nigeria write from behind the religious and attitudinal veil about issues affecting women and the nation as a whole. Even educated women are shown to be denied voices, chances or choices by their society. We see this culture of silence operating in the life of Li's mother, who represents the generation of women whose voices have been suppressed, partly because of their lack of economic power and partly because they still believe in silence as a golden rule. Li's mother lives an almost non-existent life in her own home, playing out her vital role in the shadows. A sense of realism pervades both writers' novels, in which younger women are able to express their desires and requirements only when they attain a certain socio-economic status; even then, gender inequality exists to frustrate the realization of their ambitions in the fictional societies created by their authors.

Notes

1. See Mack (1981); and Mzehemen-Andoonam (1994).
2. The report on Nana Asma'u is corroborated by Jean Boyd's research (Boyd 1989).
3. Hauwa Ali died in 1994.
4. See Iyayi (1979); Olumhese (1982); Osofisan (1979); and Fatunde (1986).

References

Adeghe, A. (1993) 'The Other Half of the Story: Nigerian Women Telling Tales', in S. Brown (ed.), *The Pressures of the Text: Orality, Texts and the Telling of Tales*, Birmingham University Press, Birmingham.

Ali, H. (1988) *Destiny*, Delta Fiction, Nigeria.

Alkali, Z. (1984) *The Stillborn*, Longman, Harlow.

— (1987) *The Virtuous Woman*, Longman, Ikeja, Nigeria.

Bamikunle, A. (1986) 'Review of *The Stillborn*', *Sunday New Nigerian*, 12 January.

Boyd, J. (1989) *The Caliph's Sister: Nana Asma'u 1793–1865: Teacher, Poet and Islamic Leader*, Frank Cass, London.

Coles, C. and B. Mack (eds) (1991) *Hausa Women in the Twentieth Century*, University of Wisconsin Press, Wisconsin and London.

Fatunde, T. (1986) *Oga Na Tief Man*, Abena, Benin City, Nigeria.

Iyayi, F. (1979) *Violence*, Longman, Harlow.

Mack, B. (1981) *Wakokin Matan Hausa: Hausa Women's Poetry*, unpublished PhD thesis. University of Wisconsin.

— (1991) 'Songs From Silence', in C. Boyce Davies, and A. Adams Graves (eds), *Ngambika: Studies of Women in African Literature*, Africa World Press, Trenton, NJ, 181–9.

Mzehemen-Andoonam, P. (1994) *Shantu Songs by Women in Kaduna State*, unpublished MA thesis.

Olumhese, S. (1982) *No Second Chance*, Longman (Drumbeat), Ikeja, Nigeria.

Osofisan, F. (1979) *Once Upon Four Robbers*, BIO, Ibadan, Nigeria.

Sabi'u-Baba, H. (1994) *A Study Of the Themes of Religion and Cu: The Fiction of*

Ibrahim Tahir and Zaynab Alkali, unpublished M.A. thesis, Ahmadu Bello University, Zaria, Nigeria.

Smith, M. (1954) *Baba of Karo: A Woman of the Muslim Hausa*, Faber, London.

Woolf, V. (1929) *A Room of One's Own*, Hogarth Press, London.

Select bibliography of contemporary female writers in northern Nigeria

Ahmed, Talatu Wada (1986) *Rabin Raina I*, Ogwu, Kaduna, Nigeria.

— (1987) *Rabin Raina II*, Ogwu, Kaduna, Nigeria.

— (1988) *Rabin Raina III*, Ogwu, Kaduna, Nigeria.

Aliyu, Sidi Hadiza (1994) *Salalar Tsiya*, SARUMEDIA, Kaduna, Nigeria.

Aliyu, Halima B. H. (1995) *Muguwar Kishiya* Al-Khamees, Kaduna, Nigeria.

Alkali, Murjanatu (1995) *Rabo Na Minallahi*, BAMAS, Kano, Nigeria.

Aminu, Hauwa (n.d.) *Kaddara Ta Riga Fata I*, Kano, Nigeria (PO Box 6478 Bompai, Kano).

Bali, Esther (1990; 1994) *Tarok Folktales*, Spectrum Books, Ibadan, Nigeria.

Dahiru, Aishatu Hajiya (1995) *Soyyaya Mai Sada Zumunci II*, SARUMEDIA, Kaduna, Nigeria.

Daneji, Hassana Ibrahim (1993) *Butulcin Masoyi*, W. F. Publishing and Computer Services, Kano, Nigeria.

Dawakin Tofa, Abdu Karima (1992) *Larai Ta Kabiru*, Gaskiya, Zaria, Nigeria.

Gasau, Jummai Hassan Nasiha (1993) *Soyyaya Mai Ben Ta'ajibi*, Bushara, Gusau, Sokoto, Nigeria.

Gwaram, Hauwa and Hajiya 'Yar Shehu (1983) *Alkalami A Hannum Mata*, Northern Nigerian Publishing Co., Zaria, Nigeria.

Habib, Mairo (1993) *Househelps: The Necessary Evils*, Ahmadu Bello University Press, Zaria, Nigeria.

Indala, Amina Ibrahim (n.d.) *Duniya Makaranta*, n.p., Katsina, Nigeria.

Isa, Zuwaira (1995) *Labarin So*, City Publishers, Kano, Nigeria.

Saulawa, Hadiza Aliyu (1993) *All That Glitters*, Kaita Commercial Industrial Press, Katsina, Nigeria.

Sherif, Hauwa Ibrahim (1990) *Ba A Nan Take Ba*, Government Printer, KTS, Katsina, Nigeria.

Umar, Hassana (1980) *Nuni Cikin Nishadi*, Northern Nigerian Publishing Co., Zaria, Nigeria.

Yakubu, Balaraba Ramat (1989) *Budurwar Zuciya*, Gaskiya, Zaria, Nigeria.

Zaharaddeen, Laila (1994) *Bari Ba Shegiya Ba Ce*, Zaharaddeen, Kano, Nigeria.

10
The onus of womanhood: Mariama Bâ and Zaynab Alkali

IBIYEMI MOJOLA

Entre la liberté et l'esclavage, il n'y a pas de compromis. (There is no compromise between freedom and slavery) *Patrice Lumumba*

Fictional narrative is often generated by life experiences, and women writers in West Africa regularly focus on women's condition in their works of fiction. Mariama Bâ's *So Long a Letter* (1980) and *Scarlet Song* (1981) and Zaynab Alkali's *The Stillborn* (1984) and *The Virtuous Woman* (1987) have made the condition of women their central concern. Both novelists were born into male-dominated Islamic African societies and both embraced the teaching profession. *So Long a Letter*, Bâ's first novel, won the first Noma Award for publishing in Africa in 1980, and Alkali's first novel, *The Stillborn*, won the Association of Nigerian Authors' award for prose fiction in 1985. However, almost a generation separates them, for Bâ was born in 1929 and Alkali was born in 1950; and Bâ is from Senegal, while Alkali is from Nigeria. In spite of the wide age gap and geographical separation, certain similarities are discernible in their perception of the condition of West African women. The manner in which women are burdened by discriminatory social, economic and religious structures, as well as possible remedies to these constraints, is of primary importance to both writers.

In *So Long a Letter*, the narrator protagonist, Ramatoulaye Fall, writes to her childhood friend, Aïssatou, an interpreter at the Embassy of Senegal in the United States. In the course of recounting her experiences since the sudden death of her husband Modou, she pours out her feelings of irritation, rancour and frustration at her husband's desertion of her and their twelve children for a second wife, Binetou, the best friend and age-mate of their teenage daughter, Daba. *Scarlet Song* contains a complexity of themes arising from the love story of Mireille de la Vallée, a French girl of noble heritage, and Ousmane Guèye, a

Senegalese from the working class. They surmount the impossible to get married and settle in Dakar. Cultural differences, nurtured by Ousmane's mother's rejection of the white woman as daughter-in-law, and by Ousmane's selfish desires, develop into conflicts: he eventually marries Ouleymatou, a semi-literate, empty-headed Senegalese, and abandons Mireille and her son. The novel ends tragically with Mireille becoming insane, destroying both her child and faithless spouse. Remaining on the level of plot synopsis, *The Stillborn* tells of the shattered dreams of three adolescent girls: Li, the main character, her sister Awa, and her friend Faku. Li and Faku rebuild their lives and find fulfilment when they learn to rely on their own efforts. *The Virtuous Woman*, essentially a story for adolescents, is a more positive depiction of the female condition, showing how the clever and beautiful Nana Ai keeps to the sound morals inculcated into her by her grandfather. She rejects every temptation to go out with men and subsequently finds a young man, Bello, whom she can love and trust.

The 'burden' of African womanhood in these texts comes from within and without, for women have internalized a socially constructed sense of self that causes them to accept, consciously or unconsciously, the role of second fiddle; Montagu writes that, '[w]omen have been so long conditioned in the environment of masculine dominance that they have come to expect the male to be dominant and the female to be subservient' (Montagu 1974: 26). In the Senegalese and Nigerian societies in which the novels are set, women are often treated as second-rate or non-beings, rarely consulted before far-reaching decisions are taken concerning their welfare. In *So Long a Letter*, Mawdo, a well-known medical doctor, marries his first cousin, Nabou, who could have been his daughter and whom he does not love, just to please his mother. The young wife is offered to him as a gift from his uncle, Nabou's father, 'to thank me [i.e. Mawdo] for the worthy manner in which I brought her up' (Bâ 1980: 48). Nabou's opinion does not count; like a simple gift, she is given away, becoming a sex object for Mawdo. As he confesses to Ramatoulaye, he uses Nabou only to satisfy his sexual desires, for he loves Aïssatou who, unlike him, cannot dissociate spiritual love from physical love and therefore leaves him.

Is it conceivable that a man's secret marriage to a second wife could be announced to his first wife as if nothing had happened? This is precisely how Ramatoulaye is treated by Mawdo, her husband's best friend, her brother-in-law Tamsir, and the Imam of his area. Returning directly from the wedding ceremony, they enter Ramatoulaye's house, all laughter: their unusual statements provoke some apprehension about her husband's safety and she asks about him with concern, only to be told, 'He has only married a second wife, today' (Bâ 1980: 56). Such treatment is meted out to a woman whom they all – her husband included – claim has served the family faithfully for a quarter of a century. To reduce Ramatoulaye further to the status of a voiceless possession, on the fortieth day after her husband's death, her brother-in-law, Tamsir, arrogantly informs her, 'After you "come out" [that is from mourning], I will marry you. You suit me as a wife' (p. 84). Not only does Ramatoulaye scornfully reject him, she also tells him that she is not an object to be passed from hand to hand.

This male – or is it societal? – perception of woman as a possession is reinforced by the narrator's comment in *Scarlet Song*, that a man's money rather than his moral qualities is all that matters to families: the bride has become a 'commodity carried away by the richest' (Bâ 1981: 203). Such sentiments are repeated in *The Stillborn*, set in a different African society, where women are also shown to be exploited and treated as inconsequential. In the father's view, '[h]e could beat Awa easily if she erred, no matter how old she was, but not Sule, his firstborn male child' (Alkali 1984: 23). Awa, aged eighteen, is the first child of the family and a primary school teacher, whereas Sule, considered a 'man-child' by their father, is still a primary school pupil. In Bâ's and Alkali's representations of society, man is regarded as the substance, while woman is treated as the shadow.

Explaining why female writers in Africa are few in comparison with male writers, Ojo-Ade writes: 'Man constitutes the majority and woman, the minority ... Minority should be contemplated in the sense of Dominated, Disadvantaged, Exploited, Excluded' (Ojo-Ade 1983: 158). This description can be applied to women's position with respect to African matriarchal practices. Expected to be a centre of happiness and companionship, marriage in West African women's novels is more often than not shown to stifle womanhood. Treated as the subordinate partner, woman is dominated and exploited, especially in polygynous marriages.

Polygyny is the epitome of female denigration, exploitation and domination in West Africa. If 'home' represents the place where one is most at peace and at ease, the polygynous home is not home but hell for the co-wives and their children as tensions reign supreme, fuelled by envy, distrust, intrigues and all sorts of destructive passions. Islam and traditional African religions sanction polygyny: only Christianity rejects it. According to the Qur'an:

> Marry women of your choice,
> Two, or three, or four;
> But if ye fear that ye shall not
> Be able to deal justly (with them)
> Then only one
>
> (Ali 1983: 100)

In practice, it is impossible to treat two, three or more wives equally. The newest wife is usually favoured by the husband even though each wife is supposed to have her 'turn'. After twenty-five years of marriage to Ramatoulaye, Modou, a lawyer turned trade unionist, marries teenage Binetou and installs her in the luxurious SICAP villa, a property jointly owned by him and Ramatoulaye. Materially and morally, he pampers Binetou and her mother, whom Ramatoulaye disparagingly refers to as 'Lady Mother-in-law' (Bâ 1980: 15). He abandons Ramatoulaye and her twelve children. According to Ramatoulaye, 'He never came again ... he forgot us' (p. 69). In spite of this, Ramatoulaye is prepared to share Modou according to the Islamic precept of equal sharing.

Modou's death reopens the wound inflicted on Ramatoulaye, as she now has ample time to reflect on married life in Senegal. Her state of mind can be fathomed from the expressions she uses to describe her feelings: phrases such as 'irritates me', 'incensed', 'to overcome my bitterness', 'my disappointment', 'my discouragement continues', underscore the pains experienced by a woman who never expected to have a co-wife.

The situation of Mireille in *Scarlet Song* assumes a tragic dimension when she learns that she has a co-wife. The modern practice of polygyny among the educated is to house the wives in different locations, but the problem of unequal treatment cannot be wished away. So it is that Ousmane completely neglects Mireille, in spite of having witnessed countless conflicts caused by rivalry among co-wives as a child: 'Children who supported their mothers were involved in their disputes and shared their deep-seated bitterness. During confrontations, the bowl of dirty water, the Madagascan stove and its embers, broken bottle ends, the saucepan of boiling water, the skimmer, the pestle were used as weapons' (Bâ 1981: 14).

The portrayal of polygynous families in *The Stillborn* follows the same pattern whereby polygyny discourages true love in marriage. On finally arriving in the city to live with Habu Adams after four years of abandonment in the village, Li finds 'an unsmiling welcome awaiting her' (Alkali 1984: 69). With each passing day, her eyes are opened by 'the bitter silences', mental and physical humiliations (her only child was conceived 'the first time he had desired her' in 'drunken intimacy'), her husband's long and unexplained absences from home: she confides in their landlady, 'He does not want me here. I know it now. He treats me as he would treat a dog, with disgust' (p. 71). It is only years later, after leaving him, that she discovers the existence of her co-wife. Likewise, her robust friend Faku, married to Garba who already has a wife with six children, soon becomes a 'gaunt-looking woman' with 'a thin haggard face', a description which reveals the whole story of the impact of polygynous life on West African women (p. 77).

In-laws, often a rapacious lot, constitute another burden for the married woman. In the Senegalese society portrayed in *So Long a Letter* and *Scarlet Song*, a wife must give, give and give – money, clothes, food – to the in-laws, who believe they have a right to their son's home and property. In the latter work, a married Senegalese woman advises Mireille on the necessity of plying her in-laws with gifts and welcoming her husband's uninvited friends very warmly to prevent a break-up of her marriage. She concludes, 'I will never insist sufficiently on the necessity of giving. Here, more than everywhere else, giving resolves many problems' (Bâ 1981: 149).

Apart from interminable giving, the wife must also welcome her in-laws with open arms at any time they come. Before the death of her husband, Ramatoulaye tolerates his sisters, who too often desert their own homes for the comfort of Ramatoulaye's. A woman's failure to accommodate them would result in the sisters-in-law refusing to touch her head on her husband's death, considered the height of disgrace and humiliation. The fear of this moment makes a wife sacrifice 'her possessions as gifts to her in-laws, and worse still, in addition to her possessions, she abandons her individuality, her dignity, becoming a thing at the service of the man who marries her. Her behaviour is conditioned' (Bâ 1980: 11).

During Modou's funeral ceremony, the younger wife, Binetou, is obliged to stay in Ramatoulaye's house 'according to the custom'. Ramatoulaye is irritated but she cannot throw her out. Her 'At last! Phew!', when Binetou departs on the fortieth day, speaks volumes for her relief after a forced cohabitation (Bâ 1980: 17). It is traditional for sisters-in-law to take care of the widow's hair while the ceremony lasts but a wife who has been 'miserly, unfaithful or inhospitable' will suffer the open disgrace of not having her hair done (p. 11), a practice which ensures that a wife seeks the favour of her in-laws. The powers accorded to mothers-in-law is particularly disturbing: 'Basking in her privileges which are never questioned, the mother-in-law orders, supervises, exacts ... She takes the best part of her son's earnings' (Bâ 1981: 111). In short, a woman within marriage can no longer lay claim to her individuality, existing to procreate and serve.

Zaynab Alkali does not dwell on the relationship between wives and in-laws, but it needs to be said that in the Nigerian context the nefarious intervention of in-laws, particularly mothers-in-law, has driven many a woman out of her home. And in some parts of Nigeria, the property of a couple is sometimes carted away by in-laws immediately after the demise of the man, even in monogamous marriages.

Whether literate or illiterate, in monogamous, polygynous, successful or failed marriages, women bear the burden of being wives, mothers and house-keepers, most often working to earn a living at the same time. In short, she is the workhorse of the family. As a teacher with two maids but twelve children to take care of, Ramatoulaye emphasizes that the working woman has double responsibilities since, even with paid domestic help, she must organize, supervise and do some work herself. Her labours are symbolic of the enormous unappreciated responsibility women shoulder: 'first to get up, last to retire, always busy working' (Bâ 1980: 34). Apart from physical chores, a mother's mental capacity is taxed to the fullest, trying to sustain the family on slim resources, settling quarrels for the children, correcting them, guiding them, attending to their educational progress and when any of them misbehaves, getting blamed for it. Interspersed with other insults, Li's father repeatedly lashes out, in Alkali's novel, 'a heathen mother can only have heathen children' (Alkali 1984: 13).

Even as children and adolescents, it is the girls, the women-to-be, who help mothers with domestic chores. As a boy, Ousmane helps his mother to fetch coal and water, empty the garbage and do other chores, but only in his father's absence; each time Ousmane is caught at it, his father thunders, 'Don't turn this kid into a sissy' (Bâ 1981: 16), echoing the views of his community to the effect that housework, regarded as menial, is fit only for women. *The Stillborn* tells the same story: in Li's family, as in other families, daughters fetch water, do the dishes, wash clothes, help the mother cook. In addition, child marriage condemns young girls to a life of domestication and denigration, while they lack the maturity to understand and cope with the complexities of marriage.

The burden borne by women often has its source in traditional practices, beliefs and prejudices which have arisen partly from myth and ignorance about the role and ability of women, and partly from a deliberate desire to subordinate women. Female subservience is not biologically produced but culturally imposed. From time immemorial, women the world over have been subjected to various degrees of physical, mental and spiritual domination, to social, economic and political exploitation.

Religious beliefs coincide very often with cultural practices which keep women in subjection. For example, before the advent of Islam, polygyny had been in existence for centuries in Africa. Li's grandfather, an animist in *The Stillborn*, marries four women. However, institutionalized polygyny, as laid down in the Qur'an, gives its adherents a justification for a practice which cannot stand rational analysis. If a man can marry two, three or four women – even if he cannot maintain them – does that not imply that he is superior to women? Other Islamic religious practices also oppress women: religion can have such a hold on women that they accept its precepts without question even when such demands are arbitrary. So Ramatoulaye willingly accepts her confinement for the mourning period, taking the purifying baths and changing her mourning clothes every Monday and Friday: 'I hope to carry out my duties faithfully. My heart agrees with the demands of religion. Nurtured, since childhood, on their strict precepts, I believe that I will not fail' (Bâ 1980: 18).

Justification for self-serving actions against women are sometimes anchored in the Islamic belief that whatever happens is God's will, as when the Imam justifies Modou's marriage to Binetou as follows: 'When almighty Allah puts two people side by side, there is nothing one can do' (Bâ 1980: 56). Tamsir, Modou's brother, adds that, according to

Modou himself, 'God has destined him to marry a second wife, he can do nothing about it' (p. 57).

Conjugal infidelity is common in men; even when a man has several wives, he still has illicit affairs. The reality is that men in general have no sexual discipline, as avowed by Mawdo: 'One cannot resist the imperious laws making eating and clothing mandatory for man. These same laws impel the "male" in other respects. I say rightly "male" to underscore the bestiality of instincts' (p. 52).

In *The Virtuous Woman*, Nana Ai, the seventeen-year-old college student, firmly rejects a lift from a car-owner whose casual manner 'suggested he was sure of his prey' (Alkali 1987: 33). Later on, Nana and her two younger companions discover that the car-owner is the secretary who is to provide them with an 'escort' to accompany them from northern Nigeria to their college in southern Nigeria. Because of their earlier encounter, he deliberately punishes them by giving them a partially crippled, poor-sighted 'old Fulani man of about seventy' for a guide (p. 34). Again, this example of male oppression of female moral virtue stems from a deflated ego and sexual indiscipline.

Ironically, women contribute in no small measure to their own burdens, as depicted by the two novelists. Mothers pressurize their daughters – under-age or adult – into becoming second or third wives for material benefits, and mothers-in-law expect their sons' wives to be their servants. Ousmane's mother's main gripe against Mireille is for selfish reasons: 'A white woman can never be a real daughter-in-law ... I who was dreaming of a daughter-in-law who would live here and replace me in doing the housework by taking charge of the house, here I am ending up with a woman who will take away my son. I will die, standing in the kitchen' (Bâ 1981: 102).

Sisters-in-law also contribute to the oppression of wives, by frequenting their brothers' houses and expecting their wives to give them royal welcomes, treating their brothers' houses like their own and remaining insensitive to the wives' feelings. Worst of all, every woman who gets married to an already married man, and every woman who accepts the advances of a married man, stands condemned as an oppressor of another woman, a usurper. Ramatoulaye's daughter, Daba, succinctly makes the point, refusing the pleas of Binetou's mother to be allowed to continue living in the SICAP villa, for she pushed her daughter into being Ramatoulaye's co-wife: 'Remember, I was your daughter's best friend. You made her my mother's rival. My mother has suffered a lot. How can a woman undermine the happiness of another woman? You deserve no pity' (Bâ 1980: 103).

Ramatoulaye sets a good example, refusing to marry the rich Daouda Dieng for two reasons: first, she does not love him and second, she cannot come between him and his family, for she understands the problems of polygyny. She demonstrates that women must refuse to be used as chattels. Aïssatou, Ramatoulaye's friend, concentrates her efforts on her work and on training her four sons, absolutely determined to avoid men in search of easy love affairs. Li and Faku in *The Stillborn* eventually realize this and take their destiny into their own hands.

Both Bâ and Alkali show that educating a woman, apart from providing her with a profession which translates into economic independence, makes her self-reliant, giving her self-confidence and self-fulfilment. Li, who of her own free will gets married at fifteen, soon finds that a woman who depends on a husband or on lovers for her livelihood is doomed to suffer. She vows 'to go back into the world and make an independent life for herself' (Alkali 1984: 85). At twenty-nine she successfully completes her Advanced Teacher's Certificate, builds a large four-bedroom house in her father's compound and, through hard work, becomes the mainstay of her family. Faku, after summoning up courage to leave her husband, 'drifted without a proper sense of direction' but eventually starts training to become a social worker and finds fulfilment (Alkali 1984: 102). Aïssatou, though already a trained teacher, returns to school to train as an interpreter and earns a handsome salary working in her country's embassy in the United States.

To free women from domination by men, a change of attitude in society must take place. According to Awa Thiam, 'to truly liberate woman, a change of mentality is indispensable' (Thiam 1978: 75). A man must discard his pervasive habit of seeing woman 'as a means of satisfying his excessive sexual propensity or a necessary complement to his social and economic functions' (Meloné 1971: 191).

Men and women are complementary. 'Femininity' in women and 'masculinity' in men are not qualities indicating inferiority or superiority. As husband and wife, man and woman should shoulder responsibilities together, think and act jointly and keep out third parties. In *So Long a Letter*, Daba and her husband Abou represent the ideal couple, affirmed by Ramatoulaye as, 'the image of my dream-couple' (Bâ 1980: 107).

Abou helps with the housework because, to him, Daba is his wife and not his slave or servant. It is in this spirit of equality between man and woman, working together, that we must see Li's decision to return to her husband, Habu Adams, who, having begged and pleaded with her to return to him, has had his legs crushed in a motor accident:

> 'You are going back to him?'
> 'Yes.'
> 'Why, Li? The man is lame', said the sister.
> 'We are all lame, daughter-of-my-mother. But this is no time to crawl. It is time to learn to walk again.'
> 'So you want to hold the crutches and lead the way?' Awa asked.
> 'No', answered Li.
> 'What then, you want to walk behind and arrest his fall?'
> 'No. I will just hand him the crutches and side by side we will learn to walk.'
>
> (Alkali 1984: 105)

Note

Throughout this chapter we have used the Mojola translation of Mariama Bâ's *Une si longue lettre* and *Un chant écarlate*, rather than the official English translation. Page references therefore refer to the French editions cited in the references.

References

Ali, A. Y. (trans) (1983) *The Meaning of the Glorious Qur'an*, Nadim and Co., London.
Alkali, Z. (1984) *The Stillborn*, Longman, Harlow.
— (1987) *The Virtuous Woman*, Longman, Ikeja, Nigeria.
Bâ, M. (1980) *So Long a Letter*. Trans. M. Bode-Thomas, Heinemann, London. Originally published as *Une si longue lettre*, Les Nouvelles Editions Africaines, Dakar-Abidjan-Lomé.
— (1981) *Scarlet Song*. Trans. Originally published as *Un chant écarlate*, Les Nouvelles Editions Africaines, Dakar.
Koroye, S. (1989) 'The Ascetic Feminist Vision of Zaynab Alkali', in H. Otokunefor, and O. Nwodo (eds), *Nigerian Female Writers: A Critical Perspective*, Malthouse Press, Lagos, Nigeria, 47–51.
Meloné, T. (1971) *Mongo Béti: l'homme et le destin*, Présence Africaine, Paris.
Mokwenyé, C. (1983) 'La polygamie et la révolte de la femme africaine moderne:

une lecture d'*Une si longue lettre* de Mariama Bâ', *Peuples Noirs Peuples Africains* 31 (Jan.–Feb.), 86–94.

Montagu, A. (1974) *The Natural Superiority of Women*, Collier Macmillan, London.

Ojo-Ade, F. (1983) 'Female Writers, Male Critics', *African Literature Today* 13, 158–79.

Thiam, A. (1978) *La Parole aux Négresses*, Denoël, Paris.

11
Narrative technique and the politics of gender: Ama Ata Aidoo's *Our Sister Killjoy* and *No Sweetness Here*

CHIOMA OPARA

Feminist literature is unquestionably as scholarly as it is political. Lillian Robinson has deftly asserted that textual analysis could elucidate the way the texture of sentences, choice of metaphors, pattern of exposition and narrative relate to ideology (Robinson 1971: 889). Differently stated, sexual politics becomes the organizing principle in the form and style of a text. The politics of gender provides the backdrop for the varied artistic devices in Ama Ata Aidoo's narratives, which can be situated within the framework of an African feminist agenda.[1] Clearly, Aidoo's narrative structure is complex and subversive. Employing the female point of view, her techniques carry her outcry against sexism. She also employs the trope of madness as she focuses on her 'mad country and her madder continent' of supposedly independent nations (Aidoo 1977: 40).

Silhouetted against this vision of a manic society are her notably sensitive women. The piteous condition of women in Ghanaian society features prominently in *No Sweetness Here* (1970) where the numerous women in the fictive world stare out at the sensible reader. Charlotte Bruner has observed that Aidoo 'writes feelingly of women in Ghana and their reaction to change' (Bruner [ed.] 1983: 14). In 'No Sweetness Here', 'Two Sisters' and 'A Gift from Somewhere', we perceive the mental agony of wives who are victims of unhappy marriages in a metamorphosing society.

Engaged in sexual politics, Aidoo reveals the prejudices that are brought to bear on Maami Ama in 'No Sweetness Here'. Bathed in pathos, she is described as 'a care-worn village woman', lonely, abandoned and abused by the entire family. The story climaxes with the death of her only child who represents an uncle, father and husband to her. As one sympathizer asks rhetorically, 'What does one do when one's only pot breaks?' (Aidoo 1970: 74). Such occasional lapses into sentimentality are found in Aidoo's works. In 'Something to Talk About on the Way to the Funeral' one of the gossips remarks, 'Oh women, we are to be pitied' (p. 122). And M'ma Asana in 'Certain Winds from the South' asks, 'Is his family noted for males that rot? No certainly not. It is us who are noted for our unlucky females' (p. 51). The negative effect of age on women is touched upon in *Our Sister Killjoy*: 'At nine a showpiece. At eighteen a darling. What shall you be at thirty? A dog among the masters' (Aidoo 1977: 42). These statements are all made to stoke our consciousness of female subjugation in Ghana and the need to change societal practices that have been compounded by postcolonial western values.

As we go through Aidoo's collection of short stories, the range of cultural repressions and prejudices is revealed. Suffice it to say that Aidoo makes a calculated effort to use female characters as both reflectors and narrators in her works. Sissie is the sole reflector in *Our Sister Killjoy*; likewise in *No Sweetness Here*, eight out of the eleven commentators are women. These speakers present the female viewpoint, while the author reveals their varied moods, frustrations and traumatic experiences in a broader frame. The plaintive voice of M'ma Asana in 'Certain Winds from the South' sounds a note of protest over the perennial female reproductive role: 'Now all I must do is try and prepare myself for another pregnancy for it seems that this is the reason why I was created ... to be pregnant for nine of the twelve months of every year or is there a way out of it all?' (Aidoo 1970: 81). In a society where maternity is obligatory, it is only logical that women should be obsessed with motherhood.

On the few occasions when a male voice is heard, it is either self-deprecating or cynical about the weaknesses of a patriarchal society. In 'For Whom Things Did Not Change', Kobina's interior monologue reveals his rancour against a corrupt system that is incapable of sowing progressive ideas in society: 'Where is the earth? Who is going to do the planting? Certainly not us – too full with drink, eyes clouded in smoke and heads full of women' (Aidoo 1970: 22).

In *Our Sister Killjoy*, we view things through the black eyes of Sissie and analyse events from her point of view. Sissie's voice is so forceful in this novel that the whole work can be said to present her attack on racism, neo-colonialism and sexism. The reader becomes aware of the world-wide oppression of women, situated in its Ghanaian context by an author writing towards an ideal of women's autonomy.

Much of the effect of Sissie's language derives from Aidoo's ability to cast her in an alien Western setting. It is noteworthy that the language in *Our Sister Killjoy* differs markedly from that in *No Sweetness Here*, which derives from the oral form and is flavoured with proverbs and transcribed vernacular idioms to bring out the local colour. In 'Something to Talk About on the Way to the Funeral', for example, the frame story is based on a dyadic conversation between women, one of whom narrates the embedded story like a typical African storyteller. Like a folkloric tale, the story is filled with repetitions, such as 'the baking business grew and grew and grew' (Aidoo 1970: 121), while the audience (or participant) inundates the story with interjections: 'But isn't this what I am coming to? This is what I am coming to ... Ah-h-h' (p. 117). This observation validates the claim that, 'female–female speech often had fewer hesitations (indicating greater ease): it had more mm/hmm's (acknowledging the speech of the other persons) and more elaborations on each other's utterances' (Thorne and Henley [eds] 1975: 24).

The dialogues of these rural women revolve round personal lives and village gossip reminiscent of Flora Nwapa's novels. Temma Kaplan holds that through gossip, women both express and find reinforcement of their thoughts, which may influence what they do (Kaplan 1982: 58). Simply put, gossip is a self-actualization process. Carole Boyce Davies on her own part asserts that 'small talk', which some straight-laced critics see as weakness in style, has now been associated with African women's oral literature (Boyce Davies 1986: 16). Aidoo translates 'small talk' into moralistic folk-song when, in 'Two Sisters', Mercy's shoes are made to sing:

> Count Mercy, count your blessings
> Count Mercy, count your blessings
> Count, count, count your blessings
>
> (Aidoo 1970: 88)

Another important observation about Aidoo's style in *No Sweetness Here* is the conversational form and the use of commentators. These literary devices enable the author to leave her stories open-ended. Robert Adams suggests that structural openness at the end of the text allows for the inclusion of a major unresolved conflict while intentionally preserving irresolution (Adams cited in Gross 1966: 362). It is Judith Gardiner's contention that works written by women are open-ended because 'the quest for female identity seems to be a soap-opera, endless and never advancing' (Gardiner 1982). Hélène Cixous also interprets open-endedness as specifically *feminine*: 'a feminine textual body is recognised by the fact that it is always endless, without ending: there is no closure, it doesn't stop and it's this that very often makes the feminine text difficult to read' (Cixous 1981: 53). While allowing for all of these critical positions, the open-endedness of Aidoo's stories demonstrates the 'irresolution' and idealistic nature of the very real quest for African women's identities.

Aidoo asks seminal rhetorical questions about male and female roles. In 'For Whom Things Did Not Change' the commentator asks: 'When a black man is with his wife who cooks and cares for him he is a man. When he is with white folk for whom he cooks and chores, he is a woman. Dear Lord, what then is a black man who cooks and chores for black men?' (Aidoo 1970: 17). There is no mistaking the irony with which the author presents Setu's husband, whom she calls 'master'; for he is a servant to both the colonial and the neo-colonial master. We become aware of the ambivalence in the conjugal division of labour. The African man claims that cooking is a feminine chore in the domestic sphere, only to engage in that same chore in the public sphere.[2]

Aidoo's poetic discourse changes in *Our Sister Killjoy* where the erudite Sissie delves into world politics. The conversational speech style of this new woman refutes the hypothesis that women can only communicate in trivial vocabulary and conservative forms of language (Bodine 1975: 131). In his analysis of Aidoo's poetic diction, Dapo Adelugba praises 'her success in creating levels of language, in matching literary grace with veracity of characterization, in suiting, for the most part, the action to the novel, the word to the action' (Adelugba 1976: 72). Aidoo combines prose, song, poetry and sketch in this novel. Perhaps she is a votary of the call for a different sphere of women's writing which feminist critics such as Elaine Showalter have been advocating (Showalter 1982). The composite of different forms in Aidoo's novel could be seen as a structural reflection of the diverse reproductive and productive roles played by women in society.

Although authorial intrusion is minimal in Aidoo's works, she succeeds in relaying her messages by means of searing irony. At Marija's disappointment over Sissie's inability to honour her dinner invitation, the latter ruminates:

> It is not sound for a woman to enjoy cooking for another woman. Not under any circumstances. It is not done. It is not possible. Special meals are for men. They are the only sex to whom the maker gave a mouth with which to enjoy eating. And woman the eternal cook is never so pleased on seeing a man enjoying what she has cooked (Aidoo 1977: 77).

When Marija explains that she sent the child to bed so that the two of them could be alone, Sissie ponders, 'It is heresy in Africa, Europe, Everywhere. This is not a statement to come from a good mother's lips – Touchwood' (p. 49). At Marija's preference for a son, Sissie remarks:

> Any good woman
> In her senses
> With her choices
> Would say the
> Same
> In Asia
> Europe ...
> So why wish a curse on your child
> Desiring her to be female?
> Besides, my sister
> The ranks of the wretched are
> Full.
>
> (Aidoo 1977: 51)

Adopting a satirical tone, Aidoo has tried to awaken female sensitivity to sexual inequality and prejudices against women in society.

Using clothing to signify African women's status in *Our Sister Killjoy*, Aidoo paints a vivid picture of women's lives in London. Decked in and doomed by their clothing, most of these women are relegated to stereotyped female professions. Their slatternliness demonstrates the subsidiary roles they play in their various families: so, by taking courses in dressmaking and hairdressing and morally supporting their husbands, who study engineering, law and medicine, they are hiding behind their husbands' identities. The close relationship between self-definition, sexual difference and costume becomes very obvious in the portraiture of these women. Unlike the progressive heroine, these women are lagging behind in the quest for self-actualization.

Aidoo's comic but sarcastic tone is a satirical tool in her works, serving to expose postcolonial inequalities. In *Our Sister Killjoy*, she directs gory humour against the 'large hearted', gullible sexist Kunle, after destroying him:

> Yes Kunle's heart stayed in
> His chest, too strong to be
> Affected by anything else,
> Still pumping under the
> Sizzling chest,
> Stopping only when
> The flames had
> Swallowed it up ...
> For it certainly would have gladdened Kunle's heart to find
> itself in the hands of the Christian Doctor.
>
> (Aidoo 1970: 107–8)

Similarly, Aidoo satirizes the nurse in 'The Message' who is full of scorn for an old woman, the representative of tradition. In the denouement, the earthiness of the old woman is pitched against the crass affectation of the nurse. By juxtaposing the traditional rural woman with the Westernized urban nurse, and exposing the antagonism between them, the author implicitly advocates female self-criticism and awareness.

In the vein of Buchi Emecheta, Aidoo's technique is deflationary towards men and inflationary towards her heroines. Male caricatures and exemplary females abound in her works. In 'For Whom Things Did Not Change', Zirigu epitomizes an African head of a patriarchal household emasculated by the incursion of Western imperialism. Kobina bluntly points out to him, 'As a man of the land and your wife's husband you are a man and therefore do not cook. As a black, not a man, therefore you can cook' (Aidoo 1970: 17). The author's wit is directed at Zirigu who, like John Nwodika in Chinua Achebe's *Arrow of God*, has joined in 'the race for the white man's money' (Achebe 1964: 169), becoming reduced in the process. While men like Zirigu degenerate to mere absurdities, Aidoo's assertive women grow psychologically and in strength, culminating in Sissie, who is the quintessential new woman. Nana Wilson-Tagoe describes her as 'a highly politicized and very aware female who tries to resolve the conflicts about her instincts and her mind' (Wilson-Tagoe 1981: 90). In fact, Sissie seems to be carrying the whole of the sky by 'carrying Africa's problems' on her shoulders (Aidoo 1977: 118). Aidoo uses her portrait to explore a binary opposition of race and gender, which is demonstrated in two episodes. The first episode takes place in Germany,[3] where Sissie is the light in every eye. Sissie beats her weak and sloppy 'opponent' Marija in a racial and cultural war. And in the second episode, which takes place in London, Sissie emerges victorious in the war of the sexes. The two episodes are woven into a unified plot to highlight the heroine's status as a prodigy.

In her effective contrasts between the modern and the traditional, and between the passive and the active, the author brings to light the conflicts plaguing women and Ghanaian society at large. In 'Two Sisters', Connie is confined literally by her pregnancy and figuratively within the household; she represents immanence, while her sister Mercy seeks transcendence from such a model of Ghanaian femininity. Confined in the precinct of the domestic sphere, Connie is the victim of her callous husband and like an angel – the madwoman's opposite in Gilbert and Gubar's seminal text (1979) – she exudes passivity and bears the mental torture precipitated by her husband's philandering. She is even impelled to sleep with her face turned to the wall to avert any possible nightmares which her pregnant form might engender. Neither the obstreperous Mercy, who descends to self-abasement, nor the inert Connie is Aidoo's ideal woman. Neither is, as it were, the author's maddened double. Perhaps in this story Aidoo has employed a double device in order to prescribe a mid-course towards female autonomy. This double technique takes a subversive turn in 'The Late Bud'. Like the biblical Mary, Yaaba has 'chosen the better part' while her sister Adwoa remains rooted to the hearth. Aidoo's maddened double might be found in Yaaba, who refuses to be confined to the domestic scene while her sister remains a prototype of the subjugated woman, relegated to stereotyped feminine roles.

These conflicts culminate in 'For Whom Things Did Not Change', where men as well as women are confused figures in an equally muddled society. In Setu, Aidoo represents a woman perplexed by colonialism and Islamic tenets: she is married to a cook, and it becomes increasingly difficult for her to distinguish between so-called wifely and husbandly duties. Even Sissie, Aidoo's heroine, is not exempt from a spate of internal conflicts. Sissie, the cardinal oppositionist to men, sometimes wishes to be a man: 'Sissie looked at the other women and wished again that at least, she was a boy, a man' (Aidoo 1977: 67). One cannot help but wonder if Sissie is suffering from an identity crisis generated by her gender or whether, in the vein of Virginia Woolf's postulate, she is aspiring towards an androgynous selfhood which would not be an interchangeable male/female but rather a fused male–female, symbolizing the author's concept of synthesis. In spite of the fact that she claims to have no womanliness in her, implying that she is infused with manliness, 'Aidoo's heroine', says Femi Ojo-Ade, 'remains a woman' (Ojo-Ade 1983: 169). One can only speculate on Aidoo's position, however, as she gives no clues to her intentions.

Adept in irony and the manipulation of language, Aidoo's work is filled with spouses, siblings, traditions, societies and sexes at variance with one another. Aidoo appears to be obsessed with the anomic state of her society. Nevertheless, she calls for a sense of temperance[4] from African women who are the victims of ingrained sexual discrimination. Aidoo does not spare women who fall prey to the 'tinsels of the West'.[5] She reveals a comprehensive, composite and pessimistic vision of society. Like her squeamish and lachrymose persona, Sissie, Aidoo sees the realization of non-sexist cultural norms as pivotal to female individuation. Promoting female bonding and financial independence, Aidoo delineates an agenda for female emancipation. Her tone is discursive and politicized: a militant female writer, she strives to arouse our consciences while taking a critical glimpse at the newly awakened African woman.

Notes

1. I have tried to distinguish between Western feminism and African feminism, which I have dubbed 'femalism' in an essay entitled, 'The Ineligible Trammels, Towards a Paradigm for Woman Consciousness in African Literature' (Opara n.d.).

2. Chinua Achebe has also discussed this conflict in *A Man of the People* (1966), where we are told that 'as long as a man confined himself to prepared concoctions he could still maintain the comfortable illusion that he wasn't really doing such an unmanly thing as cooking' (Achebe 1966: 52).

3. Peter H. Merkle has pointed out that Germany is the land of the three K's – *Kinder* (children), *Kueche* (kitchen), *Kirche* (church) – which in the nineteenth century defined the place of women in society. He further claims that in West Germany the image of women staying home, raising children, cooking and washing for the family still prevails (Merkle 1978: 129, 144).

4. In a conversation with Ama Ata Aidoo on 14 July 1992, during the WAAD conference at the University of Nigeria, Nsukka, my preconceived notion of the author's temperance and femaleness in spite of the seeming radical feminism in her works was confirmed.

5. The phrase 'tinsels of the West' has been used by a number of African writers and critics to express their disaffection with the general craving for gaudy articles imported from the West at the expense of moral uprightness.

References

Achebe, C. (1964) *Arrow of God*, Heinemann, London.

Adelugba, D. (1976) 'Language and Drama: Ama Ata Aidoo', *African Literature Today* 8, 72–84.

Aidoo, A. A. (1970) *No Sweetness Here*, Longman, Harlow.

— (1977) *Our Sister Killjoy, or Reflections from a Black Eyed Squint*, Longman, Harlow.

Bodine, A. (1975) 'Sex Differentiation in Language', in B. Thorne and N. Henley (eds), *Language and Sex*, 130–51.

Boyce Davies (1986), 'Introduction: Feminist Consciousness and African Literary Criticism', in C. Boyce Davies and A. Adams Graves (eds), *Ngambika: Studies of Women in African Literature*, Africa World Press, Trenton, NJ, 1–23.

Bruner, C. H. (ed.) (1983) *Unwinding Threads: Writing by Women in Africa*, Heinemann, London.

Cixous, H. (1981) 'Castration or Decapitation', *Signs: Journal of Women in Culture and Society* 7 (1), 41–55.

Gardiner, J. K. (1982) 'On Female Identity and Writing by Women', in E. Abel, (ed.), *Writing and Sexual Difference*, Harvester Press, Sussex, 177–91.

Gilbert, S. and S. Gubar (1979) *The Madwoman in the Attic: The Woman Writer and the Nineteenth-Century Literary Imagination*, Yale University Press, New Haven, CT.

Gross, B. (1966) 'Narrative Time and the Open-ended Novel', *Criticism*, Autumn, 362–76.

Kaplan, T. (1982) 'Female Consciousness and Collective Action: A Case of Barcelona 1910–1918', in N. O. Keohane et al. (eds), *Feminist Theory: A Critique of Ideology*, Harvester Press, Sussex, 53–76.

Merkle, P. H. (1978) 'The Politics of Sex: Western Germany', in L. B. Iglitzin and R. Ross (eds), *Women in the World: A Comparative Study*, Clio Books, Oxford, 129–47.

Ojo-Ade, F. (1983) 'Female Writers, Male Critics', *African Literature Today* 13, 158–79.

Opara, C. (n.d.) 'The Ineligible Trammels, Towards a Paradigm for Woman Consciousness in African Literature', *Dialogue & Universalism* 5 (4), 104–13.

Robinson, L. S. (1971) 'Dwelling in Decencies: Radical Criticism and the Feminist Perspective', *College English* 32, 879–89.

Showalter, E. (1982) 'Feminist Criticism in the Wilderness', in E. Abel (ed.), *Writing and Sexual Difference*, Harvester Press, Sussex, 9–35.

Thorne, B. and N. Henley (eds) (1975) *Language and Sex: Difference and Dominance*, Newbury House, Massachusetts.

Wilson-Tagoe, N. (1981) 'The Woman Writer in Africa. Her Dilemma and Her Choices: A Reading of Ama Ata Aidoo', in *Medium and Message: Proceedings of the International Conference on African Literature of the English Language*, 1, 81–90.

PART III
Popular Culture

Hausa women as oral storytellers in northern Nigeria

SANI ABBA ALIYU

Women's art of oral storytelling is as ancient as the people themselves in Hausa-speaking areas of northern Nigeria. Narrators can be located in the states of Kano, Katsina, Kaduna, Kebbi, Sokoto, Bauchi, Borno, Niger, Adamawa, Taraba, Plateau and in the Federal Capital, Abuja, where Hausa has been the lingua franca for decades. Hausa is spoken throughout the West African region and has long been recognized in Central and North Africa. Used for educational instruction in Nigeria and for radio and television broadcasts nationally, Hausa is the only language used by the Nigerian government for daily external broadcasts. Internationally, the BBC, Voice Of America, Radio Deutchewelle, Radio Beijing and Radio Moscow have regular broadcasts in Hausa. It is also employed in the judicial system, particularly in the non-Western courts spread over much of northern Nigeria.

Unlike the large number of Nigerian languages yet to be transferred to writing, Hausa has had the benefit of alphabetization for a long time. The population's early contact with Islam led to literacy in Arabic, which in turn brought about an Arabic-based Hausa script called *ajami*. Although there are Christians and animists among the Hausa, Islam predominates, and *ajami* is still used extensively for literary compositions by women and men.

Distinguishing themselves as farmers, merchants and leather-workers, the Hausa are a patrilineal people. Particularly in the rural areas, the majority of women are likely to be non-literate, married to a polygynous man and living in seclusion (purdah). In urban areas, an upsurge in the provision of Islamic education since the late 1970s has provided literacy for many married women. Increasing numbers of Hausa women are beneficiaries of Western education, moving through primary schools and on to universities; and they are now taking up careers in teaching, the civil service and the mass media.

The precolonial period might be regarded as the 'golden age' for women storytellers in Hausa areas. While such periodization is arbitrary and dangerous to a large extent, culturally distinct storytelling practices did occur before the declaration of British colonial rule over northern Nigeria in 1903. Decades of literary activities in Arabic and *ajami* predated the British colonial presence, though textual production and consumption were not really widespread, being confined to small circles of Muslim clerics and their disciples. For the vast majority in traditional Hausa society, local oral art forms had a far more pervasive influence, and women were pivotal to the rendition of imaginative narratives.

There is evidence of a strict division of labour according to gender in precolonial Hausaland. 'Male' and 'female' roles were distinguished: the art of narration itself was sub-divided, with different genres distributed along gender lines. It appears that storytelling was consigned to women, while other forms of narratives such as the *hikaya* and *labari*, perceived by male-dominated societies to be more serious, were the verbal province of the males. These forms have written, Islamic origins, unlike the *tatsuniyoyi* of the womenfolk. Considerable truth therefore attaches to the statement that Hausa women dominated oral storytelling in precolonial times, occurring in no small part because the form was viewed as 'feminine'.

Women's confinement in purdah more or less dictated that they excel as night-time narrators. When the men embarked on post-harvest migrations, leaving the women and children behind, or set off on distant errands on behalf of traditional rulers, it was only logical that the stable, domesticated women should perfect their oral artistry in weaving entertaining episodes around serious moral lessons, fulfilling their function as the children's first socializers. Being a largely non-literate community, the intellectual resources of these women still find supreme expression in the creation and imaginative retelling of stories.

Hausa women's stories are told at night: the conjunction of darkness and narration has, for a long time, characterized the storytelling situation. The particular attractions of night-time tale-telling are only too obvious, enhancing the excitement, anticipation and concentration of the gathered audience. While women tell tales throughout the year, the frequency of narration tends to peak during the rainy season which generally lasts from May to September. (The dry season offers a range of competing outdoor evening entertainments.)

Storytelling takes place indoors: women narrate within the confines of their homes. The dual dictates of Islam and Hausa cultural codes forbid women from engaging in public storytelling to live audiences outside their residences. This is not to imply that there are no professional female entertainers: however, musical entertainers, performing to fee-paying audiences, are viewed as erratic or wayward. Female musicians are seen not as role-models, but as targets of lampoon and derision. Socially respected female storytellers are firmly home-based, likely to be non-literate, old or middle-aged, married to a polygynist and living in purdah.

The targets of women's narrative endeavours are children and adolescents. The fact that tale-telling occurs indoors restricts the audience to this captive age-group, and very few adults will be present. Even among the children, there will be a preponderance of girls. Females are the most consistently present members of Hausa compounds; they rarely leave their homes in search of dry season work or Islamic education. And since storytelling is used to socialize children into adulthood, the presence of female listeners guarantees the continuity of the tale tradition. The closeness of Hausa women to children, principally as mothers and agents for the transmission of norms and values, strengthens their position as influential narrators.

With the exception of individual men who earn their living as roving entertainers, praise singers, musicians, hawkers, palace courtiers and medicine-men, the average Hausa woman is a more versatile and proficient deployer of linguistic resources than men in society. This can be explained sociologically: women have to participate in the sophisticated banter of courtship; similarly, petty trading, polygynous rivalries and child-rearing contribute to their verbal and argumentative resources.

The continuation and aesthetic refinement of oral storytelling depend upon the women. For instance, when the elaborate ceremonies associated with marriage among the Hausa are concluded, children from neighbouring compounds congregate to keep the new bride company. The bride usually leads narration sessions, aided by the contributions of her friends and applauded by the children in attendance. Hausa women, children and the marriage institution are therefore vital to the survival of oral storytelling.

In general, oral storytelling occurs for a number of reasons. Male members of society view storytelling by women as functional, facilitating the inculcation of socially desirable values such as hard work, honesty, thrift and wisdom. Stories also keep the children out of mischief as night falls. As far as female narrators are concerned, oral storytelling affords the opportunity to be very close to children, teaching them the richness of their language and culture.[1] In a predominantly oral cultural context, eloquence is cherished and cultivated, and command of the art of narration is celebrated among the Hausa as a great asset.

At storytelling gatherings, the narrator might commence with riddles and answers. Riddling performs the role of warming up both narrator and audience, sharpening their wits for the story experience. The narrator mouths the opening formula, *'Ga ta nan ga ta nanku'* ('Here is a story, here is a story'), and the audience enthuses, *'Ta zo mu ji ta'*, ('Let it come for us to listen to it'). Similarly, the conventional method for concluding stories is to pronounce, *'Takurungus'* ('This is the end of our tale'). Both the opening and closing conventions are important devices for the management of the transition into and out of the audience's imagination. The thematic import of the tales is rendered through terminal moral tags or the use of symbolism.

Narrators incorporate recognizable rhetorical structures, frequently using proverbs and songs, and Hausa stories can be classified broadly into Animal and Human tales (Pilaszewics 1985: 193). The spider (Gizo), the hero of many tales, is celebrated for his wit and cunning; many wild and domestic animals relevant to the Hausa environment also feature in the tales.

In form and theme, Hausa women's narratives have not been static. Significant socio-economic transformations have affected the contexts and frequency of oral storytelling: in particular, British colonialism dramatically altered the women's narration. Colonialism introduced money, taxes and wage employment into the peasant agricultural setting prevailing in Hausaland. Rapid urbanization and infrastructural development dragged the Hausa into the dominant capitalist system. In this tumultuous situation, conventional values and practices, including oral narration, had to be redefined. There are no indications that the colonial authorities legislated against the Hausa tradition of oral tale-telling, but attitudes to storytelling were affected by the crises and changes brought by colonial capital into Hausa societies.

Hausaland experienced an Islamic spiritual awakening in the years preceding the spread of British colonial structures. During the Shehu Usman Fodio *Jihad* against pre-Islamic ways, inherited non-Islamic artistic practices became the targets of persistent attack and criticism (Hiskett 1975: 17). With the spread of Islam in northern Nigeria, increasing numbers of Islamic schools and colleges were established. Located all over Hausaland, these institutions drew away a considerable number of actual and potential oral performers. Since Islamic learning did not favour pre-existent oral forms, the attitudes of tellers and audiences inevitably changed towards the dominant Arabic–Islamic literary and cultural practice.

The first colonial school for the sons of Emirs was established in Kano in 1911; since then, the number, type and quality of schools in Hausaland have changed considerably. The curricula of these schools excluded local cultures and narratives, being oriented instead towards English literature and culture. By the late 1930s, British colonial education had produced a literate reading constituency requiring indigenous reading materials: so the administration set up a Translation Bureau, succeeded by a Literature Bureau. The bureaux organized and issued the first set of Hausa novels in 1933, followed by a Hausa newspaper, *GTK*, in 1939. Facilitating the emergence of modern Hausa literature, the Western-style school system also contributed significantly to the shifting of loyalties away from the forms and themes of oral narratives. Educated Hausa children were more likely to be found reading Hausa or English novels than listening to female storytellers.

If British colonialism and the school system changed the context of oral storytelling, then electronic mass communication media have revolutionized it. The advent of informational and popular media, including mobile and stationary cinemas, television and radio, created an entirely new situation for oral storytellers in Hausa areas. These versatile electronic media appeal to the educated, urbanized populations of the north. Oral storytellers have to compete for audiences, pitting themselves against cinema and home video shows in the neighbourhoods. In the urban areas, women who would once upon a time have been narrating stories to children, are now likely to be showing nightly Indian films on home videos to paying audiences.[2] Children who trooped to the homes of brides in the past, still visit newly married women: they go to see the latest Indian and Hausa love videos. The technologization and commercialization of Nigerian arts and entertainments pose great challenges to Hausa women's oral traditions.

After Independence in 1960, indigenous radio broadcasting received a considerable boost: the Hausa Service of the Federal Radio Corporation of Nigeria, Kaduna (FRCN), transmitted nineteen hours daily. Women stepped on to the airwaves with a storytelling programme, *Shafa Labari Shuni* (*Making Stories Sweeter*). Broadcast daily for fifteen minutes in the mornings, with a repeat in the evenings, *Shafa Labari Shuni* has become synonymous with the Hausa service of the FRCN, Kaduna. Whereas traditional oral tale-telling was restricted to the period after dark, the modern storytelling programme reaches audiences during daylight hours.

Shafa Labari Shuni was conceived as a forum for budding, unpublished writers to broadcast their stories on air.[3] Intended to complement efforts to provide adult education and to stimulate creativity, the programme comprised a variety of stories sent in by interested listeners. Stipulating that stories had to be in the listeners' own handwriting, and excluding non-literate women from participating as a result, the radio station received several folktales and a multitude of anecdotal stories. When the flow of contributions slowed, then virtually stopped, the production team moved from reading narratives written by unknown authors to recitations of classic Hausa literary works. Colonial translations were also included: *One Thousand and One Nights* was broadcast, as well as Abubakar Imam's three-volume *Magana Jari Ce* (*Wisdom is an Asset*; 1937), Bello Kagara's *Gandoki* (1933) and Rupert East's and J. Tafida Wusasa's *Jiki Magayi* (*It is the Body that Tells*; 1933). Recently, however, the management has requested stories from listeners once again.

In the late 1980s, the Hausa narratives which inundated the FRCN, Kaduna, were of a different character, influenced by the boom in popular fiction, or 'Kano market literature', that was taking place in the most urbanized and densely populated of northern Nigerian cities. Written, printed and published by young school leavers, these Hausa 'pulp' novels and videos lack depth in form or seriousness in style, and mainly reflect the preoccupations and cultural contexts of the authors, being Hausa renditions of Indian films and English popular romantic novels. Hausa culture, values and behavioural codes are sidelined by the popular market literature, a hit with the youth but rejected by the wider society.

Contributions such as these were read on the *Shafa Labari Shuni* programme, as authors embraced popular broadcasting and continued sending copies to the radio station. Protests against the readings of Kano market literature led to their sudden cessation, and the programme has reverted to its previous classical menu. In effect, therefore, *Shafa Labari Shuni* is not really a 'folktale' rendition programme, nor is it a stage for contemporary popular fiction. Instead, written and published Hausa narratives are retold.

The continuing popularity of *Shafa Labari Shuni* has to do with its narrators: fluent, persuasive and skilled women narrate each broadcast. The presence of female storytellers is explained by the radio management team as resulting from their dominance as accomplished raconteurs in the oral setting. The voice listeners hear during *Shafa Labari Shuni* resonates with the voices of their mothers, aunts and grandmothers. What has emerged in contemporary broadcasts is therefore a coalescence of storytelling traditions, the women's narrative expertise, and the historical exigencies of Hausa broadcasting.

Shafa Labari Shuni has featured two female narrators in its short history: first to serve was Mairiga Aliyu, recently replaced by Habiba Rabiu Bako. Both narrators have been fluent and captivating, endearing themselves to the listening public as mother- or grandmother-figures and as experienced broadcasters with a more than an average competence in the Hausa language. Surprisingly, neither of the two narrators has attained a high level of Western education, possessing only an elementary school certificate. In consequence, they are not too far removed from the traditional oral context of tale-telling, obtaining considerable inspiration from it; nor are they exposed to popular fiction emanating from Europe and America. They operate most comfortably within the pro-establishment, pro-male setting of the Hausa language service of the FRCN in Kaduna.

The *Shafa Labari Shuni* programme was intended originally for adult education classes in northern Nigeria. It has transcended that now, becoming almost compulsory listening for 35 to 50 million individuals at any given time (RNK 1992: 4). The management of the FRCN claim that this is 'the most popular radio station not only in Nigeria but in [the whole of] sub-saharan Africa' (RNK 1992: 4).

The story programme has become so popular that when listeners were recently requested to send in reading materials, the response was massive. People seemed excited at the prospect of having their material read and their names broadcast on the programme. Listeners hold considerable power: their protest was responsible for the exclusion of Hausa popular fiction from *Shafa Labari Shuni*. The power of broadcasting technology has broadened the audience to include most listeners of the FRCN Hausa service. Hausa people listening to FRCN, Kaduna, have added the *Shafa Labari Shuni* programme to their cultural identity.

In the traditional oral storytelling milieu, female narrators were confined to the home, exercising their skills on children: in contrast, the female narrators on the radio have achieved almost limitless patronage. This prominence of female storytellers does not extend, however, to decision-making in male-dominated Hausa society. All of the key decisions on *Shafa Labari Shuni* are taken by men, and the women simply carry out instructions from above. Furthermore, the content of the scripts they read is frequently anti-women. Whether classical works of Hausa literature or 'pulp' fiction from Kano, the stories regularly depict women in subordinate roles, totally dependent on men for their survival in society. In spite of the storytellers' progress, it will therefore take more than female narrators to challenge the negative stereotypes of women pervading contemporary popular culture in Nigeria.

Notes

1. Group interview, Zaria, 3 June 1995.
2. Hadizalsa Waziri, personal interview, Zaria, 1 June 1995.
3. Alh. Yusuf Ladan, personal interview, Kaduna, 1 July 1995.

References

East, R. and J. Tafida (1933) *Jiki Magayi*, Literature Bureau/NNPC, Zaria, Nigeria.
Hiskett, M. (1975) *A History of Hausa Islamic Verse*, SOAS, London.
Imam, A. (1937) *Magana Jari Ce* (1–3), Literature Bureau/NNPC, Zaria, Nigeria.
Kagara, B. (1933) *Gandoki*, Literature Bureau/NNPC, Zaria, Nigeria.
Pilaszewics, S. (1985) 'Literature in the Hausa Language', in B. W. Andrzejewski, S. Pilaszewics and W. Tylech (eds), *Literatures in African Languages: Theoretical Issues and Sample Surveys*, Cambridge University Press, Cambridge.
RNK (1992) *Radio Nigeria Kaduna 1992 Anniversary Magazine*, RNK, Kaduna, Nigeria.

13
Gender politics in West African mask performance

CHINYERE GRACE OKAFOR

Ideologically and aesthetically, mask theatres are significant expressions of 'traditional' society in Africa, offering interesting points of entry into local and regional gender politics. The organization of mask performances, their production, content and execution, rest with secret cults composed of men or women; cult members are revered for their special positions, each representing not merely a character but actually reincarnating the spirits made visible through their masks. Powerful political figures, they manipulate the theatres, productions and performances in a manner that influences all levels of gender consciousness in society at large, particularly in the areas of differentiation, co-operation, discrimination and empowerment.

There are different levels of participation by men and women in mask cults across West Africa, which are organized into mono-sex, dual-sex and sexually parallel formations; and different kinds of benefit are derived by the initiates of the cults. A prominent benefit derives from members' status as part of a group which holds the power to perform and redefine vital functions in society; for while mask performers entertain, they also offer symbolic commentaries on spiritual, security and rulership issues. Likewise, the training and experiences provided by the cult are advantageous in moulding initiates for participation in the wider society.

The spiritual quality of the mask performance accords the producers a special place in those African societies where the practice still occurs. Performers rely on the mask as a medium, expressing the community's spiritual essence. Some ancestral masks represent members of the lineage who have transcended to the spirit world; others are non-ancestral masks, which might represent spirits, animals or social types. All masks disguise the actors, not merely covering them up with assumed personae, but transforming them, imbuing the dramatic character with supernatural qualities. Except in a few cases where the performance has been dislocated or has lost its social relevance, the mask character in traditional African societies is believed to possess supernatural qualities. Ostensibly, the mask performance functions to entertain spectators with a variety of dramatic pieces, including songs, dances, music, spectacles of awesome figures, and frequently a combination of all these elements in a play. For example, the *Ikaki* mask performance of the Kalabari people in Nigeria entertains through 'comic anecdotes, character sketches, music, and dance sketches all unified by the consistency of characters and the idea that furnished the theatre' (Nzewi 1981: 443). *Ikaki* is a mask character representing the tortoise, a kind of Everyman character in traditional orature. The head-piece is a wooden horizontal mask depicting the tortoise; the body costume is made of cloth that clings to the actor's body, allowing him free movement and use of the necessary stage properties, which include a boat and a tree.

Mask performances are important in the governance of societies because they serve security and magisterial functions. In precolonial Mali, the *Ton* masquerades were an 'integral and important component of the armies of kings of Segou in the eastern Bambara country', and they 'often served as a local constabulary force maintaining communal law and order' (Imperato 1980: 50). In Nigeria, the precolonial *Ekpo* mask society served as the police and law-makers for the Anang people. Severe penalties awaited anybody who dared contravene any law of the supernatural *Ekpo*, which returned to the community periodically to supervise human affairs (Etim 1983: 6–10). Masks usually carry the legal and legislative authority of the spirits they animate, constituting a vigorous and imposing presence in society. Perceiving this, French Catholic missionaries in the Cercle de Boudoukou and Protestant clergymen in Odumase, Ghana, united in their bid to destroy the *Sakara Bounou* (or *Sakarabundi*) masks; the Christians interpreted these to be synonymous with the spirits of the shrines, distracting people from Christian morality (Bravmann 1979: 47). Certain masks embody local law to the extent that they officiate as judges in disputes between parties, offering final judgements in cases that appeared previously before other courts. Power conflicts between villages are dramatized: in the *Eku* masquerade of the Igbirra of Nigeria, the ancestral spirit, *Eku*, encourages competition and bravery, assisting 'its patrician in the competition for the control and use of land and for power in the village government' (Unrug 1983: 54). The extent of their influence and the threat this must have posed to Christian missionaries are clear. Masks continue to officiate in important functions such as rites of passage, patrolling the *nkanda* initiation site of the Secco of Zaire during the passage of boys into adulthood. Encouraging obedience and respect for seniors, they 'threaten any person secretly harbouring evil intentions against one of the initiates' (Bourgeois 1980: 42).

Mask cults are training camps for initiates, who are encouraged to develop their talents in the arts. Music, dance, song, mime, acrobatics, weaving and other art forms are practised by the initiates during rehearsals. In addition, organizational and leadership qualities are developed, which is where a gender perspective gains most relevance. When, as is often the case, a mask cult is the prerogative of only one sex – usually the male – and when there is no equivalent mask cult for the opposite sex, masking becomes a source of gender consciousness and superiority. The *Kungungu* of the Yaka (Zaire), the *Mmonwu* of the Igbo (Nigeria), and the *Gelede* of the Yoruba (Nigeria) are all men's cults: membership is exclusive. Occasionally, 'special' women, who might be menopausal or the wives of senior cult members, are incorporated to perform some roles in the performance. Officially, however, the majority of the womenfolk are debarred from applying for membership.

The official exclusion of women from masking cults raises questions about the part played by mask performers in forming and reinforcing socially accepted gender expectations that confine women to roles outside positions of political and legislative authority. In many African masking communities, participation in masking is considered to be a measure of masculinity. A man who does not belong to any of the cults is regarded as female in spite of his biological sex; this condition is humiliating and degrading to men. Parents actively encourage sons to be initiated into local cults and, although they are usually apprehensive about the rumoured hazards of the process, boys aspire to be initiated, excited to join the prestigious group and achieve masculinity. In fact, overcoming the obstacles of initiation is the first mark of valour, giving boys more prestige than their non-initiated playmates, especially the girls. Enekwe's account of his first experience of children's masking illustrates these feelings: 'As I ate my Christmas meal, I was all agog with excitement mixed with fear. Nevertheless, I looked forward to my first masking experience. After the meal, I costumed myself ... I wore a raffia skirt and girded myself with a folded cloth provided by my mother' (Enekwe 1987: 9).

Enekwe's mixed feelings are part of the excitement at the prospect of performing masculine feats and becoming a hero among his male peers. Girls do not have the privilege of joining children's mask groups, and masking is therefore one of the first distinct differentiations of sex roles among children. Boys organize juvenile masquerade groups in preparation for joining the prestigious adult cults, and their new status as cultists promotes feelings of superiority over non-initiates. By the time they are initiated into the adult mask cults, their sense of superiority is enhanced, for they have attained a level of knowledge and power that excludes the uninitiated. Perhaps in response to this gender imbalance, girls' and women's dancing groups proliferate in societies with male-dominated mask cults; this activity demonstrates women's capacity as theatrical performers, albeit without the authority and credibility attaching to male masking.

Most cults are exclusively male, so their power publicly to define and interpret social roles affects the formation of gender consciousness in local communities at large. By segregating the men, cults give them the opportunity to re-emphasize, through dramatic work, societal constructions of gender attributes. Beauty, peacefulness and shyness tend to be defined as female, while aggressiveness, boldness, and courage are ascribed to men. Through iconography, mask, costume, movement and dance, female characters are shown to possess 'essentially' feminine qualities, while male characters possess masculine qualities defined by themselves: the *Buol* mask theatre of the Bakwele in Equatorial Africa (Siroto 1969: 250) and the *Eku* of Nigeria (Unrug 1983: 54) illustrate the use of mask in developing and exhibiting masculine behaviour. The masculine qualities projected through the theatre aid men's socio-political manoeuvres in the wider society outside the masking group. Among the Bakwele of Equatorial Africa, *Buol* masking is the platform for the exhibition and expression of leadership aspirations. Wealth, charisma and boldness are exhibited in mask contests which determine leadership (Siroto 1969: 250), and, through the contests, men achieve positions of influence and political authority.

Psychoanalytical studies of the sexuality of men show that the assertion of 'masculinity' tends to be a defensive reaction demonstrating the need for separateness and independence from women: in the male psyche, it is argued, women are associated with a dominating mother-figure constantly threatening to disempower men (Ryan 1985: 26). In consequence, from childhood, boys develop a kind of reverence and fear for the mother. Fear, however, is not prescribed as a masculine trait in society, so boys are encouraged to denounce and deny it, repressing it into the subconscious mind where it influences their lives. By engaging in activities and clubs that protect and enhance their masculinity, a way is created to deny this fear and overcome it. Mono-sexual male masking theatres display this separateness and give initiates a secure – fearless because womanless – environment for developing masculine traits.

The male groups are also suitable settings for the construction of men's vision of women: the submissive woman is created, offering a kind of femininity that is not a threat to the 'masculine' man. In mask performances, this ideal woman, usually given the role of mother, wife or maiden, is portrayed as beautiful, pure and peaceful. In this way, cult members selectively depict the characteristics they wish to uphold in women. These noble qualities are not, of course, the only characteristics possessed by women in African societies. In real life, the cultists see beautiful and plain, peaceful and turbulent, docile and aggressive, pure and tainted, brave and cowardly, daring and timid women. It is not in the male cultists' interest, however, to ascribe qualities to women that are marked out as masculine characteristics.

The men make efforts to observe women secretly, carving their subjective impressions into the masks. Among the *Chokwe* of Angola, when a carver is mandated to produce a female mask, he seeks out a beautiful woman whom he uses as a model. The model is unaware, or pretends to be unaware, of being observed for theatrical purposes; meanwhile the artist carves the details of her face, hairstyle, facial marks and so on, to produce a realistic portrait. He pays attention to details and: 'seizes every possible opportunity to meet her and observe her physical features including her tattoos, hairstyle, and jewelry. For this reason, the female masks are often like portraits; although they share the fundamental characteristics of all Chokwe sculpture' (Bastin 1984: 44).

Having obtained a beautiful facial mask, the producers provide a matching costume to complement its beauty. In action, the movement and dance of the character enhance the ideal of a shy and peaceful woman. In this way, the process by which the cultists create an image of womanhood can be charted: first, they translate a portrait from life into the realm of gender politics and representation; second, they re-present the portrait to audiences as an ideal, derived from the real. Ignoring the existence of aggressiveness and boldness in women, the image has been formed by selecting only those qualities which are agreeable to the masculine psyche. In cases of female deviance from the ideal type, male mask performers try to suppress 'unfeminine' qualities through satirical representations, ridiculing bold and aggressive behaviour in women.

Boldness, toughness, bravery and independence are promoted as noble qualities in male characters. Popular male characters, such as the *Mgbedike* and *Akataka* of Arondizogu and Ajalli (in Igboland, eastern Nigeria), embody strength and bravery, performing dramatic actions that instil fear in the onlooker, contrasting with the beautiful and demure maiden spirit masker (*Agbogho Mmonwu*) of the same ensemble. *Dyobi*, a similar popular male mask character of the Dogon, portrays independence through brisk movements and manipulations of his stage properties, the wooden horse, warrior's lance and gourd, contrasting with the female character, *Satimbe*, who represents a version of female beauty conceptualized by the male cultists (Dieterlen 1979: 36).

Men's mask cults service the social and political status quo by upholding the principle of gender complementarity, whereby roles are separated and shared in traditional African societies. The cultists find it necessary to discourage certain traits in women by depicting them as masculine attributes. Social control is upheld in this way: a kind of gender 'harmony' is promoted which prepares only men for leadership and the control of socio-political affairs. An Igbo proverb illustrates the process: 'There cannot be two moons at the same time.' Men are militant and bold because women are their opposite – passive, timid and peaceful, – enabling men to dominate political affairs.

Beneath the masculine show of strength lies the fear of the real woman's power. This fear is conceptualized as spiritual and is associated with the special role of women as mothers, a fascinating phenomenon for men. Among the Yoruba of Nigeria, for example, the *Gelede* elders see women as possessing the secret of life because of their role in the birth process. They simultaneously revere and fear the creative and destructive powers of women, which they cannot appropriate. The *Gelede* mask spectacle celebrates the positive and negative power of women, expressing men's fear, fascination and worship of women's difference. A *Gelede* elder explains the psychological basis of the *Gelede* mask performance, used to appease the power of women as mothers:

> The gods of Gelede are so called 'the great ancestral mothers' ... The power of the Great Mother is manifold. The ancestors, when they had a problem would assemble to determine the cause and the remedy ... and, if it is found that Gelede should be done to bring about rain or the birth of children, it should be done and it will be so. The great mother has power in many things ... [She] is the owner of everything in the world. She owns you. We must not say how the whole things works (Drewal and Drewal 1983: 7).

This explanation reveals that the creativity of women as mothers and the domineering female presence of the mother have been transformed into a sacred discourse, attempting to describe, neutralize, revere and worship the feared object. Throughout Africa, male mask spectacles stage this ambivalence. Aware of the challenging aspects of women's power, the maskers prefer to concentrate on emphasizing positive feminine qualities and usually do not discuss the negative. Ignoring how mothers can punish when provoked, the maskers tend to subdue their fear by producing beautiful maternal mask characters that dramatize the maskers' grasp on the elusive power of women.

Performances are usually before an audience in which women constitute an active part. African women understand the psychological basis of masking, sometimes knowing the identity of the masker, while denying that knowledge in words and actions. Severe penalties await anybody, male or female, who does not appreciate the spiritual dimension of masking. A second reason for their attitude of deliberate innocence is that African women understand the need for men's public display of power. A woman will allow her husband to take credit for what she has herself achieved. Ama Ata Aidoo creatively articulates this idea in her play, *Anowa* (1965). According to Kofi's wife Anowa, a strong and intelligent woman has to pretend to be less than herself 'in order for her man to be a man' (Aidoo 1965: 112). This idea facilitates an understanding of women's attitude to men's mask performances: a mother may provide material for her son to use in masking, yet she will pretend that he is a mask spirit and give him the expected respect to promote his masculine ego.

More serious than children's mask performances are adult ones, which also rely on the principle of secrecy. Among the *Chokwe* of Angola, a woman may greet the mask character animated by her husband in a special way: by offering him the gift of a hen, she indicates a special relationship with the mask, while feigning ignorance of the masker (Bastin 1984: 44). In this case, too, women contribute to the theatrical illusion, pretending that the masks are not animated by men, even when they know the identity of the actors. Ottenberg's study of West African masking corroborates this argument, because he finds that, 'members of the non-masking sex may know secrets, the individuals involved, the rituals done – where they should not – they behave as if they do not' (Ottenberg 1982: 159). In the same vein, Amankulor argues that 'women not only know the individuals who inhabit the masks, they also know that the masquerades are not spirits as such' (Amankulor 1977: 384). In *Things Fall Apart* (1959), Chinua Achebe draws from his Igbo background of the early colonial period and portrays a situation that throws light on this discussion. The occasion is the settling of a dispute in which mask spirits, *egwugwu*, officiate as judges: 'Okonkwo's wives, and perhaps other women as well, might have noticed that the second *egwugwu* had the springing walk of Okonkwo. And they might have noticed that Okonkwo was not among the titled men and elders who sat behind the role of *egwugwu*. But if they thought these things, they kept them with themselves' (Achebe 1959: 85). This event illustrates the political manipulation of women audience members to support theatrical illusions. Okonkwo's wives and other women are pretending they do not know or even suspect who the animators of the masks are. The theatrical impression remains intact.

The belief that men's masking cults are endowed with distinctive powers, which cause the ancestral spirits to emanate in mask forms, enables the maskers to perform their roles with supernatural authority. The actors and producers of the sacred masks are seen as gifted men, elevated in the society at large because of the centrality of masking and its spiritual content. The biological basis of their gender prevents women from aspiring to be in such positions; as we have seen, however, they do participate as 'silent' audiences in possession of a knowledge that they pretend not to have.

The display of the mask spectacle before women is another interesting phenomenon, important to an appreciation of the psychological basis of masking among men. Men's display of masculinity and independence is usually performed in the presence of an audience that includes women.

Women's non-involvement as producers is therefore integral to the realization of the intention of the maskers, and much of the mask display is aimed at exciting women's awe at the wonderful work of the producers. According to Ottenberg, 'much of the tension and excitement of the masquerades lies in the fact that the performance deals with male secret society or masquerade society members displaying before female nonmembers' (Ottenberg 1982: 167). Ottenberg goes further to argue that male masking and its support by women in the audience has an analogy in mother–infant behaviour. The maskers' need for maternal care and their psychological blocking of dependence are submerged in the masculine display, which nevertheless requires women's presence for the psychological effect to be achieved (p. 170). Ironically, this presence shows the men's dependence on women.

Although the discussion so far has centred on mono-sex masking cults that exclude women from membership, it must be noted that, in practice, there is hardly a men's theatre which does not require the services of women. In some theatres, women act as heralds, choruses and guides; yet their contribution is frequently denied by male cultists because of the official exclusion of women from membership. In short, their services are utilized by the family of cultists who do not recognize them officially as members. The women are 'invisible', like housemaids serving at a master's banquet. This lack of acknowledgement contradicts the evidence visible to an unbiased viewer of men's cult performances. During her research in Nigeria, Lorenz interviewed many men who denied women's involvement in masking; in consequence, she was unprepared for the reality of women's active involvement in various spheres of the mask performance (Lorenz 1989: 5).

The role of women in men's cults is sometimes fundamental to the spiritual life of the mask, and as such the mask cannot exist without the women's contribution. The role of the *Nne Ijele* (Mother of Ijele) in the *Mmonwu* masking theatre of the Igbo comes readily to mind: *Nne Ijele* leads, guards and controls the movement of Ijele, just as a mother would in real life. Among the Senufo of the Ivory Coast, the presence of the woman lineage head, *Nerejao*, 'is absolutely necessary in the founding of a new sinzinga organization' (Glaze 1975: 29). Her presence is important in invoking the spirit of the ancestress. In spite of the vital role of such women in masking, the majority of men still ignore them, since the majority of women are still excluded from the theatrical crew. Moreover, men's denial of women's participation in masking is a way of subduing women's place in their lives. Like similar denials in other spheres of activity, it shows a kind of 'autonomy (more accurately a false sense of autonomy) which is closely linked to the development of masculinity' (Ryan 1985: 27).

Masking can be a means of fostering gender co-operation. In some communities, both men and women join the same cults: such is the case among the Bambara of Mali, where the *Ton* society that produces the masks is a dual-sex cult, essentially an age grade association. The society has two leaders, one representing each gender, chosen on the basis of their organizational skills. In this way, the society encourages co-operation and leadership aspirations among initiates of both sexes. Members are also trained for roles that are socially useful: so the boys undertake farm work while the girls are mostly occupied with organizing refreshments for the group. Another interesting example of dual-sex practices among the Bambara is the twinning of members who become responsible for each other's personal welfare: the boy guards the girl's virginity until her marriage, suffering physical punishment and personal shame if he fails in his duty; the female twin takes care of the personal needs of her male twin, providing him with nourishment when he is doing the society's work. This is a way of training the young people in their future roles in the wider society. The relationship ceases when one of the twins gets married. Even as it fosters gender co-operation, the *Ton* society differentiates between male and female in the assignment of duties. Watching the mask performance, the audience of both sexes 'play an integrated participatory role with performers by reacting in a demonstrable way to satire, moralising messages, miming and dancing abilities, and the artistic talent visible in both masks and costuming' (Imperato 1980: 50).

Mask cults do exist which are exclusive to women. The *Sande* cult, first recorded by a Dutch traveller in 1668 (Richards 1974: 270), can be found in West Africa among the Vai, Gola, Shebro, Mende, Temme, Kono and Limba peoples. Hinkley's study of the *Sande* shows that the society is a significant women's organization, exercising authority throughout the areas where it exists (Hinkley 1980), operating independently and parallel to the male equivalent, the *Poro*, except in matters of common interest. Leadership is vested in the *Mojo*, who is respected for her wisdom and expertise in cult traditions, assisted by the teachers of culture and other subordinates who form a council called *Sowei*. The hierarchical structure gives the initiates an avenue for manipulation into positions of authority. Any member of the council can commission a mask: she would not wear it, leaving its animation to a talented dancer of the lower grade. The prestige of the mask, however, goes to the owner. *Sande* is popular among women because it protects and supports members, training them in the arts and empowering them for leadership and other roles in the larger society outside the cult. The sisterhood bonds formed in the cult help in promoting co-operation and progress in the larger community. According to McCormack, if a prominent *Sande* official runs for office in Sierra Leone, or supports a candidate, she can deliver blocks of votes 'by requiring Sande women to swear ... to vote for a particular person' (McCormack 1979: 37).

The women do not conceive of their position as antagonistic to the men's *Poro* cult, promoting their relationship by naming masks after male and female relations. Crucially, the women's cult does not view endurance as a masculine characteristic: instead, it is presented as a common, gender-neutral attribute. The women combine 'male attributes of force with masks representing women's power' (Hinkley 1980: 9). The *Sowo* mask represents womanhood as the women themselves conceive of it, as strong, vital, well groomed and agile. This is women's version of real beauty. As a symbol of power, it is quite different from the images of women constructed and performed by men's cults, showing African women's view of power as something they possess too. Manifestations of power in women's cults do not suppress the opposite sex, but support all, irrespective of gender. *Sowo* shows that the power of women is a unifying force, not only for women as a group but for society at large.

The *Ogbodo-Enyi* women's society in Abakiliki is a recent Nigerian mask cult, arising directly from the Nigeria–Biafra conflict of 1967–70, practised in many villages throughout the Izzi clan of the Igbo. To protect their people who were engaged in battle during the Nigeria–Biafra war, the oracle demanded the performance, and since that time women have continue to produce the mask, called *Ogbodo-Uke* in honour of an oracle called Uke. Although it is a relatively new phenomenon in the tradition of masking in the area, it has the support of the community and is acceptable to the elders. The women received the support of initiates of male cults who assisted in providing necessary stage properties for the women's initial productions. The women borrow masks from the men and use the services of men during the performance. Although these parallel or dual-sex masking cults are relatively rarer than the mono-sex male cults, they show how both genders can benefit from masking when one gender is not relegated to the background.

Masking in traditional African societies contributes to the production of social power. Men's cults, which predominate in Africa, attempt to propagate the ideology of male control by excluding the majority of women from membership and manipulating the dramatic personae to promote female passivity. As initiates, men construct idealized versions of feminine gender traits and roles, portraying them in wishful forms through masking. Women are not involved in the conceptualization processes: as audiences, however, they remain major recipients of the dramas and their messages. Mono-sex cults therefore emphasize a masculine view of society, providing a kind of theatrical indoctrination that promotes male power. In contrast, the parallel mask cults, in which men's and women's groups exist simultaneously, illustrate how masking can promote healthy gender development through segregation, co-operation and empowerment that is not discriminatory.

Women's cults indulge in politics of self-affirmation. Women cultists formulate policies and control their masking, depicting female characters as they see them rather than as male-oriented African societies would want them to be. They portray themselves as dynamic, agile and strong, traits usually portrayed as masculine in men's cult productions. The politics of membership, production and audience response therefore qualify masking not just as artistic entertainment, but as a psychological and political tool for influencing ideas in the society.

References

Achebe, C. (1959) *Things Fall Apart*, Fawcet Crest, New York.
Aidoo, A. A. (1965) *Anowa*, Longman, Harlow.
Amankulor, J. (1977) 'The Concept and Practice of the Traditional African Festival Theatre', unpublished PhD thesis. University of California, Los Angeles.
Bastin, M. L. (1984) 'Ritual Masks of the Chokwe', *African Arts* 17 (4), 40–45; 92.
Bourgeois, A. P. (1980) 'Kakungu Among the Yaka and Suku', *African Arts* 14 (1), 42–6.

Bravmann, R. A. (1979) 'Gur and Manding Masquerades in Ghana', *African Arts* 13 (1), 44–51.
Dieterlen, G. (1979) 'Masks and Mythology Among the Dogon', *African Arts* 13 (2), 34–43.
Drewal, H. J. and M. Drewal (1983) *Gelede Art and Female Power Among the Yoruba*, Indiana University Press, Bloomington.
Enekwe, O. O. (1987) *Igbo Masks: The Oneness of Ritual and Theatre*, Federal Ministry of Culture, Lagos, Nigeria.
Etim, S. N. (1983) 'Eka Ekoong Masquerade Performance in Anangland as Drama', unpublished BA dissertation. University of Nigeria.
Glaze, A. J. (1975) 'Woman Power and Art in a Senufo Village', *African Arts* 8 (3), 25–9; 64–8.
Hinkley, P. (1980) 'The Sowo Mask: A Symbol of Sisterhood', *African Studies Working Papers* 40, unpublished MA dissertation. Boston University.
Imperato, P. J. (1980) 'Bamabara and Malinke Ton Masquerades', *African Arts* 13 (4), 47–55.
Lorenz, C. (1989) 'Igbo Women and the Masquerade in Nigeria', paper presented at the American Anthropological Association Annual Meeting, November, Washington, DC.
McCormack, C. H. (1979) 'Sande: The Public Face of a Secret Society', in J. Rosette (ed.) *The New Religion of Africa*, Norwood, NJ, 27–37.
Nzewi, M. (1981) 'Music, Dance, Drama and the Stage in Nigeria', in Y. Ogunbiyi (ed.) *Drama and Theatre in Nigeria*, Ministry of Information, Lagos, Nigeria.
Ottenberg, S. (1982) 'Illusion, Communication and Psychology in West African Masquerades', *Ethos* 10 (2), 149–85.
Richards, J. V. O. (1974) 'The Sande: A Sociological Organization of the Mende Community in Sierra Leone', Baessler-Archive, Band XXII.
Ryan, T. (1985) 'Roots of Masculinity', in A. Metcalf and M. Humphries (eds), *The Sexuality of Men*, Pluto, London.
Siroto, L. (1969) 'Mask and Social Organization Among the Bakwele People of Western Equatorial Africa', unpublished dissertation. Columbia University.
Unrug, K. (1983) 'Eku Masks of the Igbirra', *African Arts*, 16 (4), 54–9.

14
Anatomy of masculine power: three perspectives on marriage and gender in Nigerian non-fiction

STEPHANIE NEWELL

Locally published non-fiction can be regarded as popular in every sense in Nigeria, influencing and influenced by the same gender debates that circulate in novels, films and other popular media. Pamphlets and paperbacks make forceful interventions in current debates about good wifely behaviour, the validity of polygyny, pre-marital virginity and household income distribution; and books of marriage guidance counselling are aimed at 'helping individuals learn new ways of dealing with and adjusting to life situations' (Fakunle 1992: 7). Echoing the emphasis of contemporary pentecostal and spiritualist movements, the majority of 'How-to' texts view marriage as a primary ordering structure, bringing stability and responsibilities into urban environments in which youths roam freely, and unmarried mothers are cut loose from their 'traditional' roles:[1] as Oladepo Fakunle writes, 'marriage is basic to the family set up and family is primary to an ordered society' (Fakunle 1992: 2).

In this body of literature, the individual, rather than the society at large, is seen to bear responsibility for successes or failures in life: in spite of anxieties about political instabilities, marriage breakdowns and juvenile delinquency, there is no real sense of social anomie in the texts. Fakunle writes, 'many undesirable elements in our society can be traced to irresponsible families' (Fakunle 1992: 23). Domestic gender relations are installed in a primary position, and non-conformist femininities are among the first to be condemned. Repeatedly, authors emphasize that households have been destabilized and families broken up as a result of women's economic independence and insistence on choosing their own marriage partners (see Fakunle 1992: 78–83). Similarly, in situations of marital crisis, urban women are presumed to have deviated from established and accepted domestic patterns. As M. S. Olayinka tells a client the instant she distances herself from Yoruba marriage conventions, 'Traditions are established to create norms of behaviour ... As you are a Yoruba woman I expect you to be familiar with some of the Yoruba cultural values and respect such traditions' (Olayinka 1987: 178).

Political reaction and dissent are censored in Nigeria: almost inevitably, aspects of them will be displaced into the field of cultural politics and interpretation. In marriage guidance books at least, women bear the brunt of the displaced political critique. They are given pivotal roles as mothers and wives, as receptacles of national morality and guardians of the children's spiritual health. Nigerian gender theories are bound up in these overtly masculine political and discursive networks. In consequence, as the discussion will demonstrate, it is difficult for Nigerian feminists to write their ways out of the dominant masculine vocabularies that confer authority on authors and boundaries around discourses.

Three of the most influential gender theorists in contemporary Nigeria are Chinweizu, Catherine Acholonu and Eze Ebisike. Given the relatively unstructured distribution networks of local publishing houses, it is almost impossible to calculate sales figures for each writer; their impact on academics, students and general readers is easier to gauge, however, as all three have started to figure as reference points in discussions of gender issues. In writing a critique of the three theorists, my aim is to contribute to these dynamic, sometimes heated debates.

Chinweizu is an ardent and controversial cultural commentator who lectures regularly at Nigerian and international venues. His book, *Anatomy of Female Power: A Masculinist Dissection of Matriarchy* (1990), is well known in Nigerian academic circles, and will be subjected to an extensive critical analysis here; its ground-breaking claims often seem to mask a reactionary, but intriguing, set of presuppositions that are symptomatic of the anxieties permeating representations of Nigerian 'masculinity' in a range of other cultural forms (see Barber 1986).

The second theorist, Catherine Acholonu, is another high-profile figure in Nigeria, having worked in higher education, campaigned to be president and participated in state-led schemes promoting rural women's welfare. Her contribution to gender theory, *Motherism: The Afrocentric Alternative to Feminism* (1995), will be analysed closely for the way it seeks to empower African women as mothers; it works within the popular gender roles and expectations that circulate in Nigeria, within many of the same conceptual parameters as Chinweizu, while arguing the opposite case and remaining ambivalent to the end.

The difficulties accompanying formulations of an African feminist position will be explored. If one follows the third theorist, Eze Ebisike, it would appear that such formulations have to occur *outside* the overtly 'masculine' master discourses prevailing in much analysis. Ebisike's discursive break-out involves the expression of a feminism that is anarchic and shattering to established gender roles. An ex-Roman Catholic priest, he is a less public figure but a no less prominent gender theorist: both of his texts, *Money Marriages: Mammon Marriages* (1992) and *She, For Greatness* (1993), can be found alongside Chinweizu's and Acholonu's texts in the University of Lagos and University of Ibadan bookshops. If they are read and absorbed by the intellectually engaged readership that their locations presuppose, all three theorists can be seen both to articulate and influence contemporary gender debates in Nigeria; and all three deserve to be studied for the ways in which they shift locally published gender discourse, from biographies, histories, and social and political analyses, into the realm of 'pure theory'.

It is into the pro-marriage environment of Nigerian non-fiction that Chinweizu launches his 'masculinist' redefinition and dissection of women's power. In *Anatomy of Female Power* he defines 'masculinism' as the concept of men's oppression by women. Paying particular attention to Nigeria, he thoroughly reorders and reclassifies gender relations: men are labelled 'machos', 'mushos' (or 'those male wives of female husbands') and 'masculinists' (1990: 124–5); meanwhile, women are labelled 'termagants', 'tomboys' and 'matriarchists' (p. 117). The scientific *double entendre* of the title, *Anatomy of Female Power: A Masculinist Dissection of Matriarchy*, contains both the female anatomical body and Chinweizu's analytical dissection of it. Female power is inscribed into the body in the form of the fertile womb, and the role of matriarch develops from women's biological capacity to give birth. In this way, he anatomizes female social roles by locating the womb as the source of women's supposed domination over men; social roles are embedded in the body, literally embodied as extensions of each gender's natural capacities. Chinweizu's analysis of society seeks to demonstrate how women have exploited this biological superiority and consolidated their power by taking over the roles of mother, cook and nurse in the household.

Redemption from tyranny can occur only in the form of 'career bachelors' who, with the author at the forefront, refuse women's bodily bribery and insist on the redistribution of household roles (p. 58).

These accusations against women's hidden power resonate with the idiom of witchcraft accusations, in which anxieties about the distribution of wealth tend to be projected on to the female body. Witches, like Chinweizu's matriarchists, 'embody all the contradictions of the experience of modernity itself, of its inescapable enticements, its self-consuming passions, its discriminatory facts, its devastating social costs' (Comaroff and Comaroff 1993: xxix). Witches are the hidden manipulators determining an individual's material well-being and physical health; they inherit abilities from their mothers, using kitchen-power and womb-power, taking a man's soul by exploiting his oral and sexual appetites. Chinweizu suggests that the female body is voracious and individualistic, operating covertly from a position within society; if the witch is an 'icon and agent of commodity value; of false representation, of unbridled circulation, and of hidden accumulation' (Apter 1993: 123), then Chinweizu's accusations might be seen to insinuate that the matriarchist is the urban, modern-day witch, with himself playing the role of witch-hunter.

Rather than promoting the marriage institution, Chinweizu blames it for men's oppression globally. *Anatomy of Female Power* is a polemic, secular intervention in Nigerian marital relations which contrasts with the domestic politics promoted in most locally published non-fiction. He attempts to resolve the threats to masculine authority posed by assertive or economically independent wives by weaving a conspiracy theory into the Nigerian social fabric: he declares that all mothers detest their sons and use their positions as child-bearers and children's primary socializers deliberately to induce a psychological and sexual dependency on the female body. Meanwhile, through clitoridectomy and punishment for expressing sexual desire, girls gain the 'enormous advantage' of physical restraint, as well as benefiting from their lessons in the arts of flirtation and pre-marital courtship (Chinweizu 1990: 29–33). Girls are trained from the outset by their witch-like mothers to seduce men with their womb-power. Roles that have been deemed potentially oppressive by feminist critics are thus reformulated by Chinweizu as a source of actual power: by adding the suffix 'power' to 'mother', 'bride' and 'wife', he transforms these subject positions into sites of women's absolute control over men (p. 14).

The matriarchal conspiracy theory petrifies the fluid, intersubjective relations within Nigerian families and societies, and refuses women's multiple, ambiguous self-definitions. In a reductive and paranoid form, this reinterpretation of the marriage institution might be seen to express anxieties about masculine identities in contemporary Nigeria. The definition of power is based on the presupposition that men are psychologically immature, dominated by their penises and brainwashed by their mothers into sexual submission (Chinweizu 1990: 16). Men are viewed as fundamentally weak. At each stage of the male life-cycle, 'female power is established over him through his peculiar weakness in that stage of his life' (p. 14). This argument removes men from positions of autonomy and responsibility for their actions, rendering them passive, trapped in patterns of sexual addiction. Men's bodies are portrayed at odds with their desire for self-control. If, as he asserts, men are pacified, manipulated and controlled 'from the womb to the tomb' by mothers and wives, the only solution is for men to abandon inherited familial formations. Sullied by female domination, the institution of marriage must be abandoned altogether (p. 111).

Having offered his diagnosis and revealed women's plans, Chinweizu attempts to re-empower masculinity by redefining it in anti-social terms, promoting an individualistic and self-reliant manhood which thrives *outside* familial and social roles. Men without homes, wives or families are re-empowered as masculinists *par excellence*.

By rejecting marriage and children, *Anatomy of Female Power* occupies a tangential relation to the masculine ideology that prevails in locally published non-fiction. From the earliest days of locally produced popular literature to the plethora of contemporary 'How-to' books, marriage has been regarded as pivotal to the attainment of adult social status;[2] and the majority of writers insist that children are crucial to the married couple's position, for 'a couple without children is looked at as an unhappy family' (Olayinka 1987: 113). Women in particular are considered to be nothing without children: S. T. Ola Akande's comment is typical, that 'a child as a gift comes to restore to a barren woman her lost dignity, her worth, and her personhood' (Akande 1986: 70).

In *Anatomy of Female Power*, human relationships are portrayed in terms of power struggles in which individual autonomy is preserved or lost: 'If the essence of power is the ability to get what one wants', Chinweizu writes, 'then women are far from powerless' (p. 11). His measurement of power also takes precedence over other power relations in Nigeria: the distribution of economic resources, military rule and religious constructions of social legitimacy are all side-lined. Believing that women are the hidden controllers of men's public, superficial enactments of authority, Chinweizu dismisses ideas that cooking for men, caring for children and relying on men's salaries are oppressive to women. As J. Lorand Matory points out in a discussion of witchcraft, postcolonial 'Big Men' are often believed to have 'women with pots behind them', like the wives described by Chinweizu, 'guiding their greedy acquisitions and providing the mystical means of their enemies' undoing' (Matory 1993: 79). Feminist analyses of oppression within marriage are inverted; instead, Chinweizu argues that this cluster of social roles has been snatched by women to consolidate their womb-power.

Almost all of the strategies specified by Chinweizu to illustrate women's power might be seen to demonstrate wives' reliance on men for economic and social sustenance. With the exception of motherhood, all of the wifely roles he describes might be interpreted as enactments of economic inferiority. Serving a man his favourite food and attracting a husband back from his 'outside wives' (see Karanja 1987) by dressing in seductive clothing are hardly the strategies of economically and socially powerful individuals. Female power is located in the very domestic attitudes and subject-positions that have been described as oppressive by feminist theorists in Nigeria (see WIN 1985). Feminism is inverted and marginalized in the text, labelled a deluded ambition to usurp male roles on the part of 'tomboys' and 'termagants', who seek public authority alongside men and sever their connection with women's real, hidden power base. Feminist women are seen to mimic men's authority, each one a 'dabbler on the turf of professional men' (Chinweizu 1990: 67) in the mistaken belief that public positions denote power. While *Anatomy of Female Power* allows for feminist politics, it belittles and derides 'emancipated' women: for, it is asserted, political power, social control and the domination of the public sphere stem from wives and mothers hiding undercover in their household lairs rather than from men and women visibly working in the outside world.

The conspiracy theory is offered as a demonstration of Chinweizu's authorial position as a 'clear-headed observer' (p. 45). He reveals, '[t]he cunning of it all is stunning! Imagine a hunt in which the huntress takes on the appearance of the prey; in which the true prey enjoys the illusion that he is the hunter' (p. 48). He has employed the familiar logic and language of witchcraft accusations, instating it in the heart of his argument as a recognizable and 'practical discourse of hidden agency' (Apter 1993: 124). Unless one is convinced by the 'if–then' and 'thus– so' logic motivating the progression of his argument, his framework collapses back into reformulations of masculine power relations. The status quo is preserved by his confident sophisms: 'women rule the men who rule the world. Thus, contrary to appearances, woman is boss, the overall boss, of the world' (Chinweizu 1990: 12).

Locally published religious paperbacks emphasize repeatedly that the man is the head of the household and husbands' domestic authority is God-given. A wife must submit and 'put everything she thinks she is, or has, under and allowing her all to be under the authority of the husband' (Idahoise 1994: 19). By inverting this conviction, writing a 'treatise [which...] shows how women rule men, and have always ruled men' (Chinweizu 1990: back cover), Chinweizu is assured of a high-impact polemical position. Employing a simple plot-line, composed of conspiracies and consequences, this unilinear narrative expresses paranoia about autonomous urban women, etching it into the depths of the female body. Female power is 'hard to see, hard to challenge, and even harder to overthrow', he says (p. 23). In spite of his anti-marital rhetoric, which is unique in contemporary Nigerian literature, his argument can be located in a discourse of masculine power. What links his text with Nigerian popular literatures is its ideological insecurity, expressed as anxieties about women's intentions, about their 'subtle, manipulative and indirect' behaviours (p. 23); in this, Chinweizu echoes directly the suspicious attitude towards independent urban women found in popular literature since the earliest texts (see Newell forthcoming a).

An anxious masculinity can be found clustered around representations of urban women in Nigerian fiction (see Boehmer 1991; Stratton 1994; Newell 1996; forthcoming). Women are portrayed as sexually deceitful and financially cunning; they disguise their money-grabbing intentions beneath beautiful 'lip-painted' exteriors. One particular surface (smiling, made-up, urban and beautiful) has become the very sign of the greed and sexual power it tries to conceal. Ever since the Nigerian 'market literature' of the 1960s, unmarried fictional heroines have threatened the stability of young men, remaining dangerously liberated, unknowable and untrustworthy until contained by marriage. Intervening narrators have set the illusion of urban women's appearances against the reality of their sexual corruption: 'beware of women', they warn repeatedly. Likewise, Chinweizu states, the 'common lesson to man is: FEAR WOMEN! ... Yes, indeed, FEAR WOMEN, and if and when they catch you, obey and serve them' (Chinweizu 1990: 100; author's emphasis). In contrast to the old market literature, however, Chinweizu suggests that marriage enhances women's conspiratorial activities, courtship being a staging post on the road to total power: in marriage, the wife has 'the power to manipulate from hidden and protected places' (p. 76). Like the narrators of popular literature, Chinweizu over-reads young women's external appearances in the effort to contain an unstable reality. Plots and conspiracies are circulating constantly. In both sets of discourses, women are suspicious entities, always conspiring and never fully embodying or expressing their authentic intentions: 'being brilliant manipulators', Chinweizu writes, 'they choose to appear stupid ... it takes great cleverness to feign such stupidity successfully' (p. 89). This duplicitous figure has become entrenched in contemporary masculinist discourse.

Single lines are extracted from women's popular songs, folk-songs and autobiographies: Chinweizu denies their status as representations within contexts. One line from a woman's calypso song, 'woman is boss' is generalized into a statement representing all women's views (p. 9); from the other side of the world, Barbra Streisand's 'Woman In Love' is manipulated into conformity with the master plan, as the line, 'I'll do any thing to get you into my world' is read as evidence of 'a clearheaded huntress [keen...] to hunt down, fetter and enslave' (p. 42). An international, essential womanhood is established, stretching from classical myth and religion to contemporary politics. Each example is narrated in an anecdotal tone that collapses myth into the time-zone of something that happened the other day; in this way, Eve's behaviour towards Adam is normalized and made historically contiguous with the Nigeria that Chinweizu describes.

Chinweizu's conception and analysis of power reverberates with the impact of the military dictatorship in Nigeria, where the presidential self is manifested, without dialogue, in the obliteration of the other's body. In *Anatomy of Female Power*, militaristic terminology is applied repeatedly to human relations: Chinweizu speaks of 'the womb's basic power, the cradle's strategic power, the kitchen's tactical power', as well as how women 'took control [in...] the most consequential coup in human history' (p. 21). He uses the language of the army, a bastion of Nigerian masculinity, and conceives of power in conflictual, territorial terms in which one partner is reduced to servitude. Focusing on the womb rather than the woman, there is no space, in this discourse, for mutual affection or negotiation.

Alongside images of warfare, dictatorship and invasion, the language of capitalist, free-market economics is applied to Nigerian gender relations. From their centres of power – the kitchen, the nursery, the womb – 'women control scarce resources, commodities and opportunities; and they distribute them ... They wield instruments of persuasion and coercion' (p. 11). The female body is not lacking, as Freud presumed in the castration theory; instead, it is a fertile territory containing the potential for plenitude. The womb, objectified into an 'it', is a scarce commodity which women wield in a bodily transaction which ensnares men – the users – in marriage, with 'no refund clause' in case it is faulty (pp. 18, 55). Turned back upon the narrator, these images of physical invasion and scarcity consolidate the impression of a threatened, unstable masculine subject unable to position himself within a dynamic, economically insecure society. His identity is under revision: he is confronted by bodily and economically independent women, assertive and self-defining. Even housewives, in this text, operate according to their own misandrous agendas, out of men's control.

In the final chapter, he attempts to bring about a fleeting liaison between masculinists and feminists, by promoting a joint battle against the 'matriarchists'. Slowly, Chinweizu has moved from a provocative, polemical position which derides the emancipatory ideals of women's movements around the world, towards an accommodation of the practical alterations to the institution of marriage that groups such as Women In Nigeria have been promoting since 1983. Fathers, he concludes, should be allowed to penetrate the kitchen and the nursery, to share domestic and childcare duties (p. 129). In their Family Code for African Women, Women In Nigeria requested a similar set of reforms: in particular, their fifth recommendation for urban women is that 'efforts should be made to abrogate the cultural definition of sex roles in terms of male/female appropriate jobs' (WIN 1985: 59; also 92–3). Chinweizu accommodates the central tenets of a feminist egalitarian politics, commenting that he is not anti-feminist, but anti-matriarchist (Chinweizu 1990: 121; 130). By ending on this note, he pre-empts feminist attempts to criticize his text as misogynous. Short of destroying the whole social order with a revolutionary masculinist movement, however, Chinweizu is unable to conceive of a secure marital environment: 'men of the world unite', he calls, 'you have nothing to lose but your macho illusions and your nest-slave burdens' (p. 130).

In her non-Christian theoretical text, *Motherism: The Afrocentric Alternative to Feminism*, Catherine Acholonu (1995) remythologizes the maternal body, loading it with organic symbols and offering it as an expression of the African essence. In Chinweizu's terms, this book might be described as an exemplary 'matriarchist' tract, for Acholonu also writes about women's 'discreet power' and states that 'motherhood is the anchor, the matrix, the foundation on which all else rests in the African society and especially the family' (Acholonu 1995: 16, 31).

The female body, which seems to destabilize Chinweizu's masculinism, is extolled and prioritized by Acholonu, filled with global and ecological significance. Interestingly, the land metaphor applied by Chinweizu to the female body recurs in Acholonu's text, in which motherism is defined according to 'the land which is her [i.e. the African woman's] womb and into which all life shall eventually be swallowed' (Acholonu 1995: 37). While Acholonu has not moved beyond the biologically essentialist conception of femininity which circulates in *The Anatomy of Female Power*, the metaphor she applies relates to elemental, organic landscapes rather than to besieged national territories. The motherland in her idealization is a no-man's-land, beyond boundaries, filled with goddesses and earth mothers; in contrast, the womb in Chinweizu's motherland is the centre of power for a cunning dictatorship which controls a scarcity economy.

Critics of male-authored African literature have often noted the discursive links between Mother Africa, ideas of a rural, precolonial African innocence and African nationalist projects (Stratton 1994; Boehmer 1991). As Florence Stratton demonstrates comprehensively with reference to Soyinka, Ngugi and other prominent African authors, the appeal to Mother Africa simultaneously silences women and authenticates political struggles over territories (Stratton 1994: 39–55). In contrast to the views of these literary critics, Acholonu is not silenced as a woman by the Mother Africa trope. Instead, she works within the cognitive categories of a masculine ideology, incarnating Mother Africa to silence feminist dissent against inherited gender roles. She describes African feminists' insistence on sexual equality and income-sharing as 'un-African' (Acholonu 1995: 26, 87, 103), and assertions that women are oppressed are simply denied and inverted; women in Africa occupy a 'privileged position' (p. 3).

When 'motherism' is defined at last, it expresses an urban woman's speculations about the lives of rural women. The 'Mother Africa' trope is preserved. Rural women's connection with agriculture and inherited social formations – the so-called folk traditions – marks them out as ideal motherists: 'The rural woman is our link with mother earth and with her rests our last hope for reunification with the indispensable mother essence' (p. 118). Acholonu reinvents peasant women as symbolic figures uncontaminated by feminism, urbanization, monogamy and technology, stating that 'the rural woman is ... innocent, unspoilt, unsophisticated in her world view, her thinking and her way of life' (p. 120). Motherism is a deeply ambivalent concept: if rural women are ideal motherists, the author refuses their political empowerment, preferring them to exist as symbolic figures in the urban imagination. Her final comment about illiteracy exposes the urban woman's conception of power, demonstrating the clash between pastoral rhetoric and the threat of an empowered peasantry: 'when you empower a non-educated person, either with information, or with privileges of choice, he/she will make wrong and dangerous uses of these privileges' (p. 129). In this particular instance, one can see how a text that set out to redefine African womanhood has replicated restrictive ideological structures.

In spite of her initial emphasis on the heterogeneity of African women's roles, references to essences and a singular, hegemonic womanhood swiftly infiltrate *Motherism*, reducing it to a series of simple binary oppositions. While white Western women occupy the position of rejected others in her discourse, Acholonu requires their presence none the less as the referential pivot against which the features of an authentic and homely African womanhood are defined. Repeatedly, Western feminism is described as being 'anti-mother, anti-child, anti-nature and anti-culture' (Acholonu 1995: 82). Ironically, there does not seem to be a great ideological distance between the arguments of Acholonu and Chinweizu. Feminism, Acholonu writes, is founded upon an interpretive error: for it is economic power, not gender, which determines social status in African societies (pp. 22, 44–5). Access to wealth is, she implies, equal to all members of society, regardless of their positions within gender, class, ethnic, familial or educational dynamics. The assertion that gender is not intertwined with economic power is problematized by Acholonu's subsequent realization that women's household and child-caring responsibilities prevent them from generating as much authority and income as men (p. 55). Unlike the mediocre man, upon whom society confers authority as a husband, father and active member of the extended family, it is only an outstanding woman – who is rich, educated, outspoken, fearless and hardworking – who can gain respect in the society described in *Motherism* (p. 44).

By stealing the popular Nigerian mother figure from masculinist discourse, Acholonu runs the constant risk of replicating restrictive, biologically essentialist attitudes towards women's social experience. She is writing to empower women, however; and several factors stop this imprisonment from happening. First, while Acholonu's interpretive categories are culturally specific, her frame of reference is global, composed of organicist and ecofeminist perspectives. 'Mother Earth is dying and she is summoning her children for help', she writes, claiming to present 'the essence of African womanhood from a new, universal perspective' (pp. 117, 3). Influenced by Vandana Shiva and the Earth Summit held in Rio, an international ideology is created which absorbs local gender stereotypes and supports her call for equality. By moving beyond the particular, Acholonu manages to evade the ideological restrictions of popular representations of women which, as we have seen, often blame bad mothers for the country's social and political ills.

Second, discursive authority and legitimacy are established through a biblical, revelatory mode of address. Writing as an African woman, Acholonu warns that a global environmental apocalypse will strike if women, the creators and sustainers of human life, are not given positions of power. Her call for women's equality is thus refused any connections with the feminist movement, which tends to be demonized in Nigeria. Her call is resituated as vital to a higher, global ideal which, once again, transcends the particularities of local gender expectations. Women's social embodiments as mothers and wives are preserved; indeed, a nurturing, self-sacrificing version of motherhood is offered as the very reason for women's political empowerment.

Third, Acholonu inscribes a web of mythological and historical matriarchs into the text, offering female role-models drawn from a sexually separatist cultural heritage.[3] The past is constructed as easily retrievable and a gendered version of precolonial history is narrated. Acholonu shows that precolonial women occupied titled positions complementing men; they exercised a public authority that paralleled men's and, like men, owned property and slaves. Moving from historical social structures into the realm of attitudes, egalitarian precolonial gender perceptions are also presented, as 'Africa's mode of perceiving reality' is documented (p. 4). If women have been powerful in precolonial Nigeria, she suggests, it is women's right to be empowered again in contemporary society.

The ambivalence of *Motherism* is ingrained in Acholonu's narration of history, which oscillates between the past and present tenses. She appears unwilling to forgo the gender-equal precolonial history she has assembled: it is suspended, awaiting restoration into the present from an ideologically loaded time-zone where 'there is always *a balance that ensures the mutual distribution of power and roles between the sexes*' (p. 17; author's emphasis). A nationalist affiliation is preserved through this formulation of a history in which the colonialists conspired to 'weaken the very foundation of the African society' by attacking African womanhood (p. 78). In this way, Acholonu further legitimizes her authorial position; she cites 'anthropological evidence' in support of her opinions and masks her insertion of interpretations with the language of historical objectivity. These intellectual self-justification strategies serve to highlight the fragility of Acholonu's enterprise to assemble a women's history and insert it into the silences and blanks in masculinist and colonial historiography.

The celebratory, inspirational style of the book betrays no sign of a victim mentality. Women's roles are idealized and affirmed, and the idea of gender oppression is denied from the outset. In an effort to reinterpret roles regarded by feminists as oppressive, familiar female archetypes and metaphors are invoked in support of the status quo: 'As wife, the woman is the deep valley that must take onto herself the burden of supporting the rest of society ... Her life is one that calls for constant sacrifice' (p. 25). The imperative 'must' occupies a pivotal position in this sentence, assisting the transition from an organic, mythopoeic register to the practical application of a gender ideology. Throughout the text, the land metaphor, followed by the imperative, fills the gaps that might otherwise be occupied by the demands of

African feminists. Mother Africa is reawakened with a flourish that would conform perfectly to Chinweizu's model of matriarchist power: 'The African feminist must reassess her position and realize her potential as the seed of the mother continent. She must align her womanhood and feminist consciousness with the traditional African ideal of womanhood ... She must respect and resume her status as mother – the mother of the family, the mother of the nation, the mother goddess of African people' (p. 108). Nigerian women are being offered alternative identities, ideal selves, in the form of mythical configurations. Such externalized images of themselves might be seen to facilitate and empower the performance of their roles as mothers.

Works by the third, and final, contemporary gender theorist to be discussed can be found beside *Anatomy of Female Power* and *Motherism* in Nigerian bookshops. Like Chinweizu and Acholonu, Eze Ebisike's books are published privately and distributed through the networks of university and private bookshops found in Nigerian towns.

Where Acholonu employed an ecofeminist standpoint in what was interpreted as an effort to transcend discourses drenched in masculinism, Ebisike situates himself within a non-culture-specific discourse: in this case, scientific universals are employed to give authority to the discussion. In the process of advocating monogamous 'middle-of-the-road' relationships in *Money Marriages* (Ebisike 1992), an ethnological map of the globe is constructed, in which cultures are biologized and redescribed in racial terms.

In *Money Marriages*, scientific discourse is employed as a neutral vocabulary to describe fixed behavioural essences. Race is the primary factor in the marriage models Ebisike describes: Caucasian genes determine 'middle-of-the-road' marriage practices, as well as industrial advances, urbanization and technological progress; 'gullible Africans' are seen to have swallowed the 'oriental opium' of bride price practices rather than following 'the progressive and modern marriage practice of the caucasian race' (Ebisike 1992: v). If race determines social practice, European colonialism and cultural imperialism are condoned implicitly as efforts to transform the 'backward' races; if 'Negroid' and 'Mongoloid' marriage traditions arise from genetically inviolable factors, however, then they are biologically programmed and can never be changed. Ebisike's discourse thus risks disallowing the very cultural transformations he advocates.

In his effort to dispel the prejudice against feminists (expressed, as we have seen, by writers such as Chinweizu and Acholonu), Ebisike tends to reproduce colonialist, evolutionary stereotypes about African ignorance and oriental sensuality, as Caucasian 'marriage without the plague of customs and traditions' is advocated (Ebisike 1992: 237). His scientific universalism seems to be blind to the historically specific status of Western marriage models.

This imprisonment within the parameters of an unacceptable ideological alternative demonstrates the conceptual difficulties of formulating anti-masculinist positions in contemporary Nigerian gender debates. In spite of its implications and drawbacks, Ebisike's anti-masculinist position is unique among the master discourses that intermingle in Nigerian publications: it stands out from the interpretive frameworks provided by Christianity, masculinity and cultural nationalism. *Money Marriages* can be regarded as radically oppositional, sliding between hegemonic discourses in search of a critical language to express pro-feminist subject positions; and, like the secular marriage guidance books that circulate in urban society, it settles on science as the least loaded, most flexible discourse. Attaching himself to a rigid, racialist biologism, however, Ebisike demonstrates the difficulties confronting feminists in Nigeria, who seek a language of self-definition unpolluted by masculinist derision. Through his scientific vocabulary, Ebisike attempts to step out of the very cultural location that necessitates his adoption of a global, universalist position. Like Acholonu, he situates his discourse in an international framework and tries to propose an objective and non-exploitative 'uniformed global marriage custom' as the ideal (Ebisike 1992: 234).

Money Marriages is described in the Preface as an 'opera. A shocker' (p. v). As an opera, it comprises short dramatic scenes, culminating in the formation of a 'Liberators' Club' by women in Lagos. As a shocker, it contains numerous detailed sex scenes between unmarried adolescents, occurring without the moral intervention of a narrator. Positive female role-models are created in the form of Azi, Ume, Chi and Ifiri, core members of the Liberators' Club; unlike authors of other locally published paperbacks, Ebisike endorses these vocal urban women, writing them into a world news conference in which Azi gave 'the best public performance of any third world woman in the living memory of the world journalists' (p. 252). Also unlike authors of other contemporary marriage guidance texts, Ebisike insists upon the absolute freedom of lovers, rejecting the controls imposed by the church, family and society: 'What's better than the freedom to marry whom you want, without anybody interfering?' he asks (p. 230). An anti-social, androgynous Utopia is described in which, strangely, the institution of marriage itself is preserved.

Bride price is the key atrocity in Ebisike's text: it stirs parental greed, causes the financial corruption of young men, commodifies the female body and introduces cash into the economy of love. Characters repeatedly voice this marital ideology, and the narrator intervenes to support them with 'stage directions'. These italicized, parenthetical intrusions carry the exegesis of the stories: he comments, 'And so bride price custom has shattered the future of two lovers ... another casualty of the vicious custom of the Igbo's demands for huge bride price for their daughters' (Ebisike 1992: 29).

The scientific conceptual framework of *Money Marriages* is marginalized in Ebisike's ardently anti-Christian *She, For Greatness* (1993), and replaced by an inspirational, prophetic language that is reminiscent of the heady religious pamphlets published by new religious movements.[4] In *She, For Greatness*, Ebisike continues to confront the Nigerian gender ideology head-on, this time without the support of fictional scenes. The positive gender-line implied by the title is not explored until the end, when a women's history is written. Most of the book is constructed from layers of nihilistic analyses, as Ebisike rereads culturally influential texts such as the Bible and the popular press and locates a long-term masculinist conspiracy against women. Anti-religious sentiments pervade every section, reaching extremes in a stream of accusations against the 'morally insane hypocrites and their undiscerning slobbering hoi polloi' in the Roman Catholic Church, and the sexual malpractices of Jesus and the Prophet Muhammad (pp. 44–69). This ex-priest insists repeatedly that Jesus, 'is a fictional character in a lying bible' (pp. 86, 151). The condemnations are not confined to Christianity, as the Torah and the Qur'an are situated alongside the Bible as 'misogynous books' (p. iv).

Revelling in the sheer joy of neologisms, Ebisike writes that the evils of patriarchy 'render women foolable, gullible, dupable, stuffable, deludable, hoodwinkable, bamboozable, humbuggable, born-yesterdayable, born-againable, etc' (p. iii). By using this comic, excessive language, he seems to be trying to express a feminist position, seeking out positive formulations about women from a language and history that discriminate against them. Often, however, the book collapses under its own linguistic excesses, making little sense beyond its lists of alliterated words and questions.

In an extended biblical exegesis that mimics religious paperbacks in an inverted form, Ebisike deconstructs each book of the Bible. Following the style of contemporary religious writers, quotations are extracted and interpreted: in this case, however, the act of interpretation includes a critical dismissal of what is viewed as an oppressive patriarchal ideology. The Bible is not regarded as existing beyond history, conveying essential truths in an unmediated form to readers, but as a deliberate misrepresentation of women by anti-feminist propagandists. St Paul's teachings, and the Christian world's refusal to acknowledge the ideologically saturated status of their Holy Book, are diagnosed as manifestations of spiritual sickness on a global scale (p. 77).

In spite of this rejection, he offers practical guidance to 'worldlings' using the language of a prophet-figure; he calls for a 'ceasefire' in the war between the sexes and presents 'new world cultural and religious scripts that will lead to world unitary government' (p. iii). Interestingly, the necessity for a primary text is retained: the Bible, which functions in religious discourse to confer authority on writers, has been replaced by new 'religious scripts' in this fundamentalist, text-centred gesture. Describing himself as an 'areligious visionary' (p. 231), Ebisike repeatedly offers the universal 'new world educational script' to readers (p. vi). While he inverts and rejects the content of Christian texts, he therefore relies on religious discursive devices for self-legitimation. The main difference, perhaps, is the writer's self-positioning in relation to the written word, for Ebisike claims the status of author rather than interpreter of the divine Text.

Perhaps the extremism of Ebisike's attack on social structures undermines the impact of this unique, anti-religious intervention in a literature dominated by Christian interpretations. *She, For Greatness* is as excessive in its idea that there is a patriarchal conspiracy against women as Chinweizu is in his idea of a matriarchist conspiracy against men. Perhaps the excessiveness of both texts can be seen to illustrate the tensions experienced by writers living in a politically repressed society. The extremism of the regime might be matched by the interpretive extremism of these cultural commentators. Instead of situating marital and familial relations in the politically turbulent and economically insecure context of contemporary Nigeria, human experience is literally domesticated, confined to the home and analysed using a rigid, absolutist language that is loaded with the discourse of military dictatorship.

Like Acholonu, Ebisike composes texts to counter hegemonic masculine representations, containing female role-models to act as 'achievement motivation' templates for Nigerian women; the impetus is one of 'de-divinizing God and gods [and...] de-patriarchising all military and sociopolitical, educational and professional, medical and judicial, family and business establishments, norms and mores' (p. 103). In seeking to retrieve a feminist position, Ebisike has exposed the culturally specific parameters that surround theorizations of gender.

In any society, frequently, and perhaps inevitably, ideas are formulated within the very master discourses that the ideas also criticize and dismiss as oppressive. As the discussion has shown, Ebisike, Acholonu and Chinweizu occupy ambivalent relationships with existing formulations of gender theory in Nigeria. In spite of their differences, marriage and motherhood are retained as primary ordering devices in each text; and, in each text, authority is gained through the construction of a version of African women's history, in which prominent Africans are named alongside figures drawn from religious and mythological archives. The lists of historically influential figures contain numerous married women: for example, in opposition to Chinweizu, Ebisike names 'Mrs Eve Adam' as 'the first woman feminist of the planet', closely followed by 'Mrs Medea Jason of Colchis [who...] stood for the freedom of all' (Ebisike 1993: 116).

In these locally published paperbacks, Nigerian women are constructed and contained by the parameters of various master discourses, including science and Christianity, both of which are underwritten by a masculine ideology. Throughout their projects to reinterpret culturally established myths and texts, the theorists work towards attaining attitudinal, rather than immediate political change. Each publication offers a set of role-models to women, constructing a heritage of strong-willed or rule-breaking women to legitimize its discourse. It remains to be seen what range of responses these writers will generate, as they further permeate academic and general debate, gaining status as figures at the forefront of contemporary gender theory in Nigeria.

Notes

1. Self-help pamphlets occupy as much space as fiction on the shelves of bookshops in southern Nigeria. Often produced by religious organizations, publications range from books on etiquette, friendship and courtesy aimed at Christian children (Hagan [ed.] 1970; Ikpong et al 1993) to marriage guidance texts and vivid testimonials about devil-worship and satanic possession. Some of the most popular Christian marriage guidance pamphlets include Adeboye (1994); Nwani (1988); and Fomum (1985). Bestselling testimonials include Oni (1987) and Uzorma (1993). They are often accompanied by an array of glossy, expensive spiritual material imported from the United States. The paperbacks are published privately, imported from neighbouring countries or printed by local church presses, and offer personal guidance to individuals, helping people to choose compatible life-partners and live in harmonious, sexually fulfilling relationships.

2. For an extensive discussion of marriage and love in Nigerian market literature, see Newell (1996).

3. This process of retrieval includes books such as Awe (ed.) (1992); Uchendu (1993); and Amadiume (1987).

4. Ebisike claims to be influenced by the Grail Movement, whose central text, *In the Light of Truth*, is written by the founder, Abdu-Ru-Shin.

References

Acholonu, C. O. (1995) *Motherism: The Afrocentric Alternative to Feminism*, Let's Help Humanitarian Project, Women in Environmental Development Series, Vol 3, Owerri, Nigeria.

Adeboye, E. A. (1994) *Journey to Marriage*, Book Ministry, Lagos, Nigeria.

Akande, S. T. O. (1986) *For Better; For Worse! A Guidebook on How to Live a Happily Married and Blessed Life and Devotional Thoughts on the Type of Home-Life God Blesses*, Vantage, Ibadan, Nigeria.

Amadiume, I. (1987) *Male Daughters, Female Husbands: Gender and Sex in an African Society*, Zed Books, London.

Apter, A. (1993) 'Atinga Revisited: Yoruba Witchcraft and the Cocoa Economy, 1950–1951', in Comaroff and Comaroff (eds), *Modernity and its Malcontents*, 111–28.

Awe, B. (ed.) (1992) *Nigerian Women in Historical Perspective*, Sankore/Bookcraft, Nigeria.

Barber, K. (1986) 'Radical Conservatism in Yoruba Popular Plays', *Drama and Theatre in Africa*, Bayreuth African Studies Series 7, 5–32.

Boehmer, E. (1991) 'Stories of Women and Mothers: Gender and Nationalism in the Early Fiction of Flora Nwapa', in S. Nasta (ed.), *Motherlands: Black Women's Writing from Africa, the Caribbean and South Asia*, Women's Press, London.

Chinweizu (1990) *Anatomy of Female Power: A Masculinist Dissection of Matriarchy*, Pero Press, Lagos, Nigeria.

Comaroff, J. and J. Comaroff (1993), 'Introduction', in Comaroff and Comaroff (eds), *Modernity and its Malcontents*, xi–xxx.

— (eds) (1993) *Modernity and its Malcontents: Ritual and Power in Postcolonial Africa*, University of Chicago Press, Chicago and London.

Ebisike, E. (1992) *Money Marriages: Mammon Marriages (Stop Mammon Marriages)*, Beteze, Lagos, Nigeria.

— (1993) *She, For Greatness*, Beteze, Lagos, Nigeria.

Fakunle, O. (1992) *Success in Marriages: A Psychological Approach*, Valuta Educational Publishers, Ibadan, Nigeria.

Fomum, Z. T. (1985) *Enjoy the Married Life*, Scripture Union Press, Ibadan, Nigeria.

Hagan, H. (ed.) (1970) *Courtesy for Boys and Girls*, Anowuo Educational Publishers, Accra, Ghana.

Idahoise, J. (1994) *How to Win the Heart of Your Husband*, Living Faith Church, Kaduna, Nigeria.

Ikpong, B. et al (1993) *Friendship Between Boys and Girls*, Daystar Press, Ibadan, Nigeria (1st edn, 1962).

Karanja, W. wa (1987) '"Outside Wives" and "Inside Wives" in Nigeria: A Study of Changing Perceptions in Marriage', in P. Parkin and D. Nyamwaya (eds), *Transformations of African Marriage*, International African Seminars 3, Manchester University Press/International African Institute, Manchester, 247–59.

Matory, J. L. (1993) '"Government by Seduction": History and the Tropes of "Mounting" in Oyo-Yoruba Religion', in Comaroff and Comaroff (eds), *Modernity and its Malcontents*, 58–85.

Newell, S. (1996) 'From the Brink of Oblivion: The Anxious Masculinism of Nigerian Market Literatures', *Research in African Literatures* 27 (3), 50–67.

— (forthcoming) 'Petrified Masculinities? Contemporary Nigerian Popular Literatures by Men', *Journal of Popular Culture*.

Nwani, U. (1988) *The Challenge of Marriage*, Central Books, Bendel State, Nigeria.

Olayinka, M. S. (1987) *Sex Education and Marital Guidance*, Lantern Books, Lagos, Nigeria.

Oni, E. (1987) *Delivered from the Powers of Darkness*, Scripture Union (Nigeria), Ibadan, Nigeria.

Stratton, F. (1994) *Contemporary African Literature and the Politics of Gender*, Routledge, London.

Uchendu, Rev. P. K. (1993) *The Role of Nigerian Women in Politics: Past and Present*, Fourth Dimension, Enugu, Nigeria.

Uzorma, I. N. (1993) *Occult Grand Master Now in Christ*, Uzorma Warfare Treatise, Book One, Benin City, Nigeria.

WIN (1985) *The WIN Document: Conditions of Women in Nigeria and Policy Recommendations to 2000 AD*, Women In Nigeria, Zaria, Nigeria.

15
Gender tempered through metal: women in metal-casting in Benin City, Nigeria

ADEPEJU LAYIWOLA

The discovery of metal art treasures in various parts of Nigeria brought cultural recognition to the country, as international art historians recognized the ancient metalworkers' high levels of sophistication and skill. Manufactured since the ninth century AD, the artefacts have attracted favourable comments: speaking of the Benin art corpus in 1919, Felix Lushan said, '[t]hese bronzes are technically of the highest quality possible' (Eyo and Willett 1980: xi). Similarly, the naturalistic bronzes of Ife prompted Leo Frobenous to suggest, rather patronizingly, an outside origin for the works (Willett 1967: 33). The *cire-perdue* (or lost-wax) mode of casting, along with the composition and choice of alloys, allow one to state with full certainty that the ancient artists had a detailed knowledge of the craft, exceeding all constructions of West African art as 'primitive' or derivative.

Of all the media used in Africa for artistic expression, metal is probably the most significant, not only because of its enduring nature, but primarily because of its social and religious significance. A brief historical overview of metal-casting is required in order to appreciate the impact made by women artists. Although no artefacts survived from the Nok village of northern Nigeria, iron slag from furnaces has been unearthed, suggesting that metal-smelting in Nigeria dates back to about 500 BC (Eyo and Willett 1980: 6). Regarded as an elite medium, metal has long been associated with prestige, royalty and enduring power. Its use was strictly dictated by the *Oba* (King) of Benin, a fact which explains the proliferation of pieces portraying royal personages and themes.

The oral tradition places the art of Ife as predating that of Benin. According to Egharevba, 'Oba Oguola wished to introduce brass-casting into Benin so as to produce works of art similar to those sent to him from Ife. He therefore sent to the Oni of Ife for a brass-smith and Igueghae was sent to him' (Egharevba 1968: 11). It is not clear if this account refers to the origin of the technique of brass-casting or the introduction of a specific object (Ben-Amos 1980: 15–17). One intriguing fact, however, is that the craft continues to be practised along the legendary Igun Street in Benin.

The *Oba* wielded power over the bronze-casters' guild, imposing restrictions on their labour and extracting oaths of allegiance. Any member of the guild who taught the craft to an outsider committed a crime punishable by death. Bronze-casting was thus rendered an exclusive, protected field of knowledge, inextricable from the site of royal power (Tunde-Olowu 1990: 39).

As far as their origin is concerned, of all the numerous guilds that existed in the ancient kingdom, the metal-casters' guild (*Iguneromwon*) was considered to be superior; its head, known as *Ine n'Igun eronmwon*, had more powers than the head of the blacksmiths (*Ine Iguekhan*). Members of the guild were all male and no record can be found of any female involvement. It was taboo for women to be seen within the foundry walls, let alone to gain enough knowledge of the craft to start working in metal.[1] Strictures and penalties have barred women from metalwork over the centuries, affecting their participation in casting, influencing the perception of them in contemporary times. Fortunately, however, the unthinkable *has* occurred: not only do women now engage fully in the art, but they also propagate feminist perspectives through their works, casting female figures which are loaded with responses to entrenched patriarchal attitudes in Nigeria.

Residual prejudices still militate against women's participatory roles in the art of metal-casting: female metalworkers practise their skills in a society whose traditional attitudes are still operational, and where vital knowledge concerning sacred aspects of the palace culture is guarded by men, and shrouded in secrecy. Inroads have been made in Nigeria by innovative artists such as Elizabeth Akenzua Olowu, and slowly women metalworkers are emerging, becoming role-models for young female artists and transforming inherited representational standards by inserting a gender dimension.

A sharp gender divide separates crafts practised by men from those practised by women (Jefferson 1973: 16). Gender differentiation in the use of artistic media has been related to a 'question of power and dominance' (Teilhet, cited in Ben-Amos 1986: 62). Access to, and the allocation of, artistic materials further manifest the biases of the gender ideology: for it is believed that the 'softer' materials used by craftswomen reflect femininity, while the 'hard' materials used by craftsmen reflect masculinity. Hard materials such as metal were 'highly rated ... for their durability, scarcity and the skill and/or technology necessary to work it and the medium's innate magico-religious properties' (Teilhet, cited in Ben-Amos 1986: 62). In line with the concept of animism, metal is believed to have innate powers capable of affecting the balance of natural and social events. Edo cosmology assigned equal status to metal, gods and royal rulers; the coolness, lustre and durability of metal were considered synonymous with the enduring nature of kingship. An Edo adage states: Bronze does not crumble, just like Kingship.

The Yoruba god of Iron is called Ogun; dynamic and present, Ogun is believed to protect anyone handling or working in metal. A god of smiths, drivers, butchers and wood-carvers, he protects and he is seen to destroy lives at will, and his bloodthirsty nature demands that before any casting operation commences, propitiation must be undertaken to avoid fatal accidents and ensure successful casts. Even among other Africans along the West Coast, this ritual must be performed before casting commences. In his novel *The African Child*, Camara Laye, the Guinean writer, recounts the ritual purification his father underwent, abstaining from sex and applying magical substances to his body before carrying out any smelting operation (Laye 1954: 29).

In many Nigerian societies, it is still widely believed that if a menstruating woman touches any magical preparation, that object loses its potency. The leading woman metalworker, Elizabeth Olowu, corroborates this view: 'In this continent of Africa, generally the furnace, bellows and smelting were regarded as sacred things and women at menstrual time [were] regarded as polluting elements. They were not allowed to touch the bronze-caster for fear of causing accidents during casting' (La Duke 1991: 24). The belief that women pollute a sanctified order shows the extent to which male authority over women has been preserved in the artistic workplace. Continuously reminded of the impending disasters accompanying any violation of the rules, women have until recently been excluded from the sacred, royal realm of metalwork.

Even in the weavers' guild, which allows for female membership and participation, men hold the positions of power. My field study revealed that the major decisions were taken by the male leaders of the guild, who bore senior rank titles such as *Okao, Obazona, Esamegho* and *Edionwere*. Such decision-making power is entrenched, part of an age-old Nigerian prejudice that is probably not restricted to the city of Benin.

In a sense, precolonial and postcolonial Nigerian society has reinforced this prejudice and male-orientation by accepting the concept of the 'sexual division of labour', in which men and women perform certain distinct tasks that are considered unsuitable, even polluting, to the opposite sex. In the context of guilds, however, men switched roles, moving within and between established guilds, while women were restricted to particular guilds and mores, reducing their functions within the structure of labour and production.

The training and employment opportunities offered by traditional precolonial societies often weighed heavily against women, illustrated particularly in the method of apprenticeship, whereby fathers would pass on their skills to male children only. Until equal education and training opportunities are made available, 'not even women themselves, still less men, can have an adequate idea of their possibilities of achievement' (Spencer 1972: 269-70). In Nigeria, while boys have been encouraged to reach the zenith of intellectual and artistic achievement, women have been trained to internalize the 'virtues' of humanity, passivity and self-effacement (Adeghe 1995: 119).

Ideologies develop from practical realities, and perhaps the idea of gender differentiation was born out of the fact that the manipulation of metal requires a great deal of physical strength, possibly beyond that possessed by women. Similarly, the amount of time required to bring a work to completion would leave little or no time for women to attend properly to their husbands and children. Improved household technologies have speeded up the time spent on chores and metal-casting techniques have increased women's opportunities in the profession. More importantly, the introduction of formal education has provided women with the tools to express themselves in all aspects of the arts.

Progress has been difficult, and early women metalworkers suffered immense discrimination. In 1981, Princess Elizabeth Olowu became the first female Nigerian metal-caster. Presently, she manages a foundry, producing works which compete favourably with pieces produced by men. Betty La Duke (1991) claims that Olowu's success can be attributed to her royal lineage. Born in 1945, the Princess is the daughter of *Oba*

Akenzua II (1899-1978). She says, 'I could never have realized my talent as a bronze caster if I belonged to the ruled class, many of whom must have died with their skills undeveloped for fear of taboos' (La Duke 1991: 31). Impelled to move into casting because of deeply felt feminist convictions, the 'desire to liberate womenfolk from the shackles of men, deprivation and taboos captures precisely the timbre of most of her works' (La Duke 1991: 23).

Olowu trespasses into a male-dominated territory. The guild of casters moved quickly to challenge her and, in defence, Olowu claimed that her father had granted her the authority to cast and to improve on the *cire-perdue* method. In support of his daughter, the *Oba* compelled the conservative Igun casters to allow Olowu access to their foundry.

In her metalwork, Olowu combines aspects of Edo cultural heritage with 'personal feelings and experiences' (La Duke 1991: 27), producing sculptures ranging from realistic to geometric stylization. In 1982, she transgressed another boundary, producing the first non-traditional view of an *Oba*. Entitled 'The Living Dead', Olowu depicts the king seated upon his throne, clad in the *Igue* festival dress. The title contains the violation for, traditionally, it is forbidden to say the king sleeps, eats or dies; such messages are ordinarily couched in allusion (Nevadomsky 1984: 41-7).

Other works by Olowu depicting female perspectives include a series of diminutive bronzes, nine to twelve inches in size, entitled 'Mother of Many'. This artistic conception culminated in a life-size edifice, 'Zero Hour', which represents a woman in full-term pregnancy, buckling under the pains of childbirth as the hour of delivery draws nearer. 'Zero Hour' is an intimate interpretation of 'a woman's life as she hovers, between life and death during labour' (La Duke 1991: 29).

Princess Olowu will be remembered as a mentor, creating an identity and outlet for women in metal-casting in Nigeria, influencing the second generation of female casters who graduated from the University of Benin in 1988. Five women, myself among them, employed the lost-wax method for the casting of brass and copper sculptures.

Teilhet observes that 'the disparities of style, technique and media between men and women artists appears to be universal' in Nigeria (Teilhet, cited in Ben-Amos 1986: 62). Indeed, this statement appears to be borne out by one striking aspect of the works produced by these women: each piece is based on a gender theme, touching various aspects of women's lives in traditional as well as contemporary West Africa, moving from women's lighter, self-admiring moods to serious reflections on survival in the face of poverty and suffering.

The significance of having children cannot be over-emphasized in Africa, influencing the female metalworkers, who depict different aspects of motherhood. A woman's social dignity and status in the home are reinforced by her ability to have children, particularly sons; as such, several ritual observances are undertaken during a woman's pregnancy to ensure safe delivery. Translated into metal, one can see charms and talismans around the waist of one seated pregnant figure; other figures depict the economic roles played by market women, or the energy and suffering of female farmers, who encounter the perennial problems of fuel and water shortages. Sculptures of the endless chores that rural Nigerian women have to undergo in fending for their families reveal the extent to which female metalworkers have moved beyond the traditional, royal themes of male casters.

More challenging pieces like 'Arise O Women' portray an African woman of the twenty-first century sounding the clarion call to her sisters; such work presents a radical challenge to the status quo, for women are not traditionally allowed to blow horns in Nigeria. If the future is invoked, history is also recast: the representation of 'Queen Idia', the mother of *Oba* Esigie in the fifteenth century, goes back into history to unearth the only woman believed to have gone to war in Benin.

Women have only just started to participate in the field of metalwork in West Africa and are beset by problems of access to materials, production and distribution. A theoretical framework has yet to be developed to accommodate the challenges and transformations brought by the entry of women to this male-dominated profession. More critical analysis is required, both by practitioners themselves and by art historians in order to appreciate and situate this innovative, challenging art form.

Note

1. Personal correspondence with Princess Egbelakame, elder daughter of *Oba* Akenzua II, December 1990, Benin City, Nigeria.

References

Adeghe, A. (1995) 'The Other Half of the Story: Nigerian Women Telling Tales', in S. Brown (ed.), *The Pressure of the Text; Orality, Texts and the Telling of Tales*, Birmingham University African Studies Series 4, 119.

Ben-Amos, P. (1980) *The Art of Benin*, Thames and Hudson, London.

— (1986) 'Artistic Creativity in Benin Kingdom', *African Arts* 19 (3), 62.

Egharevba, J. (1968) *A Short History of Benin*, Ibadan University Press, Ibadan, Nigeria.

Eyo, E. and F. Willett (1980) *Treasures of Ancient Nigeria*, Collins, London.

Jefferson, L. (1973) *The Decorative Arts of Africa*, Viking, New York.

La Duke, B. (1991) *Africa Through the Eyes of Women Artists*, Africa World Press, Trenton, NJ.

Laye, C. (1954) *The African Child*, Fontana, London.

Nevadomsky, J. (1984) 'Kingship Succession Rituals in Benin, Part II: The Big Things', *African Arts* 7 (11), 41–7.

Spencer, A. G. (1972) 'Woman's Share in Social Culture', in M. Schnier (ed.), *Feminism: The Essential Historical Writings*, Random House, New York.

Tunde-Olowu, A. (1990) 'The Igue Festival Regalia of the Oba or Benin', unpublished MA thesis. University of Ibadan, Nigeria.

Willett, F. (1967) 'Ife in Nigerian Art', *African Arts* 1 (1), 33.

Index

Abacha, Maryam, 30, 37
Abacha, Sani, 37
Abbam, Kate, 49
Achebe, Chinua, 82, 107: *Things Fall Apart*, 164; *Arrow of God*, 142
Acholonu, Catherine, 108, 171, 172, 184, 187: *Motherism: The Afrocentric Alternative to Feminism* 171, 179–83
Adams, Robert, 139
Adeghe, Ada, 117
Adimora-Ezeigbo, 2, 3, 4, 81–94: 'Agaracha Must Come Home', 89; 'Inspiration Bug', 88; 'The Missing Hammer Head', 88, 90, 91; 'The Verdict', 91; 'Who Said Dead Men Can't Bite?', 91; *Echoes in the Mind*, 84
adultery, 76, 98
Aggrey, Kwaggir, 43
Agovi, K. E., 72
Ahmed, Talatu Wada, 117
Aidoo, Ama Ata, 5, 22–6, 68, 137–46: *Anowa*, 23, 89, 163; *Changes*, 101; 'For Whom Things Did Not Change', 138, 140, 142; 'A Gift from Somewhere', 137; *No Sweetness Here*, 137–46; *Our Sister Killjoy*, 24–5, 137–46; 'Something to Talk About on the Way to the Funeral', 138, 139; 'The Late Bud', 143; 'Two Sisters', 137, 139, 143
ajami script, 149, 150
Akan system, 40, 41
Akande, S. T. Ola, 174
Akataka character, 162
Akenzua II, Oba, 195
Ali, Hauwa, 5, 117–25: *Destiny*, 122
Aliyu, Hadiza Sidi, 117
Aliyu, Sani Abba, 2, 5
Alkali, Zaynab, 5, 82, 117–25, 126–36: *The Stillborn*, 119–21, 126, 127, 128, 130, 132, 134; *The Virtuous Woman*, 119, 121, 126, 127, 133
Amadi, E., *The Concubine*, 16
Amankulor, J., 164
Amin, Samir, 36
androgyny, 144
Angola, 161, 163
animism, 193
apprenticeship, methods of, 194
Aribisala, Karen, 82
Armah, Ayi Kwei: *Two Thousand Seasons*, 83
Asana, M'ma: 'Certain Winds from the South', 138
Asante nation, 41
Asante Queen Mother, 41–2
Asma'u, Nana, 118
Association of Nigerian Authors (ANA), 81

Bâ, Mariama, 5, 126–36: *Scarlet Song*, 126, 128, 129, 130; *So Long a Letter*, 20–2, 74, 126, 127, 130, 134
Babangida, General Ibrahim, 35
Babangida, Maryam, 30, 36
Bambara people, 166
barrack culture, 29
bereavement rites, 40, 131
Better Life Programme (BLP) (Nigeria), 30, 36, 38
Biafra war *see* Nigeria–Biafra war
Bible, 186; as misogynous, 185
body, female, 172, 173, 176, 178, 179; conceptualization of, 12; treatment of, 7
Boehmer, Elleke, 7
Boyce Davies, Carole, 139
boys: and domestic work, 131; preference for, 100, 141; privileging of, 43
brass-casting, 191, 192
bride price, 98, 101, 183, 185

Brownmiller, Susan, 33–4
Bruner, Charlotte, 137
Bryce, Jane, 4
Butler, J., 107

career bachelors, 173
cassava, 4, 108, 109; association with poverty, 109; association with women, 108, 110, 112; glorification of, 110; personification of, as mother, 110, 111, 113, 114
caste, 21
Catholic church, 158, 172
chiefs, 70, 71, 72, 78
childbearing, 64, 100
childbirth, 30, 35, 162
childcare, 34, 40, 63, 118; crisis of, 38
childlessness, 18, 174
children, illegitimate, 98
Chinweizu, 6, 171, 180, 183, 184, 187: *Anatomy of Female Power*, 6, 171–9
Chokwe people, 161, 163
Christianity, 42, 64, 97, 119, 129, 186, 187; attitudes to women, 42
circumcision, female, 40
cire-perdue metalworking, 195
civil war, in Nigeria, 32, 95; effects of, 30, 31
Cixous, Hélène, 105, 140
class issues, 21, 109
Cleaver, Eldridge, 34, 36
clitoridectomy, 173
Coge, Barmani, 118
Coles, C., 117
colonialism, 4, 13, 14, 20, 25, 32, 64, 72, 74, 97, 108, 140, 143, 153; effect on women's narration, 152
cooking: as feminine chore, 140; by women, 141
corruption, in Nigeria, 121, 122

darkness, and narration, 150
deities, worship of, 16–17
democracy, 37
difference, 11
disability, rewriting of, 121
distribution of books, 1
division of labour, gendered, 95, 150, 192, 194

divorce, 1, 52, 55, 59, 64, 78, 97
Donne, John, 67
Dove-Danquah, Mabel, 67–80: 'Anticipation', 68, 70, 71, 72, 78; 'Evidence of Passion', 68, 70, 77; 'The Happenings of a Night', 68, 69; 'The Invisible Scar', 68, 70, 73, 75; 'Payment', 68, 75; 'The Torn Veil', 68, 70, 73, 75, 77
dowry, 70, 71
dress, of women, 141
Drum, 77
Dyobi character, 162

Earth Summit, 181
East, Rupert: *Jiki Magayi*, 154
Ebisike, Eze, 171, 172, 183–7: *Money Marriages: Mammon Marriages* 172, 183–5; *She, For Greatness*, 172, 185
Ebre women dancers, 85
écriture féminine, 12
education, 120, 121, 123; by women, 117; colonial, 153; Islamic, 153; of boys, 43, 60; of girls, 41, 43; of women, 118, 134, 194 (higher, 43; Western, 149, 155)
Egwugwu spirits, 164
Ekwensi, Cyprian, 82: *Jagua Nana's Daughter*, 84
Eliot, T. S., 67
eloquence, cultivation of, 152
Emecheta, Buchi, 32–4, 82, 86, 92, 142: *Destination Biafra*, 30, 32–4, 36, 38; *The Joys of Motherhood*, 3, 17–19, 20
empowerment of women, 37, 89, 180, 181
Enekwe, O. O., 159, 160
English language, 119; as second language, 106
Equatorial Africa, 160
Ezeigbo, Theodora Akachi *see* Adimora-Ezeigbo, Theodora

Fakunle, Oladepo, 170
Falola, Toyin, 36
Family Code for African Women, 178
Family Support Programme (FSP) (Nigeria), 30, 38

Federal Radio Corporation of Nigeria (FRCN), 154, 156
female body *see* body, female
'femalism', 1
femininity, 4, 6, 54, 56, 59, 63, 134, 140; social construction of, 97
feminism, 2, 11, 12, 85, 86, 96, 101, 103, 105, 106, 123, 179, 180, 181, 184, 186, 195; African, 89; eco-, 183; inversion of, 175; research, 68; socialist, 38; Western, 180
fertility, as measure of woman's worth, 18
FIDA women lawyers' association, 43
First Lady Syndrome, 36, 38
folk song, 139
folklore stories, 139
Frank, Katherine, 13, 20
Frobenous, Leo, 191
funeral ceremonies, 131

Gardiner, Judith, 140
gender, 13, 14, 26; as category of literary analysis, 11; conflict, portrayal of, 95–104; politics of, 157–69; relation to history, 12
gender relations, 194; redefinition of, 19; views of, 170–90
Ghana, 2, 3, 108, 137–46, 158; women's role in social development, 40–4
gift-giving economy, 122
girls: and domestic work, 131, 132; pressure from mothers, 133; training of, 173
'good-time girls', 7
gossip, 55, 56, 139
Graves, Ann Adams, 82
Great Mother, 163
Gwaram, Hauwa, 117
Gyamfuaa-Fofie, Akosua, 2, 3
gynocriticism, 3, 11–28

Hausa women, 5, 122; as storytellers, 149–56
Hausaland, 117
health care, 37
Hearn, Jeff, 29
housewife, stereotype of, 108

housework, 132, 133, 135, 140
housing, 58
Hurston, Zora Neale, 67
husbands, relationship with wives, 89

Idia, Queen, 196
Igbo people, 3, 4, 16, 86, 95, 96, 97, 99, 103, 108, 109, 111, 114, 167, 185; values of, 19; women of, 108 (role of, 81)
illiteracy *see* literacy
Imam, Abubakar: *Magana Jari Ce*, 154
in-laws, role of, 131, 133
income-generating activities, 99
infertility, female, 1
inheritance laws, 40
inheritance rights, 43
initiation, 159
Islam, 2, 42, 118, 122, 129, 132, 143, 149, 150, 151, 153; and fate, 122; women and, 5
Ivory Coast, 165

jealous wife, stereotype of, 87
jealousy, 57, 61, 87
Jehlen, Myra, 20
Jones-Quartey, K. A. B., 78

Kagara, Bello: *Gandoki*, 154
Kaplan, Temma, 139
Kassam, Margaret Hauwa, 5
kwashiokor, 31

La Duke, Betty, 194
law, customary, 73, 74
Lawrence, D. H., 67
Laye, Camara: *The African Child*, 193
Layiwola, Adepeju, 6
Leclerc, Annie, 105
legal system, women's redress from, 77
levirate, 97
literacy, 150, 180
localization, 107
Lorenz, C., 165
love, 1, 24, 50, 51, 52, 56, 60, 61, 62, 63, 86, 122, 127, 134; romantic, 64
Lushan, Felix, 191

Mack, Beverly, 117, 118
Mali, 166
manhood, 24; disintegration of, 19; loss of, 23
market literature, Nigeria, 176, 177
marriage, 1, 15, 21, 24, 41, 50, 51, 54, 60, 61, 63, 70, 72, 73, 74, 76, 86, 97, 98, 100, 103, 120, 121, 122, 123, 127, 128, 130, 131, 137, 153, 170–90; as means of containing men, 177; ceremonies, 151; child-, 132; conflict in, 4; early, 123; escape from bad, 101; forced, 123; Igbo, 100; infidelity in, 100; monogamous, 64, 102, 131; opposition to, 6, 23, 33, 176; refusal of, 134; successful, 102 see also remarriage
marriage guidance, 170, 171, 174, 185
Marxism, 38
masculine power, anatomy of, 170–90
masculinism, 172, 179, 184, 185
masculinity, 5, 6, 7, 29–39, 106, 107, 110, 174, 176, 178, 193
masculinization of culture, 105
mask performance, 5, 6, 157–69; *Buol*, 160; dual-sex, 168; *Eku*, 158, 160; function of, 158; *Gelede*, 159, 162, 163; *Ikaki*, 158; juvenile, 160; *Kungungu*, 159; male domination of, 160, 161; men's involvement in, 163, 164; *Mmonwu*, 159, 165; of children, 163; *Ogbodo-Enyi*, 167; *Ogbodo-Uke*, 167; *Poro*, 166, 167; *Sande*, 166, 167; *Sowo*, 167; *Ton*, 158, 166; women's involvement in, 81, 85, 157–69 (exclusive, 166)
masks: beautiful women as models for, 161; in rites of passage, 159; types of, 157
Matory, J. Lorand, 175
'matriarchism', 178, 183, 186
matriarchy, 128, 181
matrifocality, 7
matrilineal societies, 40
McCarty, Mari, 14
meaning, man-made, 105
medicine man, 75
men, 15, 181; as above the law, 77; as enemy, 13; as heads of household, 176; domination by, 96, 99, 108, 109, 156, 160, 193; in positions of power, 193; infidelity of, 101; lack of sexual discipline, 133; loss of power of, 19; Nigerian, 53; relations with, 92; sexuality of, 134, 160; values of, 74; writers, 6, 14, 26; young, socialization of, 95
Meniru, Teresa, 82
menstruation, 42
metal-casting, women in, 6, 191–7
metalworking, as elite medium, 191
Mgbedike character, 162
migration, 14, 25
military, and women, 29–39
Millet, Kate, 67
Ministry of Women Affairs (Nigeria), 37
'mirass' ritual, 20
Miss Africa contests, 44
missionaries, 158, 159
mistresses, 76
Mitchell, Juliet, 33
modernity, 100, 119
Mojola, Ibiyemi, 5
monogamy, 102, 103, 180, 183
Montagu, A., 127
Mother Africa, 6, 7, 179, 180, 183
Mother Earth, 108, 181
mother figure, 7
motherhood, 6, 40, 60, 138, 175, 179, 181, 187; crisis of, 38; meaning of, 196; reverence for, 113
motherism, 1, 180
mothers, 173; fear of, 161; pressure on daughters, 133; role of, 118, 171, 172
myth, concept of, 83

naming, process of, 109
Nana Yaa Asantewaa, 41
Nasta, Susheila, 1
Newell, Stephanie, 6
Ngugi wa Thiong'o, 71, 179
Nigeria, 2, 3, 5, 29–39, 47–66, 96, 121, 122, 126, 127, 131, 133, 149–56, 158, 160, 165, 167, 170–90, 191–7
Nigeria–Biafra war, 3, 81, 113, 167

Nne Ijele character, 165
non-fiction publication, 170–90
Nwala, T. Uzodinma, 96
Nwapa, Flora, 4, 7, 14, 15–17, 68, 82, 92, 95–104, 107, 139: *Cassava Song and Rice Song*, 4, 107, 110, 112, 113, 114; *Efuru*, 3, 15–17, 95, 97, 99; *Idu*, 95, 102; *Never Again*, 30, 38; *One is Enough*, 95, 97, 100, 101, 102; poetry of, 105–16; *Women are Different*, 100
Nweke, Therese, 51, 53
Nwoye, May Ifeoma, 4, 81–94: 'Agaracha Must Come Back', 86; 'Blessed Romance', 85; 'Dark Shadows', 90, 91; 'Men Cry Too', 87; *Tides of Life*, 84; 'Unruly Driver', 84; 'The Urhobo Dancing Maiden', 87
Nzekwu, Onuora: *Highlife for Lizards*, 83

Obaa Sima (*Ideal Woman*) magazine, 49
Odwira festival, 70, 72
Ofurun, Helen, 82
Ogot, Grace, 14, 15: *The Promised Land*, 14
Ogun, god of iron, 193
Ogundipe-Leslie, Molara, 13, 50, 53
Ogunjimi, Bayo, 3
Ogunyemi, Chikwenye, 85
Oguola, Oba, 191
Oha, Obododimma, 4
Ojo-Ade, Femi, 144
Okafor, Chinyere Grace, 3, 4, 5
Okoye, Ifeoma, 82
Okoye, Mary, 82
Okpewho, I., 107
Olayinka, M.S., 171
Olowu, Elizabeth Akenzua, 192, 194, 195: 'Arise O Women', 196; 'The Living Dead', 195
One Thousand and One Nights, 154
Onimode, Bade, 36
Onwu, Chary, 82
Opara, Chioma, 5
Opoku-Agyemang, Naana Jane, 3, 4
Ottenberg, S., 164, 165

Ousmane, Sembene, 71
Ovbiagele, Helen, 49, 51

Pampo, Hajiya Fati, 118
patriarchy, 3, 6, 14, 18, 22, 30, 32, 33, 35, 67, 86, 117, 118, 120, 186, 192
patrilineal society, 96
penis: as instrument of violence, 90; size of, 89
Pentecostal church, 42, 170
phallus, hegemony of, 30
Phillips, Maggie, 16, 18
poetry, 4, 140
political involvement of women, 44
politics: in Nigeria, 48 (impasse of, 65); of exclusion, 50
polygyny, 1, 21, 64, 71, 72, 97, 98, 128, 129, 130, 131, 132, 134, 149, 151, 170; as instrument of oppression, 101; rejection of, 74, 100
popular forms, adopted by women, 49
post-colonialism, 1, 12
praise-singers, women, 118
pregnancy, 6, 138, 143, 195, 196
property, women's rights to, 58
prostitution, 1, 120
protest, theme of, 68
proverbs, 152

rape, 33, 34, 43; marital, 101
Rawlings, Nana Konadu Agyemang, 42
religion, 16, 122; traditional, 42
remarriage, 22
resistance of women, 23
Rich, Adrienne, 30
riddles, 152
Robinson, Lillian, 137
romance, 60, 63
rural women, 180
rural-urban divide, 96

Sabi'u-Baba, Habiba, 118, 119
seclusion of women, 118, 149, 151
Segun, Mabel, 82
Sekoni, Isoken, 6
Senegal, 126, 127
sexism, 53

sexuality, 22, 24, 47, 60, 72, 173, 174; male, 32
Shafa Labari Shuni programme, 154, 155, 156
Shehu, Hajiya: 'Yar', 117
Shiva, Vandana, 181
Showalter, Elaine, 3, 26-7, 140
single parents, 51, 54, 55, 102
sisterhood, 15
slave women, 17, 18
slavery, 23
Smith, Mary, 117
Smith, Valerie, 13
song, 152
Soyinka, Wole, 83, 179
Spender, D., 109
spiritualist movements, 170
state, as father figure, 29
storytelling, 5, 149-56; female, 5; male view of, 152; oral, as 'feminine', 150; revolutionized by mass communication, 153
Stratton, Florence, 7, 179
structural adjustment programmes, 108
suicide, 25, 123
supernatural intervention, 90, 91
surnaming, process of, 108
Sutherland, Efua, 68

Taiwo, O., 107
technology, 153
theorization of African women's writings, 11-28
Thiam, Awa, 134
Third world women, representation of, 2
Times of West Africa, 69
Tofa, Karima Abdu Dawakin, 117
traders, women as, 98, 99
tradition, 119, 142; return to, 107
traditional values, 2, 40, 100
traditional village trend, 107
Treena Kwenta's Diary, 47-66
Turok, Ben, 36

Ulasi, Adaora, 82
ultrafemininity, 34
Umelo, Rosina, 82

United States of America (USA), 87, 134
unmarried women, 97
urban life, 18, 19
Uwemedimo, Rosemary, 82

Vanguard, 47-66
Verbrugge, R.R., 111
violence against women, 38
virginity, 166, 170
voicelessness of women, myth of, 92

Walker, Alice, 68
war, as masculine institution, 34
Western culture, 97
widowhood, 64
widows, 55, 97; maltreatment of, 91
Wilson-Tagoe, Nana, 2, 3, 142
witchcraft, 173, 175, 176
woman, African, as stereotype, 7, 96
womanhood, 19, 34, 39, 180; definition of, 16; notions of, 33, 126-36
womanism, 1, 81, 89
womb, as source of women's supposed power, 172, 173, 175, 177, 178; land as, 179
women: and reproduction, 32; and unhappy relationships, 76; as candidates in elections, 43; as cannon-fodder, 31; as channel of traditional wisdom, 117; as educators, 49; as focus of stories, 84; as media professionals, 53; as musicians, 151; breaking of spirit of, 76; economic independence of, 102; excluded from mask performance, 168; exclusion from masking cults, 165; exclusive masking cults of, 166; exploitation of, 109; failures of, 16; image of, 110; in media professions, 51; in metal-casting, 191-7; lack of economic power, 123; looking after themselves, 59; modern, 71; not allowed to train as ministers, 42; power of, 15; rewriting images of, 107; stereotypes of, 88, 161, 176, 177, 182; struggle for rights, 85;

subordination of, 82–3, 108, 176; taboos against, 192; traditional roles of, 32; viewed as appendages of men, 98; viewed as passive, 24, 162; young, socialization of, 95
Women in Nigeria group, 178
'women's culture' model, 12
women's magazines, 49, 50, 51, 55
women's movement, 178
women's networks, 54
writing, by women, 49, 50
Wusasa, J. Tafida: *Jiki Magayi*, 154

yams, 108, 109; association with men, 108, 112; disappearance of, 113
Yoruba people, 171, 193